INTEGRATING MINDFULNESS INTO ANTI-OPPRESSION PEDAGOGY

Drawing from mindfulness education and social justice teaching, this book explores an anti-oppressive pedagogy for university and college classrooms. Authentic classroom discussions about oppression and diversity can be difficult; a mindful approach allows students to explore their experiences with compassion and to engage in critical inquiry to confront their deeply held beliefs and value systems. This engaging book is full of practical tips for deepening learning, addressing challenging situations, and providing mindfulness practices in anti-oppression classrooms. *Integrating Mindfulness into Anti-Oppression Pedagogy* is for all higher education professionals interested in pedagogy that empowers and engages students in the complex unlearning of oppression.

Beth Berila is the Director of the Women's Studies Program and a Professor in the Ethnic and Women's Studies Department at St. Cloud State University, USA.

INTEGRATING MINDFULNESS INTO ANTI-OPPRESSION PEDAGOGY

Social Justice in Higher Education

Beth Berila

Routledge
Taylor & Francis Group

NEW YORK AND LONDON

First published 2016
by Routledge
711 Third Avenue, New York, NY 10017

and by Routledge
2 Park Square, Milton Park, Abingdon, Oxon, OX14 4RN

Routledge is an imprint of the Taylor & Francis Group, an informa business

© 2016 Taylor & Francis

Library of Congress Cataloging-in-Publication Data
A catalog record for this book has been requested

ISBN: 978-1-138-85455-0 (hbk)
ISBN: 978-1-138-85456-7 (pbk)
ISBN: 978-1-315-72103-3 (ebk)

Typeset in Bembo
by Apex CoVantage, LLC

This book is dedicated to all of my Women's Studies students over the years. You continue to inspire and teach me.

And to Amy Boland, who makes me laugh, helps me sparkle, and builds a life with me full of joy and possibility.

CONTENTS

PREFACE

I delved into yoga and meditation deeply after I earned tenure and promotion to Associate Professor. I had spent more than ten years teaching Women's Studies courses at various higher education institutions, working with hundreds of students, and tackling one social issue of oppression after another, both on campus and off. I was burned out, empty, and deeply in need of new sets of tools. I was disillusioned at how many of my students had still so deeply internalized oppressive ideologies into their sense of self even while being empowered by Women's Studies and other social justice curriculum. I wondered if those were simply lessons students had to "learn the hard way" or if there were tools missing that we needed to offer them. I had a nagging hunch that the answer was both.

After tenure, I enrolled in a 200-hour Yoga Teacher Training Program and began teaching yoga sporadically. That experience deepened my practice immensely and allowed me to begin bringing the gifts of yoga to my community. Over the next several years, the two realms of my work—yoga and Women's Studies—continued to gravitate toward one another like two parts of a magnet. However, because I was still on the academic "treadmill" of always producing and doing more, the synergy was never quite firing.

Then I found the Association for Contemplative Mind in Higher Education (ACMHE), which felt like coming home. Instead of always having to justify my interest in yoga as something so much deeper than merely "exercise" (which I so often had to do with many of my academic colleagues and administrators), I settled amongst a group of supportive people who understood what contemplative pedagogy offered collegiate learning. I participated in conferences that started with a grounding and integrated reflection. The two parts of my world started coming together even more closely.

But the social justice dimension of my work still seemed out of place in many contemplative environments. Though many of my yoga communities consist of deeply caring and even leftist people, the hard work of interrupting oppression was often not a central part of their project. I have often felt my feminist critique unwelcome in those spaces, despite the clear economic exclusion of many of the classes, trainings, and retreats. Fortunately, searching has revealed a great many people combining social justice work with yoga and meditation, including the Yoga and Body Image Coalition, of which I am a founding member, and Off the Mat, Into the World. A similar pattern emerged in other contemplative spaces. Despite the racial, ethnic, and socioeconomic homogeneity of many contemplative spaces, discussions about social justice often remained on the margins, something that I am delighted to say is changing as I write this. Leaders in the field, including those at ACMHE, are centering discussions of social justice as they move forward with contemplative pedagogy. I have great hope for the future of these conversations, which build on many historical efforts of social change that are deeply situated within contemplative communities.

After years of dong this work, I finally qualified for a sabbatical. That time was a deep gift of immersing myself in the experience of being a student, learning, practicing, and embodying these questions. Finally, the two parts of my world—mindfulness and social justice—united to provide a dynamic process of unlearning oppression that I outline in the following chapters.

At the heart of this book is my desire to help us interrupt oppression at its roots in our bodies, our hearts, and our minds. I draw on mindfulness to offer us a rich set of tools with which to navigate the complex discussions about oppression and the complicated power dynamics that exist in our classrooms and in our communities. Integrating mindfulness offers the possibility for a more empowered embodiment, which, I believe, is critical to not only interrupting injustice but also to building more resilient and vibrant communities.

As one of the first books of its kind, this book offers a theoretical grounding for how and why we need to integrate mindfulness into social justice pedagogy. But it also offers practical "how-to" tips for those teachers who want to begin doing so, along with some common challenges that can arise. I include a specific mindfulness practice in each chapter to get readers started, with more extensive options available on my web site (www.bethberila.com). I hope that this book not only offers practical tools for teachers but also opens new doors that can further the dialogue about how best to "be the change" by offering our students critical life skills.

One of the most important aspects of mindfulness is that it explicitly tells students why such practices can help their daily life and their social justice practice. Just as anti-oppression pedagogy talk about process—how you get there matters—so, too, mindfulness requires us to reflect on the meta-level. We become aware of why things happen as they do, how we got there, and what happens when we respond in one way rather than another. We learn to put our values and principles into practice: if our goal is a more just, equitable, and peaceful society, then how we get there should reflect those same goals. Mindfulness and anti-oppression both invite us to use our larger value system to determine our daily actions. Our commitment to social justice shapes the choices we make about how we engage hard conversations, how we do our own work of unlearning oppression, and how we create alternative, more empowering ways of relating to one another. Reflecting on the meta-level helps us do so.

This book is written for higher education professionals who teach about diversity issues, including Ethnic Studies, Women's Studies, Multicultural Education, and LGBTQ/Queer Studies disciplines. Faculty and staff who work in Women's Centers, Multicultural Student Services, Student Disability Services, Veterans Offices, LGBT Centers, or other student affairs offices can also benefit from the integration of mindfulness into social justice pedagogy that I outline here. Finally, those teachers who have been utilizing contemplative methods in the college classroom but have not fully explored how racism, sexism, heterosexism, or classism might shape students' experiences of those practices can learn how to better prepare themselves and their students. My hope is that, together, we can create more compassionate and effective strategies for addressing issues of oppression in our classrooms and outside of them.

What to Expect

Each chapter of the following develops a theoretical analysis of how mindfulness can complement anti-oppression pedagogy, along with "real world" examples from the social justice classroom. This book also offers a unique, practical guide to integrating mindfulness in the classroom, including specific tips and practices in each chapter. For additional practices, please see my web site, www.bethberila.com.

Chapter 1 explains the anti-oppression pedagogy framework utilized in this book and outlines the benefits of mindfulness for college students. Central parallels are drawn between contemplative pedagogy and anti-oppression pedagogy. The chapter concludes by delineating several contributions that mindfulness can make to unlearning oppression and offers tips for integrating the two modes of knowing.

The remaining chapters of this book will outline how mindfulness can prove useful to various aspects of unlearning oppression. Each chapter includes some specific tips for integrating mindfulness into our classrooms. Chapter 2 situates embodied learning as central to mindful anti-oppression pedagogy. I discuss embodiment as a vital strategy for unlearning oppression and cultivating a more empowered way of relating to one another. The chapter concludes with some tips for teachers who seek to integrate mindful embodiment practices into their social justice courses.

Chapter 3 focuses on internalized oppression, which is a common topic in social justice classrooms. I argue that internalized oppression is embodied as a form of trauma and argue that mindfulness practices that can help both students and teachers more intentionally unlearn these harmful messages about oneself and one's community.

The flip side of internalized oppression is deconstructing privilege, which is the focus of Chapter 4. That process involves dismantling the very sense of self that privileged groups have come to believe about themselves. Chapter 4 explores how mindfulness helps us do so, particularly by focusing on contemplative listening practices.

The process of unlearning oppression usually includes several difficult dialogues, in which some student responses are often characterized as "resistance." Chapter 5 argues that we need to reframe student responses of "resistance" to anti-oppression pedagogy as the inevitable cognitive and emotional dissonance that occurs when we unsettle students' deeply help worldviews and self-concepts. By looking at several common scenarios of cognitive dissonance, this chapter examines the complex responses that occur simultaneously in social justice classrooms and offers a model of mindful awareness to help students learn to productively process through the discomfort. Integrating mindfulness into social justice classes is not a silver bullet nor is it always a flawless process.

In Chapter 6, I examine some central critiques of mindfulness practices, including charges of cultural appropriation and the debate over whether these practices are secular or religious. Ultimately, I argue, these valid concerns provide fertile ground to analyze critical social justice concepts. The chapter concludes by considering different students' complex responses to contemplative practices in the classroom and offers tips for effectively handling those situations.

Finally, this book concludes with a look at how more compassionate and mindful dialogues can help us work toward a more socially just world. By better understanding our own responses to issues of oppression, we can learn to more compassionately relate to ourselves and to members of our community. We can also more intentionally engage in the work of actively unlearning oppression.

ACKNOWLEDGEMENTS

This book is possible because of the support and inspiration of a great many people. First, I want to thank the Center for Contemplative Mind in Society (www.contemplativemind.org) and the Association for Contemplative Mind in Higher Education (www.contemplativemind.org/programs/acmhe) for providing the community of support that helped me imagine this project and the forums for several earlier versions of portions of this book. Thanks to Daniel Barbezat, for urging me to write down my ideas, to Rhonda Magee, for being a leader in bringing together social justice and contemplative pedagogy, and to Jennifer Palmer and Carrie Bergman for helping me with the webinar, conference paper, and journal articles of earlier versions of this work.

Special thanks to many of my colleagues for helping me think through these ideas. I am deeply grateful to Jason Laker for encouraging me to write this book and for talking through many of the ideas in it. Many of my other colleagues at St. Cloud State University, including Jane Olsen, Kyoko Kishimoto, Glenn Davis, Mike Sharp, Lee LaDue, and Darlene St. Clair, have also provided important feedback as my ideas have taken shape. I am grateful to the SCSU Women's Studies Program and to St. Cloud State University for supporting me in this work with both financial and time resources.

Special thanks to my editor, Heather Jarrow, my editorial assistant, Karen Adler, and everyone at Routledge who helped me to prepare this manuscript.

My life partner, Amy Boland, has deeply supported me through the long process of writing this book, including many times when I was not able to play because I had to write. I owe you lots of sparkle dates this summer. Thank you, Amy, for making me laugh every day and for helping me to believe in myself. Many people in my family of choice also provided invaluable support for which

I am grateful, including Judy Sciandra, Katrina Vandenberg, John Reimringer, and Mom and Dad. Your love and support is a gift. Other critical support came from my yoga and meditation kula, without whom I could not have taken this journey.

Finally, I want to acknowledge all the amazing Women's Studies students over the years. You have inspired me, motivated me, and taught me. You have patiently participated in these mindfulness practices and provided me with invaluable feedback. You constantly remind me why I do this work. My deepest gratitude.

PERMISSIONS

Earlier versions of Chapters 1 and 6 appeared in my article, "Contemplating the Effects of Oppression: Integrating Mindfulness into Diversity Classrooms," published in the inaugural issue of the *Journal of Contemplative Inquiry* vol. 1, no. 1 (2014) by the Center for Contemplative Mind in Society (http://journal.contemplativeinquiry.org/index.php/joci/article/view/5).

Special thanks to The Center for Contemplative Mind in Society for granting permission to include it here and for the permission to include the Tree of Contemplative Practices image.

Portions of this work were also include in my webinar with the Association for Contemplative Mind in Higher Education (ACMHE), "Towards an Embodied Social Justice: Integrating Mindfulness into Anti-Oppression Pedagogy," June 5, 2014 (www.contemplativemind.org/archives/3004).

An earlier version of portions of Chapter 5 was presented with Dr. Jason Laker at the Annual ACMHE conference, "Intention, Method, and Evaluation," University of Washington, Seattle, WA, October 10–12, 2014.

Preliminary ideas for Chapter 2 were included in my poster presentation, "Engaging Our Bodies: Toward a Feminist Pedagogy of Mindfulness," International Symposia for Contemplative Studies, Denver, CO, April 26–29, 2012.

1

MINDFUL ANTI-OPPRESSION PEDAGOGY

On November 24, 2014, at 8:00 p.m. Central Time, officials in St. Louis, Missouri, announced that a grand jury would not indict Officer Darren Wilson, a White police officer, in the murder of Michael Brown, an unarmed African American teenager. Outrage, anger, and despair erupted throughout the United States. I, too, felt grief and fury in the very depth of my being. As a professor in higher education, I wondered how I was going to address this event in my courses: what were the best ways to engage in a thoughtful, critical, and caring dialogue about race relations when tensions were running so high throughout the country? It seems to me that these fraught moments are when our capacity for such dialogue so often fails us, but they are precisely the moments when we need to learn better ways of being with one another.

I entered my classroom the following morning heartsick and furious. I teach Women's Studies courses and so, of course, the grand jury's decision and its implications were highly relevant subjects for our class. We had begun the semester with discussions of the events in Ferguson, and after discussing how different bodies are raced and gendered in inequitable ways, it was time to revisit the subject. I felt unprepared to teach that day because my emotions were so raw, but my yoga and meditation practice have taught me that often such vulnerability opens a space for authentic human connection and deeper wisdom. My feminism, meanwhile, has taught me that it is my responsibility as a White anti-racist advocate to confront these issues of institutionalized racism and gendered violence in order to help students learn how to analyze and interrupt them.

So I started class by sharing the heaviness of my heart and asked students what they felt. That was the pattern in all four of my classes throughout the day: I opened with a simple, honest, and nonjudgmental description of what

I was feeling and asked them how they were. Many of my students, particularly students of color, clearly needed to express their feelings of anger, frustration, pain, and deep grief. Some students of color hollowly expressed their realization that "the system did not fail them because it was never designed to protect them" as people of color. One Black man, who rarely spoke in large group discussions, asked the class if we thought a genocide of Black men is happening. A woman of color expressed her deep fear for all the Black men in her life and her sense of powerlessness to protect them. In a later class, a young Black man asked how he was supposed to deal with police officers when he has to fear for his life in every moment of every encounter with police. Many White students expressed outrage as well. They critiqued the injustice of the verdict and condemned the deep pattern of racial profiling and police brutality against Black men. Others were notably silent, though I have learned over the years not to assume that I know what the silence means. One White man, a former police officer himself, said that while he felt that in some cases the injustice was clear, in the case of the death of Michael Brown, the facts were not so clear. "If you take race out of it," he said, "Wilson might have been truly fearing for his life." Of course, the feminist framework I teach in my classes insists that race cannot be taken out of this equation, because racial and gendered dynamics created the situation in the first place.

But his perspective, along with those of all the other students in the room, were simply a microcosm of what is happening in our communities throughout the United States at this historical moment. Nothing that was said in my classes has not been said in the broader, public conversations about police brutality, the failure of the criminal justice system, racial profiling, and the killing of Black youth in the United States. The raw emotions and the tensions were palpable in the classroom throughout the day.

The challenge for us as anti-oppression educators is to help students learn how to deeply and productively engage in these hard conversations, unpack the learned ideologies that produce inequalities in society, and learn more equitable and empowering ways of relating to one another. Fraught social issues such as the killing of Michael Brown, and the long history of deaths of young Black men that it continues, provide relevant and necessary examples to examine in social justice classes. But how to do so with intellectual nuance, analytical vigor, historical context, and empathy and compassion is still a challenge. Some students reiterate stereotypical ideas that make the conversation even more painful for those who are directly affected by the issue, while the pain and fierce fury of the latter sometimes overwhelms and seems out of place to those students who are not placing the situation within its trenchant historical context. The stakes for learning how to navigate these conversations are high, because the students in our classrooms will be shaping our societies for years to come. If they do not learn the skills in our courses, I am not sure where they will learn them.

When I was new to teaching Women's Studies courses, I struggled with how to best address instances like this one, which are all-too-common in diversity classrooms. When students inevitably make statements that are uninformed or stereotypical, I would either challenge certain comments directly in a way that often shamed the student into shutting down and refusing to learn more, or I would challenge them so indirectly that students did not realize I was trying to trouble the assumptions made. As a cisgendered woman living in a society that often shames women, I do not find shaming to be a useful or a kind pedagogical challenge, nor is direct conflict my best operational mode (Bordo 1996). But the indirect approach was also ineffective, since students often missed the point and failed to deeply examine their belief systems.

Over the next fifteen years, as I became more experienced at teaching, I grew more adept at challenging students' deeply held ideologies without alienating them from the learning process—a balance that I believe is critical for anti-oppression courses. Too much discomfort and students will simply disengage, which is not a helpful pedagogical strategy. But some discomfort is necessary, because inequalities have become normalized. It is also not enough to simply learn *about* oppression. We have to literally *unlearn* oppression: examine our role in it, dismantle deeply held ideologies, and create alternative, more empowering, ways of relating to one another. In order to achieve this outcome, students need to not merely learn the subject matter as objective content but also examine it as a social system in which *we all participate*. That participation occurs not just at the level of external behaviors but also at the level of our internal thoughts and feelings and in our ways of relating to one another. This deep inquiry often produces some necessary discomfort, but in order for it to be effective, we need to offer our students the requisite tools with which to process through that inquiry.

Though anti-oppression pedagogy highly values critical self-reflection of ideologies, power, and privilege, it often stops short of the deep reflection that mindfulness has to offer. Over the past fifteen years, I have watched many Women's Studies students become empowered intellectually and politically, only to still express self-denigrating sentiments, end up in abusive relationships, or have disordered relationships to food and their bodies. My own rather rocky path to wholeness illustrated to me that feminism, while profoundly empowering, was not enough. It sometimes failed to reach the deepest layers of self or provide all of the tools I needed to bring my feminist empowerment to a more integrated level. Those tools came to me through my yoga and meditation practice. But neither were the mindfulness tools alone enough, as too often in the Western world they remained apolitical at best or reinforced privilege and inequality, at worst. Eventually, I realized that I had to integrate feminist praxis with mindfulness in order to access the full benefits of each. The combination has proven very invaluable to my social justice teaching. This book outlines those insights, offering a model for a mindful anti-oppression pedagogy.

Some Foundational Definitions

Since this project hinges on several terms that are themselves worthy of their own lengthy discussions, I will start with some brief definitions. These concepts will be further developed throughout the following chapters.

By *feminism*, I mean an intersectional analysis of systems of oppression that examines how race, gender, class, ethnicity, and ability, along with sexual and national identities, work together to position us in complex power dynamics with one another. This form of feminism sees oppression as operating through social institutions, such as the government, the media, the educational systems, and so on. It seeks to cultivate empowerment for members of marginalized groups. The form of feminism I invoke here is a way of asking questions and a set of values, rather than a set of foregone conclusions. It does not see men and women as monolithic categories nor does it see the male/female binary as the only options for gender. Instead, this form of feminism addresses how other aspects of identity (race, religion, sexuality, class, national location, ability) shape gendered experiences.

Feminist pedagogy builds on this definition of feminism to inform teaching practices that educate the whole student. This model of pedagogy sees students and teachers as co-creators of knowledge and the classroom space as a site of knowledge production. Self-reflection is a central feature of this feminist pedagogy. Because my teaching has been in Women's Studies courses, my specific examples will come from feminist pedagogy. However, throughout the book, I argue that the mindfulness model I offer can enhance anti-oppression pedagogy in general, including critical pedagogy, anti-racist pedagogy, and queer pedagogy. I will outline these different frameworks later in this chapter.

Oppression is a system of power that subordinates some groups in order to over-empower others. It also refers to the painful and violent effects of oppression, both on individuals and on collectives. *Anti-oppression* will be used throughout this book to refer to the process of unlearning the tools of oppression and dismantling inequitable systems. For the purposes of flow, I will use the terms diversity and social justice interchangeably with anti-oppression. Obviously, all of these terms are more nuanced and differentiated, but that discussion is beyond the scope of this project. Classes such as Women's and Gender Studies, Ethnic Studies, LGBT/Queer Studies, Multicultural Education, and Sociology teach about anti-oppression.

By *mindfulness*, I mean the process by which we become more self-aware through particular practices. I will refer to these activities interchangeably as either mindfulness or contemplative practices. Some techniques are already regularly used in academic classrooms, while many are not yet widely recognized as valid academic skills. In the former category lie journaling, volunteering, storytelling, dance, and dialogue. In the latter category lie meditation, yoga, visualization, bearing witness, contemplative arts, Aikido, deep listening, and centering practices. The Tree of Contemplative Practices designed by the Center for Contemplative Mind in Society nicely depicts the interconnected array of activities that fall under the heading of contemplative practices (see Figure 1.1). Some come from particular religious or cultural traditions and, therefore, raise questions of cultural appropriation and religious belief systems, which I will discuss further in Chapter 6. For the purposes of this project, I will be focusing on secular mindfulness practices that are designed to cultivate self-awareness, embodiment, balance, clarity, and compassion. A further delineation of these techniques comes later in this chapter. First, though, I will speak to the value of integrating these practices into the college classroom.

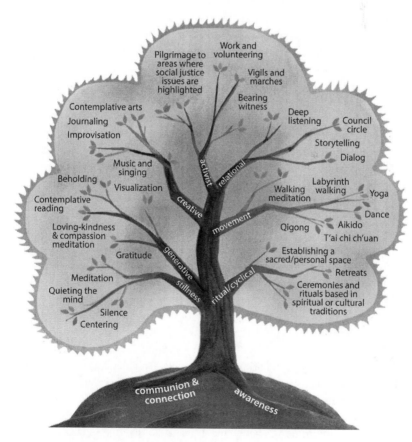

FIGURE 1.1 The Tree of Contemplative Practices

© The Center for Contemplative Mind in Society
Concept & design by Maia Duerr; illustration by Carrie Bergman

Educating the Whole Student

Over the past ten years, mindfulness initiatives have become more common, more visible, and more coordinated throughout U.S. colleges and universities (Shapiro, Brown, and Astin 2008). Increasingly, higher education is recognizing the value of integrated student learning. Some call it holistic education, which, according to Ron Miller, is "based on the premise that each person finds identity, meaning, and purpose in life through connections to the community, to the natural world, and to spiritual values such as compassion and peace" (1997, 1). Mark Nepo, author of *The New York Times* bestseller *The Book of Awakening* uses the term "transformational education," which is

> understood as educating the whole person by integrating the inner and outer life, by actualizing individual and global awakening, and by participating in compassionate communities—[it] has become a quiet but sturdy movement that encourages the recovery and development of the academy as a liberating and capacity-building environment.
>
> (2010, *vii*)

Though each concept has its nuances, all are efforts to develop resiliency and well-being in the whole student. Rather than assuming that a student's personal life is separate from the academic portion of her college experience, this vision of education facilitates the two components working more closely together. As Diana Chapman Walsh, President Emeritus of Wellesley College noted in her 2005 keynote address to The Institute on College Student Values at Florida State University,

> The issues facing the next generation globally demand that we educate our students worldwide to use all of their resources, not just their mind or their heart. The hour is late, the work is hard, and the stakes are high, but few institutions are better positioned to take up this work than our nation's colleges and universities.
>
> (qtd. in Nepo 2010, *v*)

Rather than the more traditional silo model of higher education, in which academic study remains separate from student affairs, this trend speaks to the need to not only intentionally integrate students' college experience but also to teach students how and why that integration is critical to their own well-being and that of their communities (Awbrey and Dana 2006; Palmer and Zajonc 2010). Women's Studies, of course, has long recognized the need for this integration. Women's Centers, often housed within student affairs at universities, have forged strong interdependent relationships with academic Women's Studies departments.

Similar relationships exist between Ethnic Studies departments and Multicultural Student Services offices and between Queer Studies academic departments and LGBTQ resources centers in Student Affairs. These mutually supportive partnerships provide valuable models for more holistic higher education.

Truly transformational learning, though, requires an even more fundamental integration. Feminist scholar bell hooks has called for an "engaged pedagogy," which she suggests goes further than either critical or feminist pedagogy because it emphasizes well-being and calls for "radical openness," "discernment," and "care of the soul" (1994, 15–16; 2010, 8–10). This well-being involves a knowledge of oneself and an accountability for one's actions, as well as a deep self-care, for both students and professors. Teachers, hooks argues, must be self-actualized if they are to help empower students. Engaged pedagogy is an education for how to live in the world. Discussions of holistic learning have come much further since the publication of her groundbreaking book *Teaching to Transgress* in 1994. However, the specifics that explain *how* to educate on the level of mind, body, and spirit are still up for discussion, which is where this book enters the conversation. All of these levels are critical, I argue, for social justice classrooms.

While there are many different routes to achieving holistic education and integrated student learning, this book focuses on mindfulness and contemplative pedagogy as a promising path to not only educating the whole student but, more specifically, contributing skill sets that are particularly *vital* in diversity courses. I will first define what I mean by anti-oppression pedagogy, arguing that most forms of emancipatory teaching and learning can benefit from contemplative practices. I will then discuss the benefits of mindfulness, outline important parallels between contemplative pedagogy and anti-oppressive pedagogy, and then conclude the chapter with tips for integrating mindfulness into social justice courses in order to better help students unlearn systems of oppression.

Basic Principles of Anti-Oppressive Pedagogy

Most social justice courses use some variation of what I will call anti-oppression pedagogy, the most well-known forms of which are critical pedagogy, feminist pedagogy, anti-racist pedagogy, and queer pedagogy. Each form has its unique history and dimensions, but there are some common components of each. My foundation is in feminist pedagogy, but I use the broader anti-oppression framework because mindfulness can effectively be integrated into a variety of forms of emancipatory pedagogies. It is worth establishing some of their commonalities and differences before outlining how mindfulness can enhance them.

Critical pedagogy seeks to bring radical politics to educational systems. Reflected most prominently in the work of Henry Giroux, Michelle Fine, bell hooks, Paolo Freire, Stanley Aronowitz, and Maxine Green, this pedagogy argues for the emancipatory potential of democratic learning to better the situation for disenfranchised groups. Its roots lie in James Dewey's ideas that progressive education should engage community-building and that interaction with one's environment is part of knowledge production (Darder, Baltodano, and Torres 2003, 3). These ideas were placed within a more radical framework when combined with the work of Antonio Gramsci, Michel Foucault, and The Frankfurt School (Giroux 2003a). The first two analyzed power and knowledge; Gramsci to argue that hegemony is a more effective way of achieving domination than is outright force. Through hegemony, Gramsci argued, individuals are conditioned to adopt the interests of the ruling class, even when they work against their own self-interest (Gramsci 1971). However, hegemony is always partial, opening clear fissures for resistance (Darder, Baltodano, and Torres 2003, 3). Foucault (1980) questioned the "regimes of truth" that were legitimated through institutionalized forms of knowledge production. He, like others, recognized the educational system as a site of power knowledge, but he did not see power as merely oppressive. For Foucault, power is generative as well are repressive; it produces as well as dominates. Moreover, since power is everywhere, according to Foucault, so is resistance. Critical pedagogy also draws on the critique of rational knowledge and capitalist production (both material and cultural) articulated by The Frankfurt School.

Among the other central founders of critical pedagogy is the Brazilian educator Paulo Freire, whose *Pedagogy of the Oppressed* (1970) centered questions of culture, power, and oppression within traditional models of schooling. Freire developed a model of pedagogy focused on grassroots activism, agency, and democratic, active learning. Another Brazilian, Augusto Boal, situated Freire's ideas within the context of theatre and performance to incorporate participant interaction and community reflection (Darder, Baltodano, and Torres 2003, 6; Boal 1993).

This heterogeneous theoretical base produced a few basic tenets for critical pedagogy. First, critical pedagogy seeks to empower disenfranchised groups to democratically participate in their educational process. Central to this *conscientization* is a critique of the repressive nature of traditional learning and classroom structures (Freire 1970). Many of these theorists argued that education masquerades under the guise of objectivity and neutrality that masks the underlying power dynamics (Darder, Baltodano, and Torres 2003, 11). By validating the personal experiences of marginalized groups and enabling more democratic educational spaces, this pedagogy helps schools become sites of struggle over knowledge.

Second, critical pedagogy argues that schools traditionally work against the interests of most students who are hegemonically conditioned to adopt the interests of the elite ruling class. This component challenges the myth of equal opportunity to education and instead argues that schools reproduce vastly inequitable class hierarchies (Giroux 2003b). Critical pedagogy also acknowledges that the material conditions and lived experiences of the students and teacher directly shape how and what they can know.

Rather than seeing knowledge as objective "Truth," critical pedagogy argues that knowledge is historically produced and culturally located. Students are thus encouraged to situate themselves and their experiences within historical socio-political power dynamics and to understand those dynamics as both socially produced and changeable (Darder, Baltodano, and Torres 2003, 12). This social agency is practiced both by empowering students and by revealing the fissures, gaps, contradictions, and ideologies that are embedded in knowledge production, thereby opening space for resistance. This critique is an ongoing process, since hegemony and the production of power/knowledge are also ongoing processes.

This latter component opens the door to uncertainty, undermining the emphasis on rationality and Truth that so often pervades more traditional education. "In opposition to traditional theories of education that serve to reinforce certainty, conformity, and technical control of knowledge and power, critical pedagogy embraces a dialectical view of knowledge that functions to unmask the connections between objective knowledge and the cultural norms, values, and standards of the society at large" (Darder, Baltodano, and Torres 2003, 12). It thus emphasizes the interdependence and relationality of systems and individuals, domination and liberation, theory and praxis, students and teacher.

Finally, though no less importantly, critical pedagogy centers a theory of resistance, to explain why disenfranchised groups often do not succeed in traditional educational systems that marginalize them. This resistance also opens the possibility for an oppositional consciousness, in which students actively resist their dehumanization and develop counter-hegemonic alternatives that center marginalized voices (Freire 2000). These alternatives are partly made possible by the praxis that encourages students to apply critique, analysis, and questioning to their everyday lives (Darder, Baltodana, and Torres 2003).

While critical pedagogy contributes a great deal to emancipatory learning, it has also come under some critique, most notably from feminist and critical race theorists. The majority of influential founders of critical pedagogy were men, so some of the critiques stem from a sense that they only superficially challenge the hegemony of patriarchy (Luke 1992). A deeper criticism surrounds their reification of the Enlightenment privileging of cognitive, rational knowledge (Darder, Baltodano, and Torres 2003). Feminists have staunchly argued for the importance of personal stories, biographies, and the situated nature of each individual's knowledge and experience (Darder, Baltodano and Torres 2003). Gender needs to be a category of analysis so that women and girls are included in both the content and process of education. These scholars focused on nonhierarchical learning spaces, multiple perspectives, and providing students with tools for self-empowerment (Rendón 2014).

The feminist intersectionality framework that I adopt throughout this book emerged in the context of these debates. Intersectionality argues that matrices of race, class, gender, sexuality, and national location need to be addressed, not only to challenge dominant forms of education but also to center the histories and perspectives of disenfranchised groups (Crenshaw 1991). In fact, some feminist critical race theorists have argued that important insights can emerge from the perspectives of those on the margins. Patricia Hill Collins (2000), for instance, offered the concept of "the outsider within" to explain how people from marginalized groups see the exclusionary practices of social institutions, because even when they are on the "inside," they are still marginalized by the paradigms that Other them. Those perspectives offer invaluable insights into how dominant educational systems can be deconstructed. With intersectionality, there is a greater emphasis on uncertainty, open-endedness, and relational knowledge (Luke and Gore 1992).

Feminist teaching practices draw on prominent feminist theory that argues for situated knowledges and examines the standpoint (or sitpoint) of all perspectives (Haraway 1988, Harding 2003; Garland-Thomson 2005). Because the body is such a central issue in feminism, with a focus on issues such as body image and beauty, reproductive justice, and violence against women, it makes sense that feminist pedagogy would examine the embodiment of learning, including how different bodies are constructed in the classroom (Wilcox 2009; Weller 1991). Feminist pedagogy recognizes the power dynamics in the classroom and seeks to share power between all participants (Luke and Gore 1992).

This form of pedagogy also seeks to empower students to create social change by catalyzing their agency. Here, "empowerment means not only helping students to understand and engage the world around them, but also enabling them to exercise the kind of courage necessary to change the social order where necessary" (McLaren quoted in Gore 1992, 57). Gore (1992) raises concerns about the extraordinary abilities attributed to teachers in this notion of empowerment. If power is something that is exercised, not a form of property in a zero-sum game, then empowerment in this context would need to be context-specific and grounded in particular practices (Gore 1992).

Critical race theorists expressed a similar critique of critical pedagogy, not only pointing out that many of the founding leaders were White, but also that the pedagogy failed to center the perspectives of the subordinate groups themselves, who were often communities of color (hooks 1994; Allen 2006; Bonilla-Silva and Embrick 2006; Brown-Jeffey and Cooper 2011). Anti-racist pedagogy challenges the foundation of the Western educational system as one historically grounded in White male supremacy. It troubles claims of universality and detached "objectivity" to instead argue for historically situated knowledges from multiple perspectives. In anti-racist pedagogy, like in feminist pedagogy, students are challenged to learn and unlearn paradigms at deep cognitive and affective levels—what I call our very sense of self—which is why deep emotions are often triggered in these classrooms (Wagner 2005; Blakeney 2005). Because traditional learning is seen to reinforce structures of domination, the *process* of learning how to think critically from an anti-racist perspective is critical (Wagner 2005; ARPAC 2014). This process is made explicit, for instance, by preparing students at the beginning of class that deeply held ideologies will be challenged and that students will be asked to take risks that will likely be unsettling. Anti-racist pedagogy, like feminist pedagogy, challenges participants to examine how their own identities position them in relation to the material they are learning and to the other participants in the classroom.

Queer pedagogy takes up some similar principles by positioning the identities of both teachers and student in power dynamics and by challenging the hetero-normative frameworks of traditional education (Luhmann 1998). A queer peda-gogy explores gender performativity as it is related to sexual identity and sees both as fluid and dynamic, rather than static, and challenges assimilationist frameworks (Halberstam 2003). Like the term queer itself, a queer pedagogy deconstructs the very frameworks through which we presume to know and works toward more radical alternatives (Britzman 1995; Winans 2006).

The scholar Kevin Kumashiro distinguishes between four major threads of working against oppression: "education for the Other, education about the Other, education that is critical of privileging and Othering, and education that changes students and society" (2002, 31). Many of the models of pedagogy discussed thus far include components of these different ways to challenge oppression. Many diversity classes, for instance, include information about marginalized groups and narratives told in the voices of marginalized groups, so as to more fully teach about the "Other" and to challenge the erasure of marginalized groups' experi-ences that so often pervade traditional forms of education. When marginalized groups see themselves reflected in the curriculum, they are validated in important ways. But, of course, these first two methods that Kumashiro describes have their limits, since they do not fundamentally question the paradigms that marginalize and Other in the first place. Forms of pedagogy that teach students how this privi-leging and Othering operate and what its consequences are go further toward dismantling the systems, particularly if students are taught the tools with which to interrupt the process. They can then develop the skill sets to create alternative, more emancipatory ways of relating to one another. I argue that mindfulness is an important component of this last step because it takes us beyond the cognitive into embodied transformation, at both the individual and the collective levels.

Though there are important differences between all of these forms of pedagogy, they do have some basic commonalities: 1. learning is politicized; 2. educational systems are recognized as both sites of oppression and sites of resistance; 3. students are taught to apply the concepts to their everyday lives and the sociopolitical power dynamics in which they live; 4. objective "Truth" claims are challenged as forms of domination; 5. knowledge is instead understood as historically and cul-turally specific; 6. teachers and students participate in knowledge construction; 7. the process of learning is as important as the content of learning, if not more so;

8. democratic participation is highly valued; 9. awareness and consciousness-raising is critical; 10. multiple perspectives are highlighted, often centering the experiences of marginalized groups; and 11. students are encouraged to use their learning process to actively transform society in socially just ways. Many of these forms of pedagogy examine how and where they may be complicit in the very systems they are trying to dismantle. Of course, each form of pedagogy defines some of these tenets in particular ways and centers certain aspects of identity in its mission (gender, race, class, sexuality). In doing so, each brings important dimensions to the conversation.

I believe that mindfulness offers a valuable contribution to each of these types of pedagogy. Therefore, despite the nuances in each form discussed above, I will use the umbrella term "anti-oppression pedagogy" to include all of them. Further scholarship in this area can explore the specific ways mindfulness can be integrated in the unique strategies of each form of pedagogy. But as one of the first texts in this field, this book is interested in establishing the foundation of intersections between mindfulness and anti-oppression pedagogy, explaining how and why mindfulness provides critical methods for students to unlearn oppression, and offering teachers "action" tips for implementing mindfulness practices in the classroom.

Parallels between Mindful Learning and Anti-Oppression Pedagogy

Recent efforts in contemplative education make important strides toward fulfilling hooks' call to "educate the whole student" but sometimes without the explicit social justice consciousness that is integral to anti-oppression pedagogy. However, anti-oppression pedagogy does not always help students fully *embody* their learning. In Women's Studies courses, for instance, students cultivate social awareness and feminist political consciousness. They learn how to apply the concepts from class to their own lives and the world around them. They also develop leadership, advocacy, and empowerment skills. But all of these tools have their limits if student cannot fully *embody* them. To really integrate these lessons, they need to be absorbed into our very selves, not merely learned at the level of the intellect or political consciousness.

Mindful education is one valuable way to help students fully integrate and embody the lessons of anti-oppression pedagogy. In fact, the very practice of mindfulness is a fundamental catalyst for transformation. Like feminism, mindfulness is more about process than it is about product. If, as Audre Lorde said, "the master's tools will never dismantle the master's house," then we need to learn new ways of being in the world. Integrating mindful learning into anti-oppression pedagogy lets us do just that. Contemplative practices, when integrated into the college classroom, can help students develop the ability to critically self-reflect (Barbezat and Bush 2014). They can also offer students the tools to remain present—and *embodied*—in the classroom, an idea I will examine more fully in Chapter 2.

Growing research demonstrates the vast benefits of mindfulness. Recent advances in Western neuroscience have supported what ancient yogis and meditators have long known: that mindfulness has extensive emotional, psychological, and physiological benefits. Regular mindfulness practice strengthens the immune system and eases stress. It can ease anxiety and depression, while increasing concentration and awareness (Davis and Hayes 2012; *Free the Mind* 2012; Wadlinger and Isaacowitz 2011; Williams and Penman 2011). Meditation, yoga, and *pranayama* (yogic breathing) have also been shown to decrease the effects of trauma and Post-Traumatic Stress Disorder (PTSD) (Emerson and Hopper 2011; Van Der Kolk 2014).

Mindfulness, then, can enhance the overall well-being of college students. It offers students tools that they can use anytime and anywhere to ease their anxiety and stress, which can be particularly helpful during semester crunch. Some studies indicate that regular mindfulness practice increases academic performance and enhances students' ability to relate to others (Barbezat and Bush 2014; Brown University 2014; Shapiro et al. 2011). Given the personal identity development trajectories common for most traditionally aged college students, the proven benefits to emotional intelligence also makes mindfulness particularly helpful in college. It can enable students to establish healthy life skills that can serve them long after graduation (Goleman 1994). Even if the seed does not fully take root during the college years, once students learn about mindfulness, they may be more likely to access it later in life when they find they are in need of its benefits.

However, mindfulness practices are not just dropped willy-nilly into a syllabus but are instead integrated into a pedagogy that seeks to deepen introspection and inquiry. As such, they nicely compliment more traditional modes of learning, while also enhancing students' deeper self-awareness. In fact, this type of learning recognizes the contextual nature of knowledge. In her groundbreaking book *The Power of Mindful Learning*, Ellen J. Langer distinguishes between Intelligence and Mindful Learning (1997). The former, she argues, entails a linear process of stable categories, objective facts, and learned skills that correspond to reality and moves toward resolutions. Mindfulness, on the other hand, values multiple perspectives, encourages the participant to experience control by shifting between these perspectives, and sees knowledge as fluid. Skills and information are neither inherently good nor bad; instead, the knower is encouraged to step back and reflect on solutions and outcomes to determine deeper meaning within context (Langer 1997, 110).

Though she is careful to distinguish her discussion of mindful learning from the broad-based contemporary use of the term mindfulness, her work has been influential in the field of contemplative pedagogy. Langer suggests that mindful learning generates psychological states that enable several qualities: "(1) openness to novelty;

(2) alertness to distinction; (3) sensitivity to different contexts; (4) implicit, if not explicit, awareness of multiple perspectives; (5) orientation in the present" (1997, 23). Scholar Laura A. Rendón makes a similar distinction between knowledge and wisdom. The former, she suggests, values rationality, detached objectivity and facts about the outer world but without *application* to life. Wisdom, on the other hand, "arises from personal communion and reflection on life" (2014, 90). It emphasizes self-reflection on the inner life and cultivates self-awareness. It begins with the personal space, but then expands to integrate a social responsibility (Rendón 2014, 90).

Mindful learning, then, parallels a basic tenet of anti-oppression pedagogy that recognizes all knowledge as culturally constructed and partial. Who we are shapes what we know. One goal of anti-oppression pedagogy is to make that lens visible and to try to step outside it. Both forms of learning value the *process* of inquiry as much as the results. Both, then, allow what the poet Rainer Maria Rilke calls "living the questions." In his classic book, *Letters to a Young Poet*, Rilke writes, "Do not now seek the answers, which cannot be given you because you would not be able to live them. And the point is, to live everything. Live the questions now. Perhaps you will then gradually, without noticing it, live along some distant day into the answer" (1993, 12).

Contemplative pedagogy invites student to actively situate themselves within the content of their courses and apply the concepts to their own lives, another clear parallel with anti-oppression pedagogy. As such, it takes experiential learning to a different level, one that integrates the mind and body with a more holistic value system. As Daniel P. Barbezat and Mirabai Bush, current and founding director of the Center for Contemplative Mind and Society (respectively) define it, contemplative pedagogy has a few basic goals:

1. Focus and attention building, mainly through focusing meditation and exercises that support metal stability.
2. Contemplation and introspection into the content of the course, in which students discover the material in themselves and thus deepen their understanding of the material.
3. Compassion, connection to others, and a deepening sense of the moral and spiritual aspect of education.
4. Inquiry into the nature of their minds, personal meaning, creativity, and insight. (Barbezat and Bush 2014, 11)

Contemplative practices focus on the present moment, helping students cultivate clarity about their internal experiences in any given moment. When used in an academic setting, mindfulness practices have proven to increase students' concentration, deepen their understanding, increase their emotional intelligence, sustain emotional regulation, and develop their creativity (Barbezat and Bush 2014, 22–32; Goleman 1994).

More and more educators are integrating various contemplative practices into the university classroom in order to help students cultivate presence and self-reflection.

Contemplative pedagogy uses practices that enable deep introspection into meaning, ethics, purpose, and values. They encourage reflection on our internal experience as well as our interdependence with others. Like much anti-oppression pedagogy, contemplative pedagogy challenges the objectivism and empiricism of traditional learning, suggesting that there is much more to learn than a privileging of rational knowledge and scientific methods allow. Without discounting the value of the former, contemplative pedagogy reveals the rich potential of introspection that helps cultivate the depth of our hearts with an eye toward greater sustainability. As Barbezat and Bush write, "[C]ontemplative pedagogy does not supplant or detract from rigorous analytical inquiry . . . rather, they can augment and enhance, and even transform, traditional modes of teaching and learning" (2014, 84). Just as traditional analytical education trains students how to question and perceive in nuanced ways, contemplative pedagogy helps students cultivate a nuanced discernment of their own experience. When it comes to learning about oppression, I argue, one without the other is ultimately ineffective to both understanding how oppression operates and to unlearning it.

Why Mindfulness Is Critical in Courses That Teach about Diversity

Courses that deal with oppression and diversity can greatly benefit from contemplative practices because they can help us unlearn the conditioned responses that uphold systems of oppression. Diversity classes are not just objective studies of content. They also teach self-reflective processes that invite students to examine how systems of oppression affect them and what their roles might be within those systems. Feminist and other diversity classrooms counter a one-dimensional privileging of cognition to highlight an "embodied reflexivity" in which participants learn to reflect on their own ideologies and experiences, question their ways of thinking, and imagine alternatives (Lather 1991, 48).

Contemplative practices enable students to cultivate emotional intelligence, learn to sit with difficult emotions, recognize deeply entrenched narratives they use to interpret the world, cultivate compassion for other people, and become more intentional about how they respond in any given moment. All of these abilities can transform dialogues about power, oppression, and privilege from intense reactionary debates into more relational, empathic, and reflective experiences. By integrating mindfulness into our social justice courses, we can help students learn how to navigate fraught situations in intentional, more compassionate ways. This ability is crucial not only in the academic social justice classroom but also in our broader society.

Oppression leaves its mark on our hearts, bodies, and spirits. Numerous writings by feminists, people of color, LGBT communities, colonized peoples, and people living in poverty have attested to the debilitating effects of oppression on people's very sense of self. It marks all of us, albeit in different ways, whether we are members of dominant groups or of marginalized groups. Indeed, intersectional feminist theory teaches us that while some people fit neatly in the category of "oppressor" or "oppressed," most of us hold identities across these different groups, so that we are at times marginalized and at other times privileged.

For those of us who are marginalized, the violence of oppression wounds and exhausts us. We expend a great deal of energy everyday enduring the microaggressions of oppression, while the macroaggressions may leave a powerfully traumatic mark on us. Oppression can also ooze into our very sense of self through the internalization of negative cultural messages about our group. The consequences of oppression include depression, anxiety, low self-esteem, and anger.

Oppression takes a different toll on those in the dominant groups. Though we do not suffer the same kinds of microaggressions and internalized oppression, we also do not get to live into our full humanity. While dominant groups certainly benefit from the privileges we receive, we are also disconnected from others by that very privilege. Many of my students experience a certain amount of dismay and pain when they realize that they accrue daily privileges at the expense of their classmates and community members in marginalized groups. Though some people, obviously, revel in their privilege, I believe that far more people would prefer to dismantle systems of oppression even when they benefit from them. They are often unaware of the deep and difficult work this will entail on their part, but many of my students want a more equitable world, at least theoretically.

The tricky part lies in the fact that we cannot deconstruct oppression on merely theoretical grounds. Of course, we have to engage in social transformation at the collective, societal, and institutional levels, but we also have to do it at the level of the individual. We have to get down and dirty with the hard work on ourselves and in our communities. Since oppression insinuates itself into our lived experiences and our very sense of selves, that is where some of the work lies. Anti-oppression pedagogy demands accountability for our own roles in systems of oppression, whatever those roles might be. But I find that students often feel at a loss about what to do with the intense feelings that arise or how to interrupt deeply entrenched patterns in themselves and others. Recognizing them is a first step, but I have long felt that an entire set of tools are missing from the tool belts we provide students.

Fortunately, mindfulness can help fill that gap by deepening our self-awareness on an embodied level. Rather than merely seeing patterns of oppression in the society around us or even in our external behaviors, we can begin to recognize *how* they have insinuated themselves into our selves, bodies, and spirits. We can learn to recognize the effects in our rapid heartbeat, our anger, our deep shame or sadness. We can start to recognize how we want to lash out as a defense mechanism that both protects us from external threats and gives us something to focus on besides our pain. While there is a time and place when such lashing out is a necessary survival mechanism, with deeper reflection we might find that that behavior does not serve us in every moment. Mindfulness allows us to be more intentional in our choices. In the remaining part of this chapter, I will outline some of the most critical benefits that mindfulness can bring to anti-oppression pedagogy.

The Ultimate in Applied Learning

Anti-oppression pedagogy centers around active and applied learning. Knowledge is not a static product to be absorbed by the student but rather a dynamic process in which teachers and student co-participate. The sum of what can be created in the collective process is often greater than anything that could have been produced by any one person. While there are, of course, fundamental concepts to be studied, anti-oppression pedagogy also focuses on the power dynamics of knowledge production: who has historically been excluded from that process, what gaps have resulted from those exclusions, and how understanding is altered when multiple voices are included.

Mindfulness is the penultimate form of applied learning, since it cannot be understood in the abstract. *It must be practiced.* The richness of the learning process lies in working with whatever arises, rather than from expecting prescribed or forgone conclusions. Brown University's Contemplative Studies Initiative calls this skill "critical first person inquiry" or the ability to experience something with an open mind and then step back and study the experience (Brown University 2014). This kind of engagement recognizes that learning is not merely intellectual and knowledge is not something "out there," removed from us. What mindfulness practices can bring to anti-oppression pedagogy is a more deeply *embodied* sense of this process. Just as feminist thought teaches students to analyze conventions long taken for granted, yoga, meditation, and other mindfulness practices invite students "to investigate what we assume to be true through a series of experiments, so that we may relinquish what we have been told and come to our own firsthand understanding about the nature of reality, the world, and ourselves" (Miller 2010, 23). When contemplative pedagogy is combined with feminist analysis, it offers the possibility of embodying wisdom.

Mindful learning, like anti-oppression pedagogy, teaches students an "appreciation of the conditional, or context-dependent, nature of the work and the value of uncertainty" (Langer 1997, 15). In social justice classrooms, students learn that generalizations need to be contextualized in the specificity of identity locations. For instance, though sexism and patriarchy absolutely exist, not all men have power over all women. Men of color, for instance, are marginalized in ways that White women are not and are often oppressed by White women. Mindful education encourages students to see knowledge as conditional and to examine how different perspectives offer different insights. Looking at something from a variety of perspectives not only helps students get a more well-rounded comprehension of the issue; it also helps them see that all perspectives are partial. Each has its place and each is incomplete.

Mindful learning also helps students learn to trust their own authority, because they get to test it out and examine how well a practice or theory works for them. As Langer (1997) suggests, when conditional and context-dependent learning is valued, it becomes more possible to generate alternatives, because there is a greater openness to possibility and a greater willingness to step off the beaten path.

Cultivating the Discernment to Interrupt Learned Storylines

Most contemplative practices enhance clear seeing and focus, while also enabling an ability to think on one's feet in the moment. They cultivate an ability to see things from multiple perspectives, something that is critical in anti-oppression courses. By developing compassion and empathy, they also strengthen mental and emotional health. These latter aspects of contemplative pedagogy are critical for anti-oppression classrooms, given the emotional and psychological toll oppression takes on everyone, most especially members of marginalized groups. His Holiness the Dalai Lama himself has stated that in "analytic meditation, one brings about inner change through systematic investigation and analysis. In this way we can properly use our human intelligence, our capacity for reason and analysis, to contribute to our happiness and satisfaction" (qtd. in Barbezat and Bush 2014, 84). The combination, I suggest, creates more empowering and sustainable tools for students to not only unlearn oppression but to cultivate more humane ways of relating to one another.

One of the key gifts of mindfulness is that it uncovers the mental chatter that is always present in our minds. While the exact content of that chatter differs from person to person, most of us believe our inner monologues to be "Truth" and, therefore, base our behaviors and actions on them. Mindfulness teaches us to *discern* the difference between our thoughts and our being. As Daniel J. Seigel writes in his book, *The Mindful Brain: Reflection and Attunement in the Cultivation of Well-Being*,

> Discernment is a form of disidentification from the activity of your own mind: as you become aware of sensations, images, feelings, and thoughts, you come to see these activities of the mind as waves on the surface of the mental sea.
>
> (2007, 19)

This process enables us to "disentangle" from "the chatter of the mind" by recognizing that we are bigger than our thoughts. Our thoughts and emotions are a part of us, but they are not the totality of us (Seigel 2007, 19). When we can recognize that distinction, we can bring a more analytical lens to the chatter in our minds, discern where it comes from, and make more intentional choices about how we want to be in the world. This discernment helps prevent practitioners from drowning in the sea of their emotions.

This skill becomes particularly important for interrupting systems of oppression because much of our chatter is shaped by learned ideologies. Beliefs about ourselves and others are socially produced, as are the power hierarchies that result from them. For most students, these ideologies are so normalized that they just take them for granted. Even those who are from marginalized groups, while they may recognize their oppression, may nevertheless lack the awareness to accurately name what is happening. Mindfulness can help students learn to minimize the damaging effects of oppressive ideologies on their sense of self and learn to interrupt the systems at both individual and structural levels. Similarly, students who are members of dominant groups in society are taught not to see the privileges they receive. Often they have learned a sense of superiority and entitlement that remains invisible to them. This is how systems of oppression work: when privileged students come to our classes unaware of the benefits they receive that are denied those of marginalized groups, that is the oppressive system working the way it is designed to work. Intersectional feminism reveals this process to be even more complicated, since many of us receive benefits in some ways and are oppressed in others, which manifests in similarly complex dynamics in the classroom.

Our job as teachers is to help our students develop an awareness of this process so that they can learn to interrupt the system. Most anti-oppression teachers make this the central tenet of our classes. We generally do a good job of revealing inequitable power dynamics throughout society and the ideologies that fuel them. But these learned ideologies operate at more than merely an intellectual level, so analytical awareness is not enough. Oppressive ideologies insinuate themselves into our very selves, which means that they inevitably inform that mental chatter I mentioned earlier. While many writers discuss the kinds of life experiences that inform our mental narratives, it stands to reason that some of those narratives are shaped by the oppressive ideologies that so deeply influence society and the construction of identity. Women's Studies critics, for instance, have long noted that ideologies of beauty and the devaluation of women have detrimental effect on women. Women's Studies courses help students develop media literacy and understand the effects of those portrayals on women's self-esteem and body image. This is a critical step in the unlearning process. But these ideologies so deeply inform many women's internal self-talk. It takes the capacity to recognize that negative mental chatter and the skills to interrupt it if we are to truly unearth the seeds of oppression. That means, for most of us, reworking our very wiring.

The good news is that mindfulness can help us do just that. Leading contemplative neuroscientist Dr. Richard Davidson, the William James and Vilas Professor of Psychology and Psychiatry at the University of Wisconsin-Madison, has used developments in MRI technology to measure the effects of meditation on the brain. His work reveals that, unlike previously thought, the adult brain actually has a great deal of plasticity, which means that deep cognitive changes can still occur throughout adulthood (Davidson and Begley 2012; *Free the Mind* 2012). While much of this research focuses on conditions such as PTSD and depression, on the one hand, or compassion and empathy, on the other, it reveals that deeply ingrained pathways that have become automatic can, indeed, be interrupted. They can be reworked not just on a one-time basis but in more sustainable ways. This plasticity could prove valuable in social justice classes, since oppressive ideologies that inform practices and behaviors are learned and deeply ingrained. If the storylines we repeatedly narrate to ourselves are laced with oppressive ideologies—and I argue that they inevitably are—then the ability to pause those storylines and even rewrite them can go a long way toward creating a more just world. Thus, while Davidson and his colleagues do not necessarily apply their findings about adult neuroplasticity to issues of oppression, I think they offer profound possibilities for our work as social justice teachers. This work reveals that we can choose to feed the part of ourselves that can create more empowering worlds—such as our compassion and kindness—by engaging in regular mindfulness practice. Let me reiterate here that I am *not* saying that we can "choose not to be affected by oppression." That, of course, is not possible. But we can claim some degree of agency about how deeply oppression erodes our sense of self and rework how our self relates to others. When combined with structural change, these steps can take us a long way toward creating a more just world.

Deepening Self-Reflection

Feminist and anti-oppression pedagogy mark self-reflection as a central ingredient for a transformational learning process. In this context, self-reflection usually means examining our own positionality in society, our role(s) in power systems, and an evaluation of how issues affect our personal lives. It involves questioning how we both uphold and can interrupt power systems. The reflection that contemplative pedagogy allows is an internal one that explores an individual's emotional, physiological, *and* cognitive responses. As such, it provides an added dimension to the analytical and structural analysis emphasized in anti-oppression pedagogy. If students are to really reflect on their roles in systems of oppression, they need to cultivate the tools for recognizing and understanding their internal and external reactions to that growing awareness. Like holding a camera, our positionality frames what we can and cannot immediately see. The critical self-reflection tools cultivated in mindfulness, combined with a feminist analytical understanding, helps us see that who we are shapes what we know, but it also helps us expand the lens of what we can see. This reflexivity helps students examine how their beliefs, values, and emotions affect them, enabling students "to critically analyze dominant belief systems, recognize how others have imposed limiting beliefs on them, and liberate themselves from those negative views" (Rendón 2014, 102).

I argue that mindfulness is a critical and often missing component in this self-reflection. Mindfulness invites us to reflect not only on what we are thinking but also on what we are feeling. By teaching practitioners to be more fully present in the moment, they become much more familiar with their personal responses, feelings, and thoughts. Mindfulness practices take a variety of forms, all of which develop the introspection through which we recognize, understand, and befriend our patterns. In doing so, we learn a great deal about ourselves. We become familiar with how we respond to various matters, how those responses feel in our bodies, and how they tend to manifest in our external behaviors. Just as anti-oppression pedagogy teaches how to recognize patterns in society, mindfulness teaches us how to recognize patterns in ourselves, including the mental tapes that play and the embodied effects they have. We begin to see not only what happens in our intellects but also how it rests in our bodies: what triggers our fears, resentments, and insecurities. We begin to see how we respond to those emotions: how they manifest in our bodies (rapid heartbeat, cold sweats, panic) and how we typically react to them (do we shut down or lash out?).

Mindful learning does not assume that students will take things for granted but instead invites them to engage in experiential inquiry. Contemplative practices help students cultivate the *Witness*, which allows one to be fully in an experience and simultaneously bigger than it. Rather than being entirely consumed by an experience, students are invited to have an experience and then step back and reflect upon it. As such, mindfulness takes the self-reflection that is at the heart of feminist pedagogy a step deeper. Rather than taking a teacher's word for it, students are expected to try it themselves and see what happens.

Much like feminism requires us to reflect on our own process and consider what did and did not work, mindfulness teaches us to work with whatever arises for us. There is not an ideal goal; instead, whatever resistance, avoidance, joy, or thoughts, or preoccupations arise as we meditate is precisely what we need to reflect upon. They lead us to the internal work we need to do. The Witness teaches us to accept our emotions, be with them in the present but also to be bigger than they are. It creates a distance between our basic selves and whatever we are feeling in the moment. This distance is not the same as disassociation, because we are still fully feeling our responses, but we also recognize that they *need not consume us* because they are only *a part of us.*

This mindful embodied learning is a crucial component to anti-oppression pedagogy because it teaches us how to meet our responses with clarity and compassion. Only then can we begin to unlearn these deeply embedded responses. Creating a more just society requires institutional and collective change, but it also requires the individual work of unlearning the messages internalized in an oppressive society and relearning more compassionate ways of being with ourselves and others. That work cannot be done at a merely analytical level. It MUST be done at the level of our hearts, bodies, *and* our minds.

Create a Gap between Reaction and Response

One of my yoga teachers calls this tool the "holy pause." In that pause, students can learn to accept their reactions—whatever they may be—and then thoughtfully decide how and whether to engage them. Those of us who teach about diversity issues have likely had the experience of students blurting out a statement that, intentionally or not, reinforces racism, sexism, homophobia, or some other "ism." These outbursts occur because students have learned oppressive messages from society and may not recognize how deeply those messages shape their ways of thinking. Even if they do recognize the deep ideologies, they likely will not be able to unlearn those heavily reinforced messages overnight. Indeed, given how effectively systems of oppression work, I think we should be surprised if these moments do not occur in our classroom, rather than discouraged when they do.

When these outbursts happen, the other students in the room tend to "react" back. Students might get defensive and lash out; they might become hurt and shut down; they might look to the teacher to "interrupt the moment." The level of trust and community that has been established in the class will shape how effectively the other students handle the situation. The teacher is in the position of turning the situation into a "teachable moment" that validates the responses of the students who are angry and hurt but also reaches the student who blurted the statement out. I see these kinds of situations as key opportunities for mindfulness to enhance anti-oppression pedagogy, because these moments in our classrooms also occur in our broader communities—the former is a microcosm of the latter. Helping students learn how to navigate these moments in successful ways in the classroom provides them with invaluable tools they can continue to utilize throughout their life.

Mindfulness lets us become very self-aware of what is arising for us and allows us the time to: 1. accept what we are feeling; 2. discern the situation with some clarity; and 3. determine more intentionally how we want to respond. These are crucial steps in developing more compassionate and effective social change efforts that are strategic rather than reactionary. Mindfulness creates an internal self-reflection that enables a pause between our gut reactions and our external responses. In other words, as we recognize our reactions, we also become more capable of deciding more intentionally how we might want to respond. While our automatic responses have their place and are sometimes necessary survival mechanisms, they do not always serve us. Mindfulness can help us more effectively choose what will be helpful to us and to the situation in any given moment.

Understanding the Responses of Others

When we befriend and understand our own responses, we have a better framework for understanding those of others. When mindful awareness is situated within a feminist analysis of sociopolitical power dynamics, we have a more comprehensive and sensitive way to understand WHY people respond the way they do. We can see their reactions as *the inevitable by-products of living in an oppressive society*. This understanding does not mean we excuse people's hurtful behaviors, but it does help us learn to see how systems of oppression work through and on individuals.

This brings a couple different layers of insight into the classroom. It can prevent the easy dismissal of the reactions from oppressed groups because their classmates can situate their responses within histories of oppression. For instance, women are often accused of "overreacting" to a particular sexist comment, while people of color are often accused of being too sensitive if they get angry at a comment that they experience as racist. To the classmate who just said it, it seems like a simple comment that is being blown out of proportion, so they blame the victim and reduce the significance of the comment. That situation can be reframed if we as teachers help students understand that for the member of the marginalized group, this is the thousandth time such a microaggression has occurred, so it acts like pouring lemon juice on an open wound which never gets the chance to heal because it keeps getting poked.

For the member of the marginalized group, it can be helpful to understand that their classmate is speaking from years of accumulated acculturation into systems of oppression. That does not excuse their behavior, but it does help situate it. This realization can be particularly helpful when the microaggression comes from a person they considered their ally. Perhaps this person is well-intentioned and has done a great deal of work building trust and trying to unlearn oppression. Nevertheless, they will likely reproduce systems of oppression at some point, albeit unwittingly. Depending on the level of violence of this infraction, the marginalized person might need to sever relationships with the person. But it might also be possible to recognize that the individual is a product of his/her/zir culture and that his/her/zir unlearning process is likely a lifelong process that will involve a great many mistakes. Rather than ignoring the mistake on one hand or writing them off on the other, mindfulness offers another option: holding each other accountable and having a hard conversation about why the microaggression was hurtful.

We cannot hope to have our allies unlearn their own privilege if we do not work on unlearning ours. We must start with ourselves, do our own work (whatever it is), before we can expect others to do their work. At the same time, however, I do not think it is helpful to rank oppressions. Instead, we all need to do the work simultaneously. We can learn to have more compassion for our allies who slip and fall when we recognize the myriad of ways we slip and fall, participating in microaggressions even when we strive not to do so. As a White, Western, middle-class woman, there are all sorts of ways I participate in oppression, even when I struggle daily to unlearn and interrupt my privilege. As a queer woman, I am also marginalized in many ways. Recognizing my power, privilege, and marginalization allows me to do my work and to have more compassion for others who are doing theirs. When I am mindful of the moments when I inadvertently uphold oppression, I have more compassion for those people who inadvertently marginalize me. That does not mean I do not get angry, challenge them, or hold them accountable. But it does prevent me from demonizing them, because I recognize that we are all in this together. This context helps us relate to people in more compassionate ways and helps us develop responses that neither oversimplify nor demonize the reactions of others.

Mindfulness, then, helps us strengthen our capacity for compassion. Davidson's now famous studies with Buddhist monks reveal that even when exposed to extremely disturbing stimuli, they had the ability to activate the parts of their brain responsible for compassion and empathy (Davidson 2012). Further studies by Davidson and his team indicate that compassion meditation in particular can regulate emotions and intentionally stimulate the parts of our brain responsible for kindness and compassion. Studies have shown that consistency of practice is more important than length of practice, which means that even a daily practice of ten to twenty minutes can provide positive results. (Moore et al. 2012; Ricard 2006).

One central component to mindfulness is a nonjudgmental acceptance of what is. Practitioners learn to accept their reactions, whatever they may be, as a first step toward befriending ourselves. In the context of anti-oppression pedagogy, it is important to note that *accepting our responses is not the same thing as accepting oppression*. Instead, it is a way of validating our own experiences and feelings, rather than perpetuating the violence of oppression by condemning our own reactions. Mindfulness enables us to gradually understand and befriend our experiences, which can actually serve as a tool to counter oppression. We can learn to meet ourselves with compassion, which can help heal the deep wounds of oppression. When we can meet ourselves with deep kindness and compassion, we can also more fully empathize with others, which counters the separation and Othering that uphold oppressive systems.

Tips for Integrating Mindfulness into Social Justice Courses

Since this book is focused on the praxis of integrating mindfulness into anti-oppression pedagogy, each chapter will include practical tips for doing so. In this chapter, I will address some of the responses one can expect when beginning this process of integration.

1. Colleagues and Students May Meet These Steps with Skepticism

Our colleagues in more traditional disciplines will likely scoff at mindfulness as a pedagogical tool. Its growing popularity in the West, with the scientific evidence that attests to its benefits, is certainly granting it increasing credibility. Still, we may find we need to "justify" or validate our use of it in our classroom.

Similar doubts may come from social justice colleagues and students, who see it as detracting from the "real" social justice work. They may squirm impatiently as we lead a meditation or a breath exercise, wishing we would get to the "more important" social analysis. Be prepared to sit with these reactions, explain what mindfulness offers social justice work, and invite them to give it a try.

2. Social Justice Colleagues May Dismiss Mindfulness Practices as a Way of "Protecting" Students From Doing the Hard Work of Facing Their Own Racism, Sexism, Classism, or Homophobia

As self-reflective teachers and mindfulness practitioners, it is important to carefully consider these concerns. Ask ourselves honestly if mindfulness practices are deflecting or deepening this work. Like any pedagogical tool, they can be used in a variety of ways, some of which are counter-productive to social justice goals.

However, as we will see throughout this book, when used in particular ways, mindfulness techniques can help students and teachers do the work of unlearning oppression in deeper, more embodied, ways. They also enhance emotional intelligence and resilience for our students, which are critical benefits for supporting them in continuing the work of unlearning oppression long after the end of a semester's class or even a four-year-degree.

3. The Language of Acceptance and Compassion that Informs Mindfulness Will Be Seen by Some Social Justice Colleagues as "Watering Down" the Importance of "Fighting" against Systematic Violence

I have had more than one colleague express hesitance that mindfulness will simply "coddle" privileged students and dismiss the pain and anger of marginalized students. These are legitimate concerns that anyone utilizing contemplative practices in the classroom needs to consider. However, I would argue that, when done properly, it does precisely the opposite. As Musial notes, "caring is not about coddling students, it is about being completely present with individuals" and meeting them where they are (2012, 221). I was initially disheartened when I heard that response from my social justice colleagues, but I have come to accept that we may simply disagree about the best ways to reach a common goal. I believe that mindfulness provides a deeply needed seed for sustainability in our efforts toward social change. Mindfulness offers the tools for students to learn to support themselves and one another in the experience of any emotion—anger, frustration, sadness, guilt, fear—and can help them stay present together as they work through those complex discussions in the classroom.

Emphasizing compassion and peace does not preclude battling oppression or dismantling systems. The language of compassion and peace I use here comes from socially engaged mindfulness activists from a variety of traditions, including the Vietnamese Buddhist monk Thich Nhat Hanh, the Tibetan leader His Holiness the Dalai Lama, the nonviolent philosophy of Mohatma Gandhi, the feminism of bell hooks and Audre Lorde, along with centuries of yogi and meditation scholars, many of whom addressed the inequalities of society. Drawing on both feminist pedagogy scholars and yoga philosophy, Jennifer Musial calls it a "heart-centered" pedagogy (2012, 215). Indeed, I arrived at this approach because it was a more sustainable for me. After years of teaching Women's Studies courses in the academy, I found the approach of "fighting" oppression without the complementary ingredient of compassion and healing left me feeling like I was doing more violence to myself and others—constantly challenging without having the capacity to rebuild more equitable and socially just alternatives. I see social justice, mindfulness, and anti-oppression pedagogy as supporting each other as we seek to create empowering alternatives and support our students in doing this work for the rest of their lives.

4. Talking About Oppression May Be Seen as Disturbing the "Peace" of Mindfulness Spaces

Some mindfulness colleagues may express frustration that we are bringing critique and social issues into the supposedly "peaceful" realm of meditation and yoga. They might bristle at being challenged on their privilege. This accusation is nothing new for those of us who do this work. What is unique about this context is that too often these practices are seen as "escapes" from life that should remain removed from critical analysis. While I do believe that there are some ways of being that require modes of inquiry other than intellectual critique, I also believe that mindfulness spaces need to address social justice concerns if they are truly to live up to their potential. As Rendón writes, "When all we do is focus our self-awareness without a concomitant emphasis on social consciousness and action, what remains is a self-serving, individual blindness to world needs" (2014, 9). For instance, those of us who discuss racism, sexism, or homophobia in yoga studios are often accused of being disruptive, as though these issues are not already in those spaces and too often are not named. The claim that the yoga studio is people's "escape" from the harsh realities of life does not hold when U.S. yoga studios are so predominantly White, heteronormative, and middle- to-upper class. More and more activists, including the Yoga and Body Image Coalition, an organization in which I am member, are raising these conversations in order to make those spaces more inclusive and more informed. The integration of mindfulness and social justice is a dialectical and mutually transformative process.

5. Some Students Will Dislike Some of the Practices

No mindfulness practice is a silver bullet that will meet all the needs of every student. We should be skeptical of anything that claims otherwise. It is helpful to prepare students ahead of time that some practices will resonate with them more than others and to create spaces to discuss what did and did not work for students after each practice. That also means integrating a range of practices so that hopefully something will resonate with each student. Alternatively, a class might focus on one or two particular practices so as to develop depth and consistency throughout the semester. In the latter case, students should be informed of that expectation at the very beginning of the semester, in time for them to drop the class if they are unable to participate in the practices for any reason. It is also incumbent on the professor to work with students to make the practices accessible for everyone if they are required for the class; that may mean offering alternatives for some students.

6. The Pressure to Place Content over Process in Limited Class Time

This is a tricky one, often informed by our own internalized paradigms as teachers that the content is actually more important than this "out-of-the-box" mindfulness practice. Our students and colleagues cannot be expected to accept the value of these practices if we doubt them ourselves (believing in their value is not the same thing as suggesting that they are silver-bullet, universal fixes). So we must try to resist the urge to cut mindfulness practices in favor of devoting more class time to content. (I myself have been guilty of doing this, but when I do, the mindfulness practices do not have their desired effect.)

The best way of countering the content-over-practice paradigm is to clearly articulate the value of the process itself. Explain why and how you are using mindfulness in the classroom and why it brings such valuable contributions to social justice work. Help students see that often, the "resistance" that arises in doing the practices is precisely the material we need to work with, just as the "resistance" that arises in working against power and privilege often highlights the exact power dynamics we are trying to dismantle. The teacher can facilitate reflective discussions about the process itself, thereby modeling the experiential process.

Unlearning oppression in the college classroom usually produces some intense discussions, and I believe that teachers have an ethical responsibility to prepare students for the affective rawness that can emerge through this kind of pedagogy and to provide them with tools to handle it. Class discussions can flow more effectively if participants are able to recognize, understand, and be accountable for their own reactions. Contemplative practices offer the tools to do just that. When learned and practiced effectively, mindfulness also offers more compassionate alternatives to the ways that people often engage the challenging conversations about diversity. As such, I believe they are a necessary addition to diversity classrooms. Neither anti-oppression pedagogy nor contemplative education are enough on their own, but their integration can provide a powerful recipe for enabling social transformation through the learning—and unlearning—process.

Mindfulness Practices

Each chapter will include at least one specific mindfulness practice related. This first one focuses on developing more general mindful awareness, as we first need that before we can move it into the more complicated and fraught context of anti-oppression work.

Mindfulness Check-In

Read the directions over first before starting so that you do not have to interrupt your inward focus to read. If it would make it easier for you to have a guided meditation, you can record yourself reading the directions or use the MP3 of this meditation on my web site. Have a notebook and pen handy for the follow-up reflection activity.

Find a quiet space where you can sit with minimal distraction for 5–7 minutes. Dim the lights, light a candle (or use a battery operated one if candles are not allowed), turn off the music, silence your cell phone, and minimize any other noises.

Take a good seat. You might want to sit up on some blankets or a cushion so that your pelvis tilts slightly forward and your knees angle down a bit. Alternatively, you can sit on a chair, making sure your feet are flat on the ground and only your lower spine is resting against the back of the chair. Your palms can be open or closed, resting gently on your upper thighs or knees.

Take a few deep breaths. Feel the breath move all the way through your lungs and into your belly as you inhale. Exhale from your belly through your lungs and out your mouth. As you breathe three or four times, imagine your breath wiping away all the thoughts of the day and bringing your attention to the here and now.

Now let your breath return to normal.

Once you feel fairly present, turn your attention inward. What are you feeling right now? Can you detect the emotions that are swirling through you? Do you notice worry? Excitement? Anger? Joy? Fear?

Where do you notice the emotions in your body? Do they rest in your heart? Your head? Tension in your shoulders? A fluttering in your belly? See if you can find them in your body. Do they have color or texture? Are they cool and blue or fiery and rough?

Try to familiarize yourself with your emotions and how your body holds them. Most importantly, try not to judge them. You are allowed to feel whatever you feel. At this point, we are just trying to recognize them. We'll work more with them later.

Try not to get caught up in the storyline of thoughts. Just notice the thoughts and let them go, like a leaf floating by on a river. Take note of the emotion behind the thought and then let it go.

As we move toward the close of our meditation, take 4–5 deep, cleansing breaths. With each breath, gradually move your attention back outward, maybe gently inviting some movement back into your fingers and toes. When you are ready, open your eyes.

Journal Reflection

Allow yourself to sit quietly for a moment, digesting your experience and returning to the outer world. Then journal for a few minutes to record your experience. What did you notice about your emotions: color, texture, location. If none of that stood out to you and your observations were to merely name the emotions, that's OK, too. Jot that down.

Where do you think some of these emotions come from? Here it is OK for you to follow your thoughts. Unlike in meditation, where we want to stay with the visceral emotions, in your journal, it would be helpful for you to discern where some of the emotions come from. For instance, if you noticed a solid knot in your belly during your meditation, in your journal, you might explore what is causing that feeling.

Simple Practices to Cultivate Mindfulness

1. Declare the classroom a "Cell phone–free space." Students are not to check their cell phones during the class. While many faculty members have this rule anyway, the purpose here is to prevent distractions and multitasking that can impede full presence.

2. Pause and breathe in between each comment. Rather than the usual non-stop flow of a class discussion, implement a "pause and breathe" pattern. Students

are to listen to the speaker, then turn inward, breathe, and reflect on what the person said. Only then can the hands go up for the next comment.

3. Journal: add a journaling piece to the previous step. Have students jot down a few notes about their initial reactions to whatever was just said. The idea here is not for them to write down thoughts, but rather felt sense: the emotions that arise, what is happening in their body, their gut reactions.

References

Allen, Ricky Lee. "The Race Problem in the Critical Pedagogy Community." In *Reinventing Critical Pedagogy*, edited by César Augusto Rossatto, Ricky Lee Allen, and Marc Pruyn, 3–20. New York: Rowman & Littlefield, 2006.

Anti-Racist Pedagogy Across the Curriculum (ARPAC). Workshop. Maple Grove, MN, August 4–8, 2014.

Awbrey, Susan M. and Diane Dana. *Integrative Learning and Action: A Call to Wholeness.* New York: Peter Lang, 2006.

Barbezat, Daniel P. and Mirabai Bush. *Contemplative Practices in Higher Education: Powerful Methods to Transform Teaching and Learning.* San Francisco, CA: Jossey-Bass, 2014.

Blakeney, Aida M. "Antiracist Pedagogy: Definition, Theory, and Professional Development." *Journal of Curriculum and Pedagogy* 2, no.1 (2005): 119–132.

Boal, Augusto. *Theatre of the Oppressed.* Translated by Charles A. McBride. New York: Theatre Communications Group, 1993.

Bonilla-Silva, Eduardo and David G. Embrick. "Racism Without Racists: 'Killing Me Softly' with Color Blindness." In *Reinventing Critical Pedagogy*, edited by César Augusto Rossatto, Ricky Lee Allen, and Marc Pruyn, 21–34. New York: Rowman & Littlefield, 2006.

Bordo, Susan. "The Pedagogy of Shame." In *Feminisms and Pedagogies of Everyday Life*, edited by Carmen Luke, 225–241. Albany: State University of New York Press, 1996.

Britzman, Deborah. "Is There a Queer Pedagogy? Or, Stop Reading Straight." *Educational Theory* 45, no. 2 (June 1995): 151–165.

Brown-Jeffy, Shelly and Jewell E. Cooper. "Toward a Conceptual Framework of Culturally Relevant Pedagogy: On Overview of the Conceptual and Theoretical Literature." *Teacher Education Quarterly* 38, no. 1 (Winter 2011): 65–84.

Brown University Contemplative Studies Initiative. "Contemplative Studies Initiative." Accessed November 24, 2014, www.brown.edu/academics/contemplative-studies/.

Collins, Patricia Hill. *Black Feminist Thought: Knowledge, Consciousness, and the Politics of Empowerment*, 2nd ed. New York: Routledge, 2000.

Crenshaw, Kimberle. "Mapping the Margins: Intersectionality, Identity Politics, and Violence Against Women of Color." *Stanford Law Review* 43, no. 6 (July 1991): 1241–1299.

Darder, Antonia, Marta Baltodano, and Rodolfo D. Torres. "Critical Pedagogy: An Introduction." In *The Critical Pedagogy Reader*, edited by Antonia Darder, Marta Baltodano, and Rodolfo D. Torres, 1–23. New York: RoutledgeFalmer, 2003.

Davidson, Richard J. "Investigating Healthy Minds." *On Being* with Krista Tippett, American Public Media. June 14, 2012, www.onbeing.org/program/investigating-healthy-minds-richard-davidson/251.

———— with Sharon Begley. *The Emotional Life of Your Brain: How Its Unique Patterns Affect the Way You Think, Feel, and Live—and How You Can Change Them*. New York: Hudson Street Press, 2012.

Davis, Daphne M. and Jeffrey A. Hayes. "What are the Benefits of Mindfulness?" *APA Office of CE in Psychology* 43, no. 7 (July/August 2012): 64. www.apa.org/monitor/2012/07–08/ce-corner.aspx.

Foucault, Michel. *Power/Knowledge: Selected Interviews and Other Writings, 1972– 1977*. New York: Vintage, 1980.

Free the Mind: Can You Rewire the Brain Just by Breathing? Directed by Phie Ambo. Danish Documentary, 2012.

Freire, Paulo. *Pedagogy of the Oppressed*. New York: Herder and Herder, 1970.

Emerson, David and Elizabeth Hopper. *Overcoming Trauma Through Yoga: Reclaiming Your Body*. Berkeley, CA: North Atlantic Books, 2011.

Garland-Thomson, Rosemary. "Feminist Disability Studies." *Signs* 20, no. 2 (2005): 1557–1587.

Giroux, Henry. "Critical Theory and Educational Practice." In *The Critical Pedagogy Reader*, edited by Antonia Darder, Marta Boltodano, and Rodolfo D. Torres, 27–56. New York: RoutledgeFalmer, 2003a.

————. "Education Incorporated?" In *The Critical Pedagogy Reader*, edited by Antonia Darder, Marta Boltodano, and Rodolfo D. Torres, 119–125. New York: Routledge-Falmer, 2003b.

Goleman, Daniel. *Emotional Intelligence: Why It Can Matter More Than IQ*. New York: Bantam Books, 1994.

Gore, Jennifer. "What Can We Do for You! What *Can* 'We' Do for 'You'? Struggling Over Empowerment in Critical and Feminist Pedagogy." In *Feminism and Critical Pedagogy*, edited by Carmen Luke and Jennifer Gore, 54–73. New York: Routledge, 1992.

Gramsci, Antonio. *Selections from the Prison Notebooks*. New York: International, 1971.

Halberstam, Judith. "Reflections on Queer Studies and Queer Pedagogy." *Journal of Homosexuality* 45, no. 2–4 (2003): 361–364.

Haraway, Donna. "Situated Knowledges: The Science Question in Feminism and Privilege of Partial Perspective." *Feminist Studies* 14, no. 3 (Autumn 1988): 575–599.

Harding, Sandra. *Feminist Standpoint Theory Reader: Intellectual and Political Controversies*. New York: Routledge, 2003.

hooks, bell. *Teaching Critical Thinking: Practical Wisdom*. New York: Routledge, 2010.

————. *Teaching to Transgress: Education as the Practice of Freedom*. New York: Routledge, 1994.

————. *Feminist Theory: From Margin to Center*. Boston, MA: South End Press, 1984.

Kumashiro, Kevin. *Troubling Education: Queer Activism and Antioppressive Pedagogy*. New York: RoutledgeFalmer, 2002.

Langer, Ellen J. *The Power of Mindful Learning*. Cambridge, MA: Da Capo Press, Perseus Books, 1997.

Lather, Patti. *Getting Smart: Feminist Research and Pedagogy With/In the Postmodern*. New York: Routledge, 1991.

Luhmann, Susan. Queering/Querying Pedagogy? Or, Pedagogy Is a Pretty Queer Thing. In *Queer Theory in Education*, edited by William Pinar, 120–131. New York: Routledge, 1998.

Luke, Carmen. "Feminist Politics in Radical Pedagogy." In *Feminisms and Critical Pedagogy*, edited by Carmen Luke and Jennifer Gore, 25–53. New York: Routledge, 1992.

———— and Jennifer Gore. "An Introduction." In *Feminisms and Critical Pedagogy*, edited by Carmen Luke and Jennifer Gore, 1–14. New York: Routledge, 1992.

Miller, Richard. *Yoga Nidra: A Meditative Practice for Deep Relaxation and Healing*. Boulder, CO: Sounds True, 2010.

Miller, Ron. *What are Schools for? Holistic Education in American Culture*. Brandon, VT: Holistic Education, 1997.

Moore, Adam, Thomas Gruber, Jennifer Derose, and Peter Malinowski. "Regular, Brief Mindfulness Meditation Improves Electrophysiological Markers of Attentional Control." *Frontiers in Human Neuroscience* 6, no. 18 (2012), www.ncbi.nlm.nih.gov/pmc/articles/PMC3277272/.

Musial, Jennifer. "Engaged Pedagogy in the Feminist Classroom and Yoga Studio." *Feminist Teacher* 21, no. 3 (2012): 212–228.

Nepo, Mark. Foreword. In *The Heart of Higher Education: A Call to Renewal, Transforming the Academy Through Collegial Conversations*, edited by Parker J. Palmer and Arthur Zajonc, v–xvii. San Francisco, CA: Jossey-Bass, 2010.

Palmer, Parker J. and Arthur Zajonc, *The Heart of Higher Education: A Call to Renewal, Transforming the Academy Through Collegial Conversations*. San Francisco, CA: Jossey-Bass, 2010.

Rendón, Laura I. *Sentipensante (Sensing/Thinking) Pedagogy: Educating for Wholeness, Social Justice, and Liberation*. Foreword Mark Nepo. Sterling, VA: Stylus, 2014.

Ricard, Matthieu. *Happiness: A Guide to Developing Life's Most Important Skill*. Translated by Jesse Browner. New York: Little, Brown, 2006.

Rilke, Rainer Maria. *Letters to a Young Poet*. New York: Norton, 1993.

Shapiro, Shauna L., Kirk Warren Brown, and John A. Astin. *Toward the Integration of Meditation into Higher Education: A Review of Research*, edited by Maia Duerr. Northampton, MA: The Center for Contemplative Mind in Society, 2008.

————. "Toward the Integration of Meditation into Higher Education: A Review of Research Evidence." *Teachers College Record* 113, no. 3 (2011): 493–528.

Siegel, Daniel J. "The Science of Mindfulness." Accessed November 24, 2014, www.mindful.org/the-science/medicine/the-science-of-mindfulness.

————. *The Mindful Brain: Reflection and Attunement in the Cultivation of Well-Being*. New York: W.W. Norton, 2007.

Van Der Kolk, Bessel. "Restoring the Body: Yoga, EMDR, and Treating Trauma." *On Being* with Krista Tippett, American Public Media. October 30, 2014. www.onbeing.org/program/restoring-the-body-bessel-van-der-kolk-on-yoga-emdr-and-treating-trauma/5801#.VHY27VxjRBU.

Wadlinger, Heather A. and Derek M. Isaacowitz. "Fixing Our Focus: Training Attention to Regulate Emotion." *Personality and Social Psychology Review* 15, no. 1 (2011): 75–102.

Wagner, Anne E. "Unsettling the Academy: Working through the Challenges of Anti-Racist Pedagogy." *Race, Ethnicity, and Education* 8, no. 3 (September 2005): 261–275.

Weller, Kathleen. "Freire and a Feminist Pedagogy of Difference." *Harvard Educational Review* 61, no. 4 (Winter 1991): 449–475.

Wilcox, Hui Niu. "Embodied Ways of Knowing, Pedagogies, and Social Justice: Inclusive Science and Beyond." *NWSA Journal* 21, no. 2 (Summer 2009): 104–120.

Williams, Mark and Danny Penman. *Mindfulness: An Eight-Week Plan for Finding Peace in a Frantic World*. Foreword by Job Kabat-Zinn. New York: Rodale Books, 2011.

Winans, Amy E. Queering Pedagogy in the English Classroom: Engaging the Places Where Thinking Stops. *Pedagogy* 6, no. 1 (Winter 2006): 103–122.

2

BRINGING THE BODY BACK IN

You can't dominate a people without separating them from each other and from themselves. The more people get plugged back into their bodies, each other, the more impossible [it] will be for us to be dominated and occupied. That is the work right now.
—Eve Ensler (2013)

Mindful education not only echoes many of the principles of anti-oppression pedagogy, it also deepens them by bringing an embodied layer into the learning process. More precisely, it highlights the embodied layer that is always present for us but that often remains buried deep below our thinking mind. The legacy of the Western mind/body dualism places much greater emphasis on the intellect than on most other aspects of our being. As we saw in Chapter 1, trends toward holistic learning call for a more well-rounded and inclusive education (Brown University 2011; Palmer and Zajonc with Scribner 2010; Shapiro, Brown and Astin 2008). As important as these calls are, they still tend to refer to student lives inside and outside the classroom, rather than to workings of power and ideology inside and outside the individual and between the individual and the collective. While much education seeks to be transformative, social justice courses, in particular, urge participants to "walk the talk," which means that our belief systems inform our choices. We also teach students how to collectively organize, so that they learn how groups and individuals make change in their communities. Mindful anti-oppression pedagogy posits that there is yet another layer of change that is necessary: one that is embodied and that requires learning to turn within in order to effectively transform both ourselves and the larger collective.

Reclaiming embodiment is critical for well-being, resilience, and the ability to make healthy and informed choices in life. Resilience, in the words of yoga teacher and therapist Hala Khouri, means "knowing that we're going to be OK even if our circumstances aren't perfect.... Resilience is falling and keeping your breath while you fall" (personal communication, November 14, 2014). The reclamation of embodiment is even more critical in social justice contexts because oppression is held in our bodies, our hearts, our psyches, our spirits, *and* our minds. As the epigraph to this chapter from feminist Eve Ensler (2013) notes, Othering requires dehumanization, which entails disconnecting ourselves from our embodied experience. Once that step is accomplished, it is much easier to do violence to people, who then often need to remain disassociated from their bodies in order to survive the trauma of that violence. Part of the work toward social justice, then, *requires* a re-connection to ourselves and to others, so that our profound interdependence is both revealed and treasured.

If we only ask students to learn about oppression at a conceptual level, then we are missing two-thirds of the journey. Whether we are a member of a marginalized group, a member of a dominant group, or (more likely) both, the ideologies and power dynamics that uphold systems of oppression are embedded in our very being. Before we can unlearn them, we have to unearth them, but, like an invasive weed, their roots are strong and stubborn. Addressing this process at the layer of the intellect is a critical step, but we need to dig much deeper to dismantle oppressive messages that lie deep within us. Do we teach students how to understand what they are experiencing? Do we teach them to discern why they might be having particular reactions and why other people, with different identities, might have different ones? Do we give students adequate language for understanding their responses, both intellectually and in an embodied way? Do we give them tools for skillfully processing and sitting with those reactions? I do not think we can effectively unlearn oppression if we do not engage this first two-thirds of the journey, and I certainly do not think that we can dismantle systems of oppression without engaging it. It is the *process of unlearning* that will enable new ways of being, and both stages of that—the unlearning and the creation of new, liberatory possibilities—are *embodied* processes. This chapter will first define embodiment, then briefly situate this discussion within feminist theories of body knowledge and cultural disembodiment. The latter part of the chapter will explore the value of embodied learning for a mindful anti-oppression pedagogy.

Revealing Embodiment in Our Classrooms

First, let us explore a scenario that highlights how these dynamics might play out in our classroom. Like all the scenarios included in this book, this one is a composite of numerous class discussions I have had over the past fifteen years. As such, it is hypothetical and yet representative. This one revisits the moment that opens this book.

It is the morning after a grand jury decision announced that Darren Wilson, the White police officer responsible for the killing of Michael Brown, an unarmed African American youth, would not be indicted on any charges. Students attend my Introduction to Women's Studies class. Many of them feel a sense of relieved anticipation, because they are aching to talk about the issue. Few, if any, have had discussions about it in their other classes, and they need to discuss it. They know this class will be a reasonably safe space in which to have the conversation, because there has formed a rich and fairly friendly community in this Women's Studies class. Other students file in preoccupied with daily college concerns. They are unaware of both the grand jury verdict and the privilege that allows them to remain oblivious to this most recent occurrence in the racial tensions in the United States.

I start the class with an honest statement of my own rawness, anger, and heavy heart at this unjust verdict. I ask what others feel. Some students of color jump right into the conversations, their bodies and gestures animated with their frustration and anger. Other students of color slump back in their chairs, and when they speak, their voices echo the hollowness and loss of hope that render their bodies limp. Some students of color sit contained but wired, listening carefully but unable to stop bursts of statements periodically during the discussion. One woman, who has described herself as biracial, recounts her discussion with her father about this issue. She starts to cry as she describes her dismay and pain when her father asks her why she is so upset, because, he says, she is White. She is part White, she acknowledges, but she is biracial, and it is the latter identity that society sees. She tears up at the pain of her dawning realization that all these years her father has not noticed her positionality in society. A Black man turns to me and says under his breath that his mother called him after the verdict to make sure he is OK. I notice that he chooses to say this to me, not to the entire class.

Many White students in the room also express their outrage, their gestures also animated, while others listen actively, looking up details on their cell phones and adding information to the conversation. I wonder if the urge to research is a way to avoid the raw emotion in the room. I can see the mouths of some White students harden and their bodies begin to tighten as they work up the courage to say what is on their mind against the current of the discussion. One White woman says she is dating a man who is in training to become an officer, and she has spent a lot of time with officers. She says she gets angry that all officers are judged by the actions of these few, because the people she knows are good people. Before she can even get the words out of her mouth, another White student animatedly says that police officers cannot keep getting away with killing people with no consequences, and the first White student sits

(Continued)

back in her chair, her guard up and her withdrawal noticeable. Other White students just keep their heads down. It is hard to tell if their slumped shoulders and their looks of consternation are the result of their pain at the injustice, their discomfort at the challenges to White privilege, their dislike of conflict, or something else entirely. Throughout the room, emotions are high, but they are also getting expelled in some important ways. Nothing is said in this classroom is that is not being said in the broader public sphere.

As this scenario illustrates, embodied reactions are in our classrooms whether we acknowledge them or not. Indeed, the tendency of much higher education is to disembody our students and to privilege objective knowledge rather than the subjective experiences of course material. While most social justice courses challenge this myth of objectivism to instead assert that the personal is political and urge students to connect course material to their everyday lives, mindful anti-oppression pedagogy goes a step further by situating embodiment as a critical site of both knowledge and transformation.

So what exactly is embodiment? Sherry B. Shapiro, author of *Pedagogy and the Politics of the Body*, defines embodiment as "the process by which the body becomes a vehicle for socialization" (1999, 24). Peter McLaren describes embodiment as "the terrain of flesh where ideological social structures are inscribed" (qtd. in Shapiro 1999, 24). Embodiment, then, refers to the imprints and manifestations of power, ideology, and socialization on our very bodies. According to Diana L. Gustafson, author of "Embodied Learning: The Body as an Epistemological Site," embodiment is interested in how we know what we know at the level of the heart and the body, rather than the merely static, cognitive, mostly cerebral focus of more traditional, Eurocentric, and androcentric knowledge (1999, 250). It is a turning inward to better discern the complexity of the outer world and a recognition of their deep interdependence. The yoga teacher Tara Judelle, whose teaching is greatly informed by Body Mind Centering and the work of Bonnie Bainbridge Cohen, understands embodiment to "be the way our particular domain of consciousness (which [she sees] as a fluid continuous energetic field) coalesced into a particular, identifiable form" (personal communication, November 29, 2013). In other words, the various layers of our energy bodies both reflect and shape our consciousness. Mindfulness allows us to better understand all of those layers of being and knowing. Peter Levine writes that:

> *Embodiment is about gaining, through the vehicle of awareness, the capacity to feel the ambient physical sensations of unfettered energy and aliveness as they pulse through*

our bodies. It is here that mind and body, thought and feeling, psyche and spirit, are held together, welded in an undifferentiated unity of experience.

(2010, 279, emphasis in original)

The layers of sensation, feeling, and even the workings of our internal organs all constitute embodiment. For most of us, all but the most intense of these workings remain at the automatic or unconscious level. We may, for instance, become aware of our internal organs when they cause pain, cease to work, or change dramatically, but otherwise we often remain oblivious to them. For instance, we are constantly processing sensations through our skin, but we are most likely only aware of the most notable ones (such as touching a hot stove or a cold ice cube). That selective awareness makes sense, as it would likely be overwhelming to notice every single bodily sensation. But the selectivity is often unconscious—we do not consciously *choose* which ones we notice. Helping students learn to know themselves more fully and providing them with both the framework to understand where their embodied experiences come from and the skill sets to more compassionately and intentionally process their embodied experiences will take us much further down the path of social justice. Mindful anti-oppression pedagogy makes this process visible, *consciously experienced*, and open to critical inquiry.

Mindfulness, when combined with anti-oppression pedagogy and social justice course content, can help us more fully understand the layers of our experiences and discern how sociopolitical power dynamics have produced them. As Gustafson notes, "embodied learning" blends both more traditional ways of analytical knowing and the insights that come from turning inward and reflecting on our own, embodied experiences (1999, 250). This form of learning is often more empowering because it both values marginalized voices and lets participants better understand their own role in knowledge production. Social justice courses provide critical analysis with the former, and as such, it is an important contribution to mindfulness initiatives. The mindful anti-oppression pedagogy model I delineate in this book enables a more liberatory space within higher education, a social institution that is both a site of oppression and a site of resistance. In the next two sections, I will draw on feminist theory and pedagogy to establish why embodied mindfulness is such an essential addition to anti-oppression pedagogy. Though I argue throughout this book that mindfulness is a critical component to anti-oppression pedagogy in general, my own background is in Women's Studies, so I will draw on those contributions throughout the next sections.

Body Knowledge

Feminist theory and pedagogy have established two key tenets that lay the foundation for the embodied learning outlined in this chapter. First, the body itself is a site of knowledge, and second, we often have to counteract the powerful disembodiment that pervades Western culture in order to tap into that knowledge. I will examine each of these tenets in turn and then discuss how embodiment informs mindful anti-oppression work.

Feminist pedagogy tells us that knowledge is not something that exists outside of us but, rather, something that we participate in producing. Not only are our bodies biological entities situated in the material world and given meaning in particular cultural contexts but, even further, we learn something from our bodies themselves (Bordo 1993). The body has long been a subject of interest for feminists, who have studied how the body has been portrayed and regulated in culture(s) (Butler 1999). Michel Foucault noted that disciplinary practices regulate and normalize our bodies, in particularly gendered ways, as feminists Susan Bordo and Sandra Barky have added (Foucault 1979; Bordo 1993; Bartky 1988). From early women's health movements to reproductive rights to advocacy to end violence against women, feminist movements feature the body as central to justice for women (Davis 1997, 2).

Feminist theories of the body have challenged the disembodied patriarchal gaze to instead argue that the material body is constructed through social power dynamics that are deeply gendered, racialized, classed, and shaped by heteronormativity. By challenging the Cartesian mind/body split and the patriarchal disembodied self, feminists have instead explored women's experiences with their bodies. Much feminist activism centers on women's bodily experiences as part of their identities and social locations. As a focal point for gender power dynamics, the body is "a subject inscribed by the cultural meanings and values of our time. The body is a vehicle for understanding oppression, resistance, and liberation" (Shapiro 1999, 15). Not only has the body become a tool through which to create and recreate one's identity, it also generates our sense of what we can and should be (Davis 1997, 10).

However, scholarship on the body is often removed from the material body, leaning safely on the side of disembodied theory. Even some feminist work, while making powerful interventions into our understandings of the gendered normalizations of the body, nevertheless seems ambivalent about embodied experience (Davis 1997, 10). I have taught several courses on feminism and the body and am constantly struck by the challenge of connecting the intellectual work with our actual material experience. Students will share their personal experiences of rape, eating disorders, body image, or reproductive rights, so they become energized by the connection of the theory to their own lives. But they do not often take the further step to inquire into their internal, embodied experiences. My deduction is that they do not have the tools to do so. They have internalized years of cultural disembodiment, which is only reinforced by the clear message that higher education is more interested in their intellect than any other aspect of their being.

The feminist scholar Sherry Shapiro has posed the provocative question, "How can we understand through our embodied knowledge what it might mean to live freer and more empowered lives?" (1998, 9). This is particularly critical for women students who are so often disassociated from our bodies. Some women survive traumas in their lives by disassociating and becoming disembodied. Sometimes women implode as they internalize the degrading messages to such an extent that they manifest as eating disorders, addictions, or negative self-perception. While Women's Studies empowers many women to reclaim their sense of self, I argue that women are often still left with a lack of tools with which to relate in healthy ways to our own bodies. I argue the same is true for most students, whether they are members of dominant groups or marginalized groups in society. We cannot assume that students (women, men, or gender queer) know how to cultivate a more *empowered embodiment* or to *embody empowerment*. If one is successfully disengaged from one's body, one often does not know the full extent of it. Shapiro describes a parallel experience as a dancer. She notes that in the dance world, the body is often seen as a tool. She writes that as a dancer, she did not initially understand her body as a source of insight about her identity or position in the world (Shapiro 1998).

By developing mindful critical first-person inquiry skills, students learn to see and feel how gendered, racial, sexual, economic, and ableist power dynamics shape their bodily experiences. They also learn tools to cultivate oppositional, more empowered bodily experiences. As we integrate mindful education with anti-oppression pedagogy, we can help students learn how to connect with their bodies in more holistic and empowered ways. Students can then begin to see how they can reclaim their bodies from the cultural ideologies that have co-opted them. They will also cultivate greater capacity to craft their own narratives about their experiences.

Feminist pedagogy tells us that we need to take into account differences between participants: identities are positioned differently in power dynamics, which means that different bodies will likely produce different insights. So it is not just that any contemplative practice will result in a different experience but also that our identities will likely shape what we produce. The insights produced from our embodied experiences will be as diverse as the participants in the room. The dynamic exchange that results can produce exciting new directions for class discussion. As students turn to their own bodies for insights that they situate within social justice analysis, they begin to understand themselves and the course content far more deeply. The idea that the body itself is a powerful epistemological site for understanding not only our own positionality but also our commonalities and differences from others is something educators can actively enhance.

Reinhabiting Our Bodies as Sites of Knowledge

The feminist maxim that the personal is political is perhaps most true around the body. We all have one. The body is not merely an intellectual subject matter; we actually inhabit our bodies and have relationships with them, albeit in unexamined and even vexed ways. Our bodily experiences are shaped by the ideologies, belief systems, and power dynamics of the societies in which we live. It is important to note here that when I speak of the experiences of women, people of color, or LGBT communities, I am not advocating an identity politics that says members of these groups have an essentialized and monolithic experience. Rather, I am invoking Gayatri Chakravorty Spivak's (2008) notion of "strategic essentialism" to aver that our lived experiences are shaped by how we are positioned within socio-political power dynamics, which, in turn, shapes what we know. That knowledge can be informed by broader political awareness of experiences outside of our own, which is a key component of social justice education: to help us both understand our own lived experience and to see ours in complex relation to those of others.

Bodies are often considered something we "have," objects that exist in the service of cognitive goals (Ellsworth 2005, 27). In traditional higher education, learning is sometimes seen as content to be known and then taught, rather than as a dynamic process in which we engage. Feminist and anti-oppression peda-gogy helps counter this one-dimensional privileging of cognition to highlight an "embodied reflexivity" in which participants reflect on their ideologies and experiences. Gustafson describes this reflexivity as "a self-conscious, critical, and intense process of gazing inward and outward that results in questioning assump-tions, identifying problems, and organizing for change" (1999, 249). Feminist ped-agogy attends to not only the content that is learned but also the learning process itself. Thus, the body, as Bordo notes, "is seen as the vehicle of the human making and remaking of the world, constantly shifting location, capable of revealing end-lessly new 'points of view on things'" (1993, 144).

Feminist praxis highly values the recognition of shifting points of view, argu-ing that sociopolitical positionality shapes our perceptions of the world. The layer of embodiment enables students to self-reflexively experience how they inhabit the world. As that layer becomes integrated with the content and analytical skills of anti-oppression pedagogy, students can better empathize with and understand other perspectives. This angle adds another layer to what Elizabeth Ellsworth (2005) calls "new pedagogies of sensations." She writes that,

> Pedagogy as "sensation construction" is no longer merely "representa-tional." It is no longer a model that teachers use to set the terms in which already-known ideas, curriculums, or knowledges are put into relation; rather to the extent that sensations are "conditions of possible experience," pedagogy as sensation construction is a condition of possible experiences of thinking.
>
> (2005, 27)

While Ellsworth focuses her work on architecture and media, the argument could also apply to our experiences of our own bodies. *Embodied learning is generative*:

students become co-creators of knowledge by recognizing the body as a dynamic epistemological site. If we look at the Tree of Contemplative Practices by the Center for Contemplative Mind in Society included in the previous chapter, we can see the diverse range of mindfulness exercises that actually *generate* knowledge, including journaling, performance exercises, dance, and meditation (2011). These practices invite participants to turn inward and listen to their bodies, hearts, and minds. Anti-oppression classrooms offer opportunities to practice using these tools in a way that counteracts cultural disembodiment, along with the ability to reflect on the experiences that are generated. When we write, dance, or otherwise create from the body, we never know what kinds of knowledge might emerge. Mindfulness teaches us to be fully present so as to be open to this creative process. The combination of students with differently positioned identities and bodies in any given classroom is a vibrant and dialectical opportunity for co-creation. Students develop critical awareness about the body as well as critical thinking about the social justice subject matter.

This process requires an openness, an ability to tune in to our "inner vibe" and to allow ourselves to just create. No editing, no judging; just being and manifesting. That creative stage will be familiar to artists, but for many students in academic classrooms, they will have to unlearn standard modes of performance that require mastery to instead embrace what hooks (1999) calls "radical openness." As hooks notes, the liminal space of the margin can become a site of resistance and alternatives, not merely a place of oppression and despair. When knowledge is generative, we do not always know what will come of it. We have to be open to possibility and "go with the flow," be in the present moment, and interact with each other to produce something together.

Excavating the Deeper Roots of Oppressive Ideologies

Higher education, with its emphasis on intellectual learning, epitomizes the "I think, therefore I am" maxim. The Cartesian mind/body split has long placed a great deal more value on the mind at the exclusion of the body. But, as Levine notes, we are motor creatures before we are thinking creatures, so a more accurate maxim might be, "I prepare to move, I act, I sense, I feel, I perceive, I reflect, I think, *and* therefore I am" (Levine 2010, 318, emphasis in original). Audre Lorde asserted something similar, revising the Cartesian motto to read "I feel, therefore I can be free" (1984, 100). Our bodies are brilliantly complex systems that operate in a myriad of ways *beneath* the layers of our consciousness and *before* we have rational thoughts. A primary focus on the intellect only scrapes the surface of how oppression works, which allows it to remain deeply entrenched in our very beings. Like a dandelion weed, we can snip off the yellow flower and even get the top of the root that lies just beneath the soil, but the root system of oppressive ideologies have burrowed so far down in us that we have only created a temporary fix; soon, it will reemerge, possibly stronger, and we will have to go through the weeding process all over again. If that is all we do, then all of our energies are repeatedly spent on superficial, even reactionary measures, never allowing us to get to the deeper work of unearthing the strong root structure that actually keeps the effects of oppression in place. Of course, at this stage, the focus on embodiment remains at the individual level. Oppression is enacted upon us by structures, so change needs to interrupt those institutional levels. But we also need to heal the effects on our very selves.

While the dandelion metaphor has its limits, I find in instructive nevertheless. If we focus primarily on the parts of the oppressive system that have already risen to the surface, then we are missing its deeper root structure. That conceptual level is critical, of course (I, for one, learn much more effectively when I understand *why* I am doing something). But, it will have limited effectiveness in actually dismantling systems of oppression unless we go deeper

That deeper layer is embodiment. Most contemplative practices invite us to reflect on our experiences, but in order to do that, we first need to become aware. How do we know when we are happy, afraid, or angry? What does that feel like in our bodies? What sensations arise that we then characterize as particular states of being? What conceptual storylines do we attach to those sensations, and how can we tease apart our labeling of those bodily sensations from the tainting ideologies of oppression itself?

Emotional states shape our bodies and vice versa. Maybe we have slumping spines and a caved in chest or maybe we have muscles that are often spring wired for action. For instance, in my late twenties, my relationship with my first lesbian partner was crumbling and I was trying desperately to hold onto it in ways that spiraled me into depression. I flew to a friend's wedding and met another friend, a massage therapist, whom I had not seen in quite some time. She immediately commented on how shut down I looked. I had assumed that she could just "sense it," but she noted that it was actually held in my body: my shoulders were rounding forward and I was literally turning in on myself. My body was a marker of a difficult time in my life, both reflecting and carrying the disturbance I was unsuccessfully trying to process. This example was simply at the breakup of a significant relationship (significant because it was my first committed lesbian relationship, the one I had come out into). Imagine how much more deeply the effects of enduring oppression throughout one's life have inscribed themselves on and through our bodies. It leaves its mark on our minds, our hearts, our muscles, and our skeletons (Fay 1987).

I have already noted that many feminists situate the body as a site of knowledge. Scholar Sara Ahmed goes even further to note that the borders of our bodies and subjectivity are defined, in part, by what she calls "the cultural politics" of emotions (Ahmed 2004). While emotions are typically understood as internal experiences, she notes, they take on meaning in cultural and political ways. Indeed, often emotions serve to draw boundaries between "us" and "them," wherein those who are marked as "others" are made responsible for "our" feelings. "Feelings do not reside in subjects or objects, but are produced as effects of circulation" (Ahmed 2004, 8). This circulation both reflects and reproduces power dynamics. It also helps explain why discussions about oppression are so hard and what function that fraughtness serves. "Emotions are not 'in' either the individual or the social, but produce the very surfaces and boundaries that allow the individual and the social to be delineated as if they are objects" (Ahmed 2004, 10). She goes on to say, "these feelings not only *heighten tension*, they are also *in tension* . . . even when we have the same feeling, we don't necessarily have the same relationship to the feeling" (Ahmed 2004, 10, emphasis in original). How does this work? When we experience pain, she suggests, that sensation gets transformed from "'it hurts' to 'you hurt me' which might become 'you are hurtful' or even 'you are bad'" (Ahmed 2004, 28). This process occurs not just at the level of the individual, Ahmed argues, but also at the level of communities, passed along through genera-tions. Quoting Kai Erickson, Ahmed goes on to write, "collective trauma involves 'a blow to the basic tissues of social life that damages the bonds attaching people together'. . . . The skin of the community is damaged, but it is a damage that is felt on the skin of the individuals who make up that community" (Ahmed 2004, 34). Ahmed's analysis puts my own discussion of embodiment within the larger context by placing our individual bodily experiences within larger sociopoliti-cal relations. It helps explain how our internal experiences shape our relations to others in our communities and why it is so important to find ways to disrupt our habitual ways of making meanings. Though Ahmed would likely not embrace my mindfulness approach because of its presumed "internalness," I believe that it offers us different ways of understanding and relating to one another. In the words of John A. Powell (2014), "we're constantly being constituted" through our inter-action with each other. Mindfulness helps us become aware of our experiences and to recognize the myriad of ways we are interconnected.

Levine suggests that we get as much information from our internal organs as we do from the outer sheath of our body, though many of us in the Western world are unaccustomed to hearing or validating this information. While our muscles, our joints, and our visceral organs are constantly sending us a great deal of information, we are often oblivious to it until it reaches the point of illness or vast dysfunction. Our body itself operates through this vastly intelligent system, though most of it does not reach our conscious cognition.

Physical sensations, both internal and external, are a large part of who we are, what we experience, and how we make sense of the world. Thinking helps us understand the world and categorize it in various ways. But the influence of the Western Cartesian model means that the innate body intelligence is often overlooked. Certainly, only a few notable disciplines in higher education pay any attention to the body, and while Women's Studies is one of them, even there, much of the scholarship remains more cerebral than it is embodied. Given the extent to which oppression works somatically, emotionally, and cognitively, an awareness of our embodiment is key to anti-oppression work.

Cultivating Embodied Awareness

Increasing this layer of awareness is an important first step to reclaiming our embodiment. In his book, *Body Sense: The Science and Practice of Embodied Self-Awareness*, psychology professor Alan Fogel defines embodied self-awareness as "the ability to pay attention to ourselves, to feel our sensations, emotions, and movement online, in the present moment, without the mediating influence of judgmental thoughts" (2009, 1). Awareness, then, is a pathway to being fully embodied. Levine distinguishes between the types of awareness that every living creature has, and "self-awareness," which only humans have (2010). The former allows animals and humans to be alert to their surroundings in order to survive. The latter, however, gives humans a sense of themselves as individuals, as separate selves with distinct thoughts, feelings, and needs. Levine further distinguishes between awareness and introspection: "*awareness is the spontaneous, and creatively neutral, experiencing of whatever arises in the present moment—whether sensation, feeling, perception, thought, or action. In contrast, introspection is a directing of our attention in a deliberative, evaluating, controlling, and not infrequently, judgmental way*" (Levine 2010, 289, emphasis in original).

Fogel makes a similar distinction between "thinking about the self," which he calls "conceptual self-awareness," and the feeling self of embodied self-awareness. The latter, he suggests, involves "**interoception**—sensing our breathing, digestion, hunger, arousal, pain, emotion, fatigue, and the like—and the **body schema**—an awareness of the movement and coordination between different parts of the body and between our body and the environment" (Fogel 2009, 10–11, emphasis in original). He goes on to say that whereas "conceptual self-awareness" is a mental process, "[e]mbodied self-awareness involves being in the **subjective emotional present**, being able to actually feel one's sadness or pain, for example, without judgment and without trying to escape from it" (Fogel 2009, 11). Thus, while conceptual self-awareness is rational, abstract, and based in language systems, embodied self-awareness is "spontaneous, creative, open to change," and based in the "sensing, feeling, and acting" experience of the present moment (Fogel 2009, 31).

Much of what we do in anti-oppression classrooms, I argue, is closer to introspection than it is to awareness. Though feminists talk of "consciousness raising" or "raising awareness," we often mean an analysis that brings with it evaluation, critical thinking, and even judgment. These forms of analysis are crucial to social justice work, but they are not the kind of awareness that enables and informs embodiment, at least not as a first step. Contemplative awareness is much closer to Levine's first definition of awareness because it focuses on cultivating inquiry and observation with a sense of curiosity and wonder. One can be an expert on the sociopolitical factors that cause something to happen and still not know how it manifests deep in one's body or why it produces certain responses in others. One can understand the theory of patriarchy without being fully present in the moment of its eruption within oneself. To undo the system, we need both parts. We need to see the larger system at work and try to dismantle it, but we also need to be present with how it takes form within ourselves and our neighbors at any given moment. Once we can do the latter, we can begin to cultivate the equanimity to make different choices about how to engage it (wherever that is possible). This latter component is what mindful education can bring to anti-oppression pedagogy.

Typically, this form of awareness requires an excavation of sorts. Most of us have aspects of our embodiment that we recognize, but far more remains hidden. "It is a descent into the parts of our being that are alien, that we might prefer not to deal with" (Levine 2010, 291). Yoga teacher Tara Judelle says, "yoga teaches me that my body is a tool for experiencing consciousness. There is no experience of reality without this body AND everything I experience is subject to the felt sense of this body" (personal communication, November 29, 2013). Another yoga teacher, Anna Guest-Jelley, notes that, in her experience teaching students, "if the mental/emotional work isn't complemented with a physical component of some kind (like yoga), then it isn't as effective or sustainable as it could be" (personal communication, December 21, 2013).

For anyone who has taught diversity classes, the deep manifestations of oppression are easily evident. As students demystify the status quo and reveal the systematic power relations that sustain oppression, they learn to look at the world through a different lens. As they begin to ask who benefits from the system as it is and who is marginalized by it, they are challenged to examine their own places in this system. The process is an unsettling one. It is not uncommon for students to experience a variety of reactions in these classes, from anger to fear to outrage to alienation to empowerment. These reactions are usually shaped by their positionality in power dynamics and their life experiences. When a student breaks into tears after a class about sexual assault, for instance, that response does not occur mainly at the level of the mind. In fact, it is often precognitive. Discussions about oppression at the college level often challenge students to experience emotions that they may not yet know how to express, explain, or understand.

These reactions are embodied manifestations of the deep tendrils of oppression. They are inevitable steps in the process of excavating how our very sense of self has been invaded by systems of oppression and move toward the embodied healing of unlearning those systems. In diversity courses, students are taught to recognize and interrupt discriminatory mental patterns, such as catching themselves when they make automatic assumptions about a person of color based on stereotypes or when they judge a woman as unattractive because of her body type and size. But each of these intellectual decisions is accompanied by embodied experiences that often precede the intellectual label. It is those earlier steps that mindful education helps us explore.

Levine (2010) developed a model he calls SIBAM to explain these different ent layers, which incorporate the neurophysiologic, the somatic, the behavioral, and the cognitive aspects of the human experience. This model recognizes that bodily motor actions usually precede cognitive ones, so this approach is more of a "ground-up" or "inner to outer" process than a "top-down" or "mind-down" one. SIBAM refers to Sensation-Image-Behavior-Affect-Meaning. It is worth outlining his model at some length (Levine 2010, 138–154).

Sensation refers to our actual physical sensations (Levine 2010). Multiple types of receptors send information through nerve impulses to the Thalamus in the upper brain, which then distributes the information as necessary, often below our consciousness (Levine 2010).

The **Image** channel refers to not only our visual perception but also to all external sensory impressions that we incorporate into our sensory memory. These include our most familiar senses (taste, touch, sight, smell, and sound) through which we relate to the external world (Levine 2010).

Behavior involves the outer expression or response to these stimuli, including gestures, posture, emotions, and autonomic signals (both cardiovascular and respiratory). Levine also refers to visceral behavior in this category, which comes from the gastrointestinal "gut" actions and archetypical behaviors, which emerge from a deep collective unconscious (Levine 2010).

The **Affect** channel, according to Levine, refers to the "felt-sense" or the "sensation-based feeling." This includes categorical emotions such as anger, fear, joy, and love (Levine 2010).

The final Step is Levine's SIBAM model is the **Meaning** channel, which refers to the "labels we attach to the totality of our experience—that is, to the combined elements of sensation, image, behavior, and affect" (Levine 2010, 151). Essentially, this layer is the culmination of the previous four steps. These are the cognitive interpretations we attach to the sensations and images that have come before.

The meanings we develop may or may not serve us in the present moment. For instance, if we have experienced oppression or trauma in the past, the sensations that evoke that memory may produce the conclusion that "the world is not a safe place" or that "people are out to get me" or that "I am unlovable" (Levine 2010, 151). If we are indeed living in an unsafe environment, this conclusion is likely a survival mechanism. But if we are no longer in a trauma-likely context or if we have areas in our community that are safer for us, these meanings we attach to certain sensations may not serve us in every moment.

More importantly for anti-oppression work, when a meaning we attach to the first four steps in the SIBAM process becomes crystallized, then it is not flexible, revisable, or even adaptable. The conclusions become foregone, predetermined to the point of being at best automatic and at worst retrenchable. They become what some call "premature cognition" because they are habitual and often limiting prejudgments (Levine 2010, 151). In moments of trauma, these "prejudgments" (which are often negative), enable our survival. But when they are no longer useful, they can do us harm, and we cannot easily unlearn them.

I argue that in a system of oppression, this premature cognition is learned behavior that perpetuates inequitable power dynamics by inducing us to participate in them, sometimes without even knowing it. So, for instance, if women get into positions of leadership but then act as patriarchal "gatekeepers" that prevent other women from advancing unless they conform to patriarchal norms of behavior, those women leaders may not realize that the model of leadership they are adopting have been shaped by power. Similarly, when a White person simply expects to be respected and noticed, she/he/ze might not notice the entitlement s/he/ze has internalized as a result of the privilege granted to him/her/zir by institutionalized racism.

The mindful anti-oppression model I propose offers us the opportunity to slow down this SIBAM process, reflect on what is happening, and make more flexible decisions. "When cognition is suspended long enough," Levine notes, "it is possible to move through and experience flow via these different channels . . . of Sensation, Image, Behavior, and Affect. Then it is probable for *fresh new* Meanings to emerge out of this unfolding tapestry of body/mind consciousness" (Levine 2010, 151, emphasis in original). Since unlearning oppression involves not simply stopping certain behaviors but actually creating new, more empowering ways of making meaning and relating to one another, we need to engage in a process that will lead to those new meanings.

I believe a main goal of anti-oppression pedagogy is to dislodge these more crystallized beliefs and replace them with more adaptive, situation-specific ones, so that we can more intentionally choose which ones will best serve ourselves and more liberatory goals at any given moment. This process will allow us greater emotional intelligence and resilience. The way we do this begins with becoming aware of our sensate processes. We cannot start at the layer of meaning making, in the SIBAM model, nor can we stop at the layer of the behavioral. Though these layers are likely the first to be unearthed, we need to dig deeper still. The point here is not to simply reverse the Cartesian model to privilege the body over the mind but rather to more fully integrate them into the unified system that they are. That integration requires first recognizing the deeper layers of embodiment, exploring them, and then enabling all the layers to more productively work together.

For most of us, this process will take a great deal of time. Like cognitive critical thinking, this is a skill that we need to develop gradually and with compassionate patience. But unlike the rapid flow of ideas, this process is typically much more incremental; in fact, embodiment often requires us to suspend our thinking mind in order to sink into our felt experience without storylines. Eventually, we will attach meanings to at least some of our felt experiences, but we also need to learn to temporarily suspend that part of our brain in order to reflect on other aspects of our being. The more we practice this ability, the more we are able to stay with our embodiment and focus our reflection on certain aspects of our sensations. The repetition of this process is crucial; mindfulness is not achieved in one activity but, rather, is cultivated over time. Fogel notes that "this practice effect happens because the brain learns from each experience of embodied self-awareness. Neural learning is reflected in the physiological changes in the nerve cells and their connections. Practice leads to the growth of an increasing number of interconnecting fibers that can synapse between cells" (Fogel 2009, 61). Fogel compares this process to wearing a path in a grassy field. The first couple times, we have to work harder, but eventually the pathway will be worn and easy to follow. "These increasingly entrenched pathways [in our brain] make it easier for information to travel along the same routes in the future," which is how habits and memories are formed (Fogel 2009, 61).

Recent advances in Western neuroscience have confirmed what Eastern meditation leaders and yogis have long known: that mindfulness actually changes the brain. Davidson's groundbreaking research on experienced meditators has proven several significant conclusions. It reveals that adult brains have neural plasticity and can change, which means the more we practice mindfulness, the more we forge new pathways in our brain that can fire the areas in our brains responsible for empathy and compassion (Davidson 2011). Using modern MRI technology, Davidson and his team performed a number of experiments on Tibetan monks who had meditated for thousands of hours. Despite being exposed to traumatic and highly disturbing stimuli, he found much higher levels of activity if the left prefrontal cortex, which is responsible for positive emotions, than in the areas of the brain responsible for stress, anxiety, and other more "negative" emotions. The neural activity of the seasoned monks also far outpaced that of the novice monks who were also tested. In this and several other experiments, Davidson concluded that regular mental training with mindfulness techniques can produce positive changes in the parts of our brain responsible for compassion and a desire to alleviate the suffering of others (2011).

When Embodiment Is Unsettling

Admittedly, it can be an overwhelming process to learn to sink into our bodies when we have long been disconnected from them. Because one characteristic of embodied experience is spontaneity, we have much less control (at least initially) over what we feel than we do over our more rational cognition (Fogel 2009). This lack of control can be unpredictable and frightening, but it is also the place for much of our personal growth. The most transformative moments may be quite unsettling, which is all the more reason for us to develop tools in less stressful moments so that they are available to us in more intense ones. For some of us, that will require overcoming barriers that we have built as a protective survival technique; when those barriers start to come down, the flood of sensate emotions can overwhelm us. I would argue that some of this already happens in diversity classrooms—students often get angry, cry, or get so overwhelmed that they shut down. The goal here is to give students a language to understand their reactions and the *skills* to process them. For some students, what comes up may require professional help that is beyond the scope of the classroom. However, I would suggest that we tread on this boundary anyway, such as when we discuss eating disorders, racial profiling, queer bullying, or sexual assault. When we approach the more intense units in my Women's Studies classes, I always warn students that these issues hit close to home and urge them to talk with me or the Counseling Center if the class discussions bring things up for them. It is not uncommon for students to approach me, at which point I connect them with the appropriate campus resources to support them.

In any real discussion about oppression, the embodied sensations will come up for many of our students (and ourselves as faculty and staff). We need to help students cultivate the mindfulness tools that allow them to sit with and process through their reactions at an embodied as well as at the intellectual level. Mindfulness develops the skills discussed in Chapter 1, including critical reflection, focus, and attention, all of which are highly valued in college learning. But it also cultivates invaluable skills for working through the complex physiological and emotional responses that inevitably arise when working through issues of oppression. While not all students feel these tough emotions, and certainly not all of them experience their responses like a kind of trauma, nevertheless I think we can agree that a range of complex emotions arise in discussions of oppression. Those of us who have been targets of oppression have some serious healing that needs to be done, and often we have to learn to reclaim our embodiment as a first step in that healing. Those of us whose privilege is challenged in these classrooms likely feel a disturbance of a different kind, but one that also needs to be met with effective skills if we are to continue with productive unlearning of oppression. I will talk more about this latter issue in Chapter 4. Suffice it to say here that mindfulness offers students the ability to witness their responses (whatever they are) and make more intentional choices about whether or how to engage them.

Levine notes that a key aspect of processing traumatic memories is "cultivating the ability to hold a dual consciousness with an emphasis on the sensations, feelings, images, and thoughts that are unfolding in the *here and now*. When this is done, fragmented sensory elements, which make up the core of trauma, become gradually integrated into a coherent experience" (Levine 2010, 297, emphasis in original). Healing, he notes, is not about fully remembering the traumatic events so much as it is about integration so as to move "out of fixity and fragmentation into flow and wholeness" (Levine 2010, 298; van der Kolk 2014b). One of my goals as a feminist teacher is to dislodge the fixity of oppressive ideologies in order to help students move toward being more integrated, whole, and compassionate beings. The embodiment piece is the missing part of the puzzle. In fact, it adds a different dimension to the dual consciousness that it is often discussed in anti-oppression circles. Anti-racist pedagogy, for instance, notes that double consciousness occurs when people of color understand themselves both from their own individual perspective but also from the dominant White paradigm; they have learned the dominant system so well that they see themselves through "white eyes" as a survival mechanism (Fanon 2008). Of course, this also leads to internalized racism, as I will discuss in Chapter 3. When we bring Levine's definition to bear on this latter one, what we see is that we can learn to distinguish between the learned, internalized lens of the dominant society and our present, here and now experience. The more we can do that, the more we can choose more intentionally how to respond and gradually begin to unlearn those dominant messages.

Accepting and Trusting Our Internal Responses

The yogic traditions tell us that we possess an innate wisdom that guides us and that offers us a wealth of innate resources upon which we can draw to meet life's challenges. In order to do so, we have to learn to live in the NOW. When I was first beginning my yogic studies, I would hear tenets like this one and my feminist voice would retort, "That's all fine and good for people with privilege. Sure, they have all these resources. But oppressed groups cannot simply *choose* to meet structural barriers of institutionalized oppression by drawing on their inner resources." I would then scoff away, disillusioned by the platitudes expressed by the often White, middle-class, Western woman yoga teacher. There remains, unfortunately, some truth to this critique of the Western yoga circuit. However, the deeper my yoga studies progressed, the more I realized what was at the heart of these teachings. The ancient yoga philosophers were certainly not immune from inequalities, though they lived in a very different system in ancient India than I live in today. But the principles they discovered and wove into the system of yoga remind us that our embodied being is healthiest and wisest when it is an integrated one. In the present moment, when we can listen to our vast, inner self, we learn that our validation comes from within, not from external authorities, and we reconnect with our own inner stability (Miller 2010, 23). When we can draw on all of the resources of our mind, body, and spirit and learn to listen to our innate intelligence, we find more wisdom than we expect. Ideally, that wisdom helps strengthen our emotional intelligence and inner resiliency by undermining the ideologies and drive for power that fuel systems of oppression. I, for one, need to embrace that hope for humanity if I am to keep doing the social justice work that can be disillusioning in its slow pace. For me, yoga, like feminism, is a way of being in the world.

Even if one chooses not to embrace that philosophy as a worldview (like I have chosen to embrace feminism as a world view), the science of embodied wisdom is still highly relevant. How many women doubt themselves because they have internalized sexist messages? How many queer youth deny their sexuality and their budding queer sense of self because society tells them it is "abnormal"? This ability to learn to listen to and trust one's own inner compass is a vital skill to surviving oppression. The way I am invoking this idea here does not deny that large-scale oppression exists nor does it place the responsibility for fighting oppression squarely on the individual. I still argue that systematic and collective institutional shifts in power need to happen. But I also see the everyday effects of oppression on my students, and I have searched for skill sets to offer them that would allow them to cultivate more resilience to those damages. I have also wondered how best to meet each student in my classroom. Students come into anti-oppression courses in very different places of power, privilege, and familiarity with the material.

Much research has shown that experiential learning is more effective than rote learning and that active learning is more effective than the "banking model" of education (Freire 1970). These insights are well-recognized in anti-oppression pedagogy, and they become even more important when we apply them to our own embodied present moment. When one is engaged in mindfulness, one goes through a variety of experiences, some uncomfortable, some distracting, and some transformative as "negative patterns of conditioning are burned away by the fire of discriminative wisdom" (Miller 2010, 16). We have to learn to allow whatever arises to just be in order to work through it and as we do so, we learn more about ourselves. We also become less attached to any given reaction, because the more we sit in meditation, the more we realize how quickly sensations pass. Rather than getting fully invested in our frustration, confusion, fear, or anger, we learn to notice it, let it be, and watch it pass.

This inquiry is important in anti-oppression work because the various reactions students have are results of their conditioning and positioning in systems of oppression. When a White student feels waves of shame or indignation when their White privilege is challenged, how they meet those feelings will inform how or whether they engage the discussion in a fruitful way. Similarly, when in an Hmong American student waves of inadequacy and pain arise because of her internalization of the model minority myth, she might become overwhelmed unless she has the tools to put those feelings into perspective. These skills, of course, are developmental behaviors as well; just as we go deeper and deeper into our unlearning of oppression the more we study this material, we also tend to go deeper and deeper the more we practice mindfulness skills. My point here is that in order for students to effectively do the work of unlearning oppression, they need to learn to be present with whatever they are feeling and learn to examine how their responses are shaped by their position in oppressive power dynamics.

I am not interested in using mindfulness as an escape tactic to let people avoid the hard feelings that are an inevitable part of this unlearning process, but I am interested in equipping students with adequate tools to be able to handle the range of emotions that might arise. I am also invested in keeping students in the conversation, rather than having them shut down or avoid the work of confronting oppression. In order to have that happen, I think we need to effectively prepare them to do so.

The nonjudgmental awareness of mindfulness is critical in the initial stages of embodiment. This can be tricky in anti-oppression pedagogy. Most diversity classes contain the basic premise that injustice and oppression are not acceptable. The condemnation of the violence of oppression is inherent in the concept of social justice. So when Fogel (like most mindfulness practitioners) calls for us to be aware "without the mediating influence of judgmental thought," we might raise some objections (2009, 1). After all, we do not want to just accept oppression, right? Of course not. At the intellectual, political, and societal levels we want to condemn and resist oppression. However, at the level of embodiment, this judgment is counter-productive. When we resist our embodied experience, it tends to become stronger. If we make ourselves the enemy by condemning what we feel, we have a much harder time unlearning oppression, because our judgment actually works like nutrients that feed it.

Moreover, few of us in the West are actually aware of what we are experiencing at an embodied level, which means we would be judging it before we even understand it (van der Kolk 2014a). More than likely, that judgment would be shaped by systems of oppression rather than by compassionate social justice. In other words, our embodied experiences are often our gut, automatic reactions. If oppression is embedded deeply in our beings, then those gut reactions are very likely shaped by oppressive ideologies (Johnson n.d.). Since they happen so automatically, we are often unaware of how that process works (Van de Kolk 2014b). To layer judgment on top of them would be to either feed the roots of oppression within our very selves or layer social justice condemnation on top of them, neither of which helps in the unlearning process. Instead we need to allow ourselves to accept our embodied experiences, whatever they are. It is no accident that virtually all mindfulness practices guide practitioners to meet their experiences with curiosity and compassion. We have to first become aware of our responses and learn to understand them before we can hope to change them. This early part of the process cannot happen if we automatically judge our responses. To accept our responses with compassion is NOT the same thing as accepting oppression. On the contrary, it is a critical first step to dismantling oppression as it operates within our very beings.

Resources and Tools

Few students come to the classroom adept at being mindful. We need to help students learn to cultivate the tools for developing and sustaining this embodied self-awareness. Fogel (2009) outlines the nature of mindful embodiment skills, so I will take a moment to summarize a few of them and then relate them to anti-oppression pedagogy.

First, embodiment offers resources to be present with one's subjective bodily experience (Fogel 2009, 24). In the classroom, that means that students learn to sit with whatever arises for them emotionally, physically, cognitively, or psychologically. Mindfulness teaches us how to be with intense emotions without clinging to them, judging them, or pushing them away. This can be an important antidote to the more typical survival mechanism of simply disembodying in the face of oppression. Though, of course, we may need to still disassociate in more intense moments of violence, the ability to be present with our embodied experience is an invaluable tool for the daily, cumulative microaggressions many of us face. This skill is also important for the feelings of confusion, disillusionment, fear, and anger that can arise for dominant groups when their privilege is challenged (a topic for Chapter 4). Since many of us straddle both dominant and marginalized groups through different facets of identity, the ability to navigate these responses requires first the ability to remain present with them.

In order to remain present, we need to slow down long enough to do so, which is the second benefit of embodiment that Fogel (2009) describes. Contemporary U.S. culture is a frenetic one and college environments are even more so. Students juggle an unheard of amount of responsibilities, particularly during the latter part of a semester. Between classes, work, student organizations, family life, and their social networks, students are always multitasking, something that is only increased by our modern means of communication. The ability to simply BE and not DO is rare. I find that in the beginning of the semester, when I first introduce meditation, many students have a hard time with it. They fidget, make mental lists, think of all the things they should/could be doing, and get impatient. This, of course, is a very normal response to early meditation. But as the semester progresses, while some students still remain in that first state, many of them long for the stillness meditation offers. In fact, by midterms, I often have students requesting that we meditate because, they say, it is the only moment of stillness they have. I remind them that they can create that space for themselves at any moment; they do not need me to meditate. But the fact that they make this request is a sign that they have not yet learned how to slow down, a skill that comes with regular meditation. If they cannot even learn to set aside a planned moment of stillness, there is little chance that they will be able to slow down in a moment of intense response. Regular sitting (in meditation or other forms of mindfulness practice) develops our ability to do so, so that we can call on that skill in unplanned moments. Without the former, that skill will not be accessible for the latter. This capacity sometimes requires "coregulation" by someone who can help the individual come back to their emotional present and/or draw on their resources more effectively (Fogel 2009, 23). While Fogel is talking about coregulation by a therapist, I would argue that our community members, our teachers, and our mindfulness or yoga teachers are important coregulators for students learning to become embodied in healthy ways.

The fourth benefit of embodiment, according to Fogel (2009), is the ability to verbalize what is happening *without losing connection with one's embodied present*. Essentially, this is the ability to reflect without losing connection to our embodiment (Fogel 2009). This is one place in the process where body and mind are unified, so that students can use their cognition while remaining fully embodied. This skill is related to the next benefit Fogel describes, which involves establishing links and boundaries between ourselves and those around us. Here, students learn to draw more effective boundaries between what is their work and what is someone else's responsibility, which can be particularly useful in anti-oppression classrooms. Members of marginalized groups often get frustrated when they are constantly asked to educate others about themselves or when they are expected to take care of members of the dominant group as they confront the pain of an oppressive system. Clearly learning what is our work as members of marginalized groups and what is our work as members of dominant groups can be a critical step in lessening that burden. For instance, at a recent Anti-Racist Pedagogy workshop I attended, we did "racial identity caucusing" near the end of the workshop. People of color went into one room to talk about how internalized oppression affects them, while the White participants went into another room to discuss how internalized superiority (the other part of racialization) affects us. The rationale for this separation, the facilitator explained, was to enable each of us to do our work in safer spaces so that we did not get in each other's way. In other words, it is not the job of people of color to bear witness or be involved in White people interrupting our own racism; it is also not the job of White people in community movements to participate in the work of people of color as they try to dismantle the deep roots of internalized oppression. This is a strategic separation, not an essentialist one. But it is, at times, strategically useful for each group to focus on particular work that needs to be done. In order to be clear on what that work is, this step of establishing links and boundaries is helpful.

Mindful embodiment also develops self-regulation, which means cultivating the ability and responsibility to bring oneself back to balance and restoration (Fogel 2009, 24). This skill is a critical step in healing from oppression, because while we cannot control the systems of power that circulate around us, we do want to have some agency over our own selves. Working to create institutional change is a long haul, which it is not particularly helpful in moments when we are directly experiencing oppression. Self-regulation is a skill we can draw on to survive and heal internally, so that we can better take care of ourselves and work toward becoming whole. I find it is so important to teach young feminists this skill, and it is one that I did not learn until I found yoga. Years of practicing feminism had still not adequately helped me develop this skill.

Notice that the progression Fogel (2009) outlines moves from first being aware, then being able to verbalize, then being able to connect to others and differentiate from them, and then to stages of empowerment. This, too, is a parallel with social justice work, since agency and empowerment is a primary goal of both. When we can self-regulate, there is a greater chance of "reengagement," which Fogel describes the "ability to remain in the subjective emotional present of embodied self-awareness while experiencing the world with empowerment, triumph, and assertiveness" (2009, 24). Not only does reengagement enable greater agency, it "also includes a growing empathy with others and an ability to be in touch with others while staying in one's own" embodied present (Fogel 2009, 24). This reconnection is important for building community in the classroom. It is also a critical skill to learn how to have empathy for others even while disagreeing with them and learning how to relate to others, even in fraught moments, without losing one's self-aware embodiment.

Finally, there is the "letting go," which "includes being able to 'step off the treadmill' of life to take care of yourself, the acceptance of your limits, a sense of compassion for others, and the ability to let yourself get lost in pleasurable creativity and self-discovery," without losing one's embodied self-awareness (Fogel 2009, 24). This stage can only come after the previous ones. This "letting go," then, includes the ability to "pick one's battles," so as not to get caught up in fighting oppression every minute of every day. If we are committed to social justice, we often feel the responsibility to do so, and there are moments, of course, where we cannot choose not to resist oppression because we are being targeted by it. But we will quickly burn out if we pick every battle, especially if we do not have good restorative self-care practices. I often advise young feminists that it is not self-indulgent to have a regular self-care routine. Audre Lorde reminded us that "[c]aring for myself is not self-indulgent, it is self-preservation, and that is an act of political warfare" (1988, 131). In fact, there is no way we can do social justice work for the long haul if we do not take care of ourselves. We will become depleted and ineffective at what we do. Generally, when we are exhausted, we do not make the best choices and sometimes may unintentionally make situations worse.

When we take the time to take care of ourselves, we can remain more balanced and, therefore, more effective in social transformation. In addition, this "letting go" allows us do our own work of self-discovery, which is important for us to "walk the talk." We cannot expect others to do the hard work of unlearning oppression if we are not also doing our own. The exact nature of our work will vary from person to person, but we all have work to do. That work needs to be done at the deep level of embodiment, not just at the level of the intellect, and it cannot be effectively engaged if we are always multitasking, running, and refusing to be still.

Embodied learning allows individuals who are often marginalized in educational spaces to claim their internal experience. Particularly if their voices and experiences are excluded in higher education, they may not feel accustomed to bringing their fully embodied selves into the classroom. While this has been an important survival mechanism, it dramatically impacts how they can learn and certainly makes it impossible to be fully present in the college community (hooks 1994). To learn to recognize and claim one's subjective internal experience within this climate is a form of empowerment. It is also risky, because to learn to be reconnected with our body requires being vulnerable in a fraught environment. Mindfulness practices are critical forms of self-support and empowerment precisely *because* we can turn to them in moments of danger. They can be deep sources of learning in safe spaces, but they can also provide self-sustenance in times of direct oppression. They allow us to develop the "dual consciousness" that Levine describes, in which we can remain present in our present subjective experience while also recognizing the deeply entrenched patterns that oppression provokes. This mindful dual consciousness enables agency and self-care for the individual, which is an important step for resiliency and for working toward social change.

Because embodied learning requires an inward focus, I can hear some critics expressing concern at the focus on the individual here, particularly given the ways marginalized groups are outnumbered on many college campuses. Won't this focus on the individual self perpetuate the centering of dominant voices, some might ask? It certainly could, if mindfulness initiatives are not informed by anti-oppression pedagogy. It is not enough to work at the individual level. Change needs to happen at both the structural and collective levels as well. But I argue that the partnership of the two acknowledges the complex selves that are already in our classrooms and allows us to more fully address how they already do and do not learn. It also allows us to help students learn the skills of better addressing the range of responses that arise in discussions about oppression, so that we can more effectively build a collective, engaged, community dynamic, both in our classrooms and on our college campuses. The process of mindful learning is a critical partner to the longstanding work of Ethnic Studies, Women's Studies, and other social justice-oriented disciplines. For it to be an effective partner, however, mindfulness communities also need to do their own anti-oppression work, a topic I will address further in Chapter 6. Integrating mindful education into anti-oppression pedagogy and recognizing the important of embodied learning in higher education are two important steps toward structural change. As more and more people on college campuses practice mindfulness, the likelihood of creating community that deeply honors one another's humanity increases; both of these are essential to a more socially just climate.

Tips for Integrating Embodiment into Our Classrooms

As with all the chapters in this book, I will conclude this one with some specific, practical guidelines for adopting these principles in our classrooms.

1. Reclaiming Our Embodiment Is a Slow and Often Unsettling Process.

To become embodied, for many of us, means to counter a lifelong process of disembodiment. It requires learning new skills and practicing them constantly, in the face of the barrage of cultural messages that encourage the opposite. Reconnecting with our embodiment will not happen in a semester. It may not even happen in the four or five years one is at college. Particularly if students are only exposed to mindfulness in one or two college courses, this process will likely be two steps forward, one step back. I find it is helpful to prepare students for that reality. The more transparent we can make the process, the more effective it will be. That means giving students a language with which to make sense of what is happening. We can explain the prevalence of cultural disembodiment as a tool oppression. As we establish that awareness, we can also prepare students for the range of successes and missteps they might expect as they try to reconnect with their experiences of embodiment.

2. Model Our Own Process for Students, Rockiness and All.

As teachers, we are powerful role models and mentors for our students. They look to us for guidance and leadership. Over the years, I have increasingly realized that revealing my own journey toward embodiment and unlearning oppression is deeply instructive for students. The more honest I can be about the progress and missteps I have made, the more it seems to give them permission to be with their own journey, whatever that may be. Both my yoga practice and my feminist journey have taught me that authenticity is much more profound than is a false storyline of flawless success. None of us has the answers to ending oppression; if we did, oppression would no longer exist. What we have is a deep commitment to combating oppression, theories of how it works, and, often, more years working against it than many of our students. Sharing the insights we have learned along the way—including the lessons we learned the hard way—can authorize students to be honest about their own paths.

An important caveat here: this vulnerability will be easier and safer for some faculty and staff than it is for others. For instructors from marginalized positions, this vulnerability may seem risky (Kishimoto and Mwangi 2009). As a White woman, I am received differently when I talk about racism than are my colleagues of color. Though I am a queer woman, my gender performance is fairly normative, which means that I am received differently than are my more gender queer colleagues. I recognize, as I offer this advice, that marginalization places some faculty in more tenuous positions than others. Each teacher, therefore, will need to determine the degree to which he/she/zir shares his/her/zir path with students. When possible, though, I find that sharing our experiences is deeply instructive, both for the teacher (who gets yet another chance to reflect on our journey) and for the students (who see that their mentor has experienced uncertainty as well.)

This tip is meant to model self-reflection and inquiry with compassion for any missteps that may occur. It is not meant to be presented as a definitive map. Each participant needs to find his/her/zir own path with various mindfulness strategies. The process of how we engage and inquire is as important as any particular steps we might take. It is that process that teachers can model in valuable ways.

3. Recognize That for Some Participants, Their Body Is Not Their Friend.

Most of us in the West, I would argue, have to disrupt some level of disembodiment. But for some, this process is made more complicated by their sense that their body is a battleground. If a student has been sexually assaulted, for instance, she may not be ready to reconnect to her embodiment, and if she tries to do so, the encounter will likely not be a positive one. As teachers, there is no way we can know the complex history of each of our students. But I always assume that a range of such realities are in the room, and I try to create the conditions for everyone to engage in various ways without having to advertise to their classmates what they are feeling.

As I will argue in the next chapter, I see oppression as a form of trauma. Trauma survivors often experience their embodiment as deeply painful and fraught. Increasing work is being done in the field of mindfulness as a path toward healing from trauma, but some of that work is beyond what we can do in the average classroom (van der Kolk 2014a). Moreover, in any given course, students will have a variety of embodied experiences that are shaped by their cultural locations. Some students will not be ready to sink into their embodiment or may not feel safe doing so in the classroom. Some may need additional support of counseling services, depending on where they are in their healing process.

One important way of handling these issues it to prepare students for that reality. Let them know the range of reactions that might arise and why. Give them a lens for making sense of those reactions. Offer mindfulness practices for handling various reactions in the moment and campus services for assisting students outside of class. (It is often helpful to notify our colleagues in those campus services if we know a student may be coming to them for additional support.) Offer students who are not yet ready to engage in particular embodiment practices (such as yoga) alternative options. Even being able to in tune enough to their own needs to discern which embodiment practice they wish to choose is a big step in the right direction.

4. As Teachers, We Can Guide but We Cannot Control the Direction or the Pace of Students' Journeys.

Our job as teachers is to provide students with skill sets and critical analysis to understand social justice and to apply their learning to their everyday lives. We provide a language and a lens for students to more fully engage and understand what they experience in the world around them. But we cannot dictate what they do with that information. I tell my student that I do not expect that they "become feminist" in my classes. I do expect that they be able to articulate a feminist analysis and explain why feminists take the positions that they do, but I cannot require that they embrace any particular politics. Similarly, I can teach them mindfulness skills and the context for how they work, but I cannot control the degree to which students actually engage them.

What we can do, however, is help students to "release limiting views about themselves" (Rendón 2014, 1). Systems of oppression produce narrow boxes for ourselves and one another. The more we reveal that and offer students more freedom to make their own choices, the more they will be willing to experiment with more liberatory definitions. That recognition does not mean that "anything goes." I am quite clear, in my Women's Studies courses, about my condemnation of oppression and my analysis of what causes it. But I am also clear that there are many ways to work toward a more socially just world, each with its strengths and limitations. As strongly as I believe in feminism and as deeply committed as I am to practicing mindfulness as a path to a better world, I do not believe that I can impose those particular beliefs or strategies on students. Instead, I teach them as options. I make clear that the process matters and try to empower students to find the process that empowers them. This openness, I find, takes us further down the path toward a more liberatory community than would any more prescriptive formula.

Integrating mindfulness with anti-oppression pedagogy not only recognizes the body as a site of experience and knowledge, it also validates "the body's capacity to transform (rather than simply enact and reproduce) oppressive experience" (Johnson, n.d., 11). In the next chapter, I will further examine oppression as a form of trauma, particularly as it is internalized, and I will offer ways that mindfulness can be productively brought into social justice classes in order to help students interrupt those demoralizing narratives and cultivate empowerment.

Mindfulness Practices

Body Scan

Find a comfortable seat. You may sit in a chair or on the ground. If seated on the floor, it may be helpful to have a cushion or blanket underneath your pelvis to give it a little bit of a tilt. If seated in a chair, have your feet firmly planted on the ground and the lower part of your back supported by the chair. As you inhale, extend up through your torso, broadening across the front of your chest and drawing your shoulder blades on your back. Extend up through the top of your head, then soften into that posture. Your eyes can be closed or open and softly gazing at a spot on the floor a couple feet in front of you. Your hands can be resting on your thighs, palms open or gently closed.

Start by taking a few deep breaths, filling your lungs then your belly on an inhale, letting each exhale wash away your stress. With each deep breath, bring your awareness to the present moment.

Gently direct your attention to the top of your head, your forehead, your eyes. Imagine each exhale like an ocean's tide, wiping away any tension that might be there. Allow your eyes to soften. Breathe a few deep breaths here.

Then gently move your awareness to your jaw line, your chin, your mouth. With each exhale, invite your jaw to release any tension that might be held there.

Direct your attention to your neck and shoulders. Notice if you feel any tightness in that area, and invite those muscles to tighten. Breathe gently with your attention here for a few breaths.

Then direct your attention to your heart center and mid torso, breathing in and out to the rhythm of your heartbeat.

Move your awareness down to your hip and pelvis region. Notice if you feel any tightness or sensation there. Direct your breath to that area of your body and invite it to soften.

Then direct your awareness to your thighs and knees Notice any stiffness there. With each breath, let your body relax.

After several breaths at your knee and calf region, bring your awareness to your ankles and your feet. Feel the earth rest beneath them, gently grounding you with each breath.

Then take in your whole body. Notice if any part of you is calling out for attention. If it is, then gently direct your breath to that area and try to give yourself what you need. Take 5–6 breaths here.

To close the meditation, take a few deep breaths, rub your hands together and place them over your eyes. When you are ready, open your eyes, softly removing your hands as you become accustomed to the light.

References

Ahmed, Sara. *The Cultural Politics of Emotion.* New York: Routledge, 2004.

Bartky, Sandra Lee. "Foucault, Femininity and the Modernization of Patriarchal Power." In *Feminism and Foucault: Paths of Resistance*, edited by Lee Quinby and Irene Diamond, 61–86. Boston, MA: Northeastern University Press, 1988.

Bordo, Susan. *Unbearable Weight: Feminism, Western Culture, and the Body.* Berkeley: University of California Press, 1993.

Brown University. "The Rationale Behind Contemplative Studies." *Brown University Contemplative Studies Initiative.* Accessed December 24, 2011, www.brown.edu/Faculty/Contemplative_Studies_Initiative/rationale.html.

Butler, Judith. *Gender Trouble: Feminism and the Subversion of Identity.* New York: Routledge, 1999.

Center for Contemplative Mind in Society. Accessed December 24, 2011, www.contemplativemind.org/practices/tree.html.

Davidson, Richard. "Investigating Healthy Minds." *On Being* with Krista Tippett, American Public Radio. Accessed December 24, 2011, http://being.publicradio.org/programs/2011/healthy-minds/.

Davis, Kathy. "Embody-ing Theory: Beyond Modernist and Postmodernist Readings of the Body." In *Embodied Practices: Feminist Perspectives on the Body*, edited by Kathy Davis, 1–26. Thousand Oaks, CA: SAGE, 1997.

Ellsworth, Elizabeth Ann. *Places of Learning: Media, Architecture, and Pedagogy.* New York: Routledge, 2005.

Ensler, Eve. "A Second Wind in Life: Inhabiting the Body After Cancer." *On Being* with Krista Tippett, American Public Radio. 5 March, 2015. Accessed June 8, 2015. www.onbeing.org/program/a-second-wind/6050.

Fanon, Franz. *Black Skin, White Masks.* Translated by Richard Philcox. New York: Grove Press, 2008.

Fay, Brian. *Critical Social Science: Liberation and Its Limits.* New York: Cornell University, 1987.

Fogel, Alan. *Body Sense: The Science and Practice of Embodied Self-Awareness.* New York: W.W. Norton, 2009.

Foucault, Michel. *Discipline and Punish.* New York: Vintage Books, 1979.

Freire, Paulo. *Pedagogy of the Oppressed.* New York: Herder and Herder, 1970.

Gustafson, Diana L. "Embodied Learning: The Body as an Epistemological Site." In *Meeting the Challenge: Innovative Feminist Pedagogies in Action*, edited by Maralee Mayberry and Ellen Cronan Rose, 249–274. New York: Routledge, 1999.

hooks, bell. *Yearning: Race, Gender, and Cultural Politics.* Brooklyn, NY: South End Press, 1999.

———. *Teaching to Transgress: Education as the Practice of Freedom.* New York: Routledge, 1994.

Johnson, Rae. "Oppression Embodied: The Intersecting Dimensions of Trauma, Oppression, and Somatic Psychology." *Academia.edu.* Accessed January 24, 2015, www.academia.edu/629607/Oppression_Embodied.

Kishimoto, Kyoko and Mumbi Mwangi. "Critiquing the Rhetoric of 'Safety' in Feminist Pedagogy: Women of Color Offering an Account of Ourselves." *Feminist Teacher* 19, no. 2 (2009): 87–102.

Levine, Peter. *In an Unspoken Voice: How the Body Releases Trauma and Restores Goodness.* Berkeley, CA: North Atlantic Books, 2010.

Lorde, Audre. *Burst of Light: Essays.* Ann Arbor, MI: Firebrand Books, 1988.

———. *Sister Outsider: Essays and Speeches.* Berkeley, CA: Crossing Press, 1984.

Miller, Richard. *Yoga Nidra: A Meditative Practice for Deep Relaxation and Healing.* Boulder, CO: Sounds True, 2010.

Palmer, Parker and Arthur Zajonc, with Megan Scribner. *The Heart of Higher Education, A Call to Renewal: Transforming the Academy through Collegial Conversations.* Foreword by Mark Nepo. San Francisco, CA: Jossey-Bass, 2010.

Powell, John A. "Preconference Opening Keynote." International Symposium for Contemplative Studies. Mind & Life Institute. Boston, MA, 2014. Accessed February 18, 2015, www.mindandlife.org/international-symposium-contemplative-studies/.

Rendón, Laura I. *Sentipensante (Sensing/Thinking) Pedagogy: Educating for Wholeness, Social Justice, and Liberation.* Foreword Mark Nepo. Sterling, VA: Stylus, 2014.

Shapiro, Shauna, Kirk Warren Brown, and John A. Astin. "Toward an Integration of Meditation into Higher Education: A Review of Research." *Center for Contemplative Mind in Society.* October 2008. Accessed June 8, 2015. www.contemplativemind.org/programs/academic/MedandHigherEd.

Shapiro, Sherry B. *Pedagogy and the Politics of the Body: A Critical Praxis.* New York: Garland, 1999.

———. "Toward Transformative Teachers: Critical and Feminist Perspectives in Dance Education." In *Dance, Power, and Difference: Critical and Feminist Perspectives on Dance Education*, edited by Sherry B. Shapiro, 7–22. Champaign, IL: Human Kinetics, 1998.

Spivak, Gayatri Chakravorty. *Outside the Teaching Machine.* New York: Routledge, 2008.

Van der Kolk, Bessel. *The Body Keeps Score: Brain, Mind, and Body in the Healing of Trauma.* New York: Viking Adult, 2014a.

———. "Restoring the Body: Yoga, EMDR, and Treating Trauma." *On Being* with Krista Tippett, American Public Media. October 30, 2014b/. Accessed January 12, 2015, http://onbeing.org/program/restoring-the-body-bessel-van-der-kolk-on-yoga-emdr-and-treating-trauma/5801#.VMJ7tlxjRBU.

3

RECOGNIZING AND UNLEARNING INTERNALIZED OPPRESSION

In order to be whole, we must recognize the despair oppression plants within each of us . . . [a]nd we must fight that inserted piece of self destruction that lives and flourishes like a poison inside of us, unexamined until it makes us turn on ourselves in each other. . . . [W]e can lessen its potency by the knowledge of our real connectedness, arcing across our differences.

—Audre Lorde (1984, 142)

Courses that teach about power and diversity usually address the issue of internalized oppression, which occurs when a member of a marginalized group begins to believe the negative messages about his/her/zir group that pervade the culture in which s/he/ze lives (Reynolds and Pope 1991; Szymanski, Kushubeck-West, and Meyer 2008). When a woman constantly tells herself that she is too fat or when a gay man believes that he is a "freak" because he is not attracted to women, internalized oppression is at work. The negative perceptions of their group so saturate society that they cannot help but breathe it in like smog (to use Beverly Tatum's metaphor, 2006). It is one of the most insidious forms of oppression because it eats a person from within. Often the messages are so deeply ingrained that it is hard to discern them, much less disrupt them. They start at a young age and usually become embedded in one's sense of self, particularly if the messages are not balanced or interrupted by positive counter messages (Tappan 2006). Unlike blatant types of oppression, such as hate crimes, internalized oppression is harder to pinpoint as a source of violence because we have learned to accept it as "truth" (Hilpato-Delgado, Payan, and Baca 2013). Many students will say that they are immune from these negative messages, but few of us are because they work most powerfully in our subconscious, below our levels of awareness.

Internalized oppression is a critical point to study in diversity courses, not just as objective knowledge but also as a dynamic presence in our classrooms. If a large percentage of the population suffers from internalized oppression in various ways and to various degrees, then we can assume that it is affecting how our students—and we as teachers—are present in the classroom. It also informs why conversations about oppression are so loaded. Anyone who has taught courses about oppression knows that if class discussions are authentic, then they are also hard. People have a variety of responses to the subject matter, responses that are shaped by their subject positions and lived experiences, which result in myriad reactions to the issues. Part of our job as teachers is to help students learn to recognize the role internalized oppression plays in their own lives. As students learn to do so, they can also learn to recognize and navigate how different positionalities shape class discussions. Just as importantly, we need to help students learn the tools to disrupt the damaging messages of internalized oppression within themselves.

These messages are harmful and self-destructive, but because internalized oppression operates below the surface, they can be difficult to actually *unlearn*. Contemplative practices are critical in that process. Knowledge about the concept alone is not enough. We need to offer students practices to understand and befriend their own deep reactions and to cultivate compassionate space so that they can learn to be more intentional about their responses. This skill will ultimately prove invaluable not only to having deeper, more productive discussions in the classroom but also as a life skill. In order to elucidate how contemplative practices can play that transformational role, we need to better understand internalized oppression.

What Is Internalized Oppression?

Internalized oppression results in a devaluation of one's own group. It becomes a kind of "hidden injury" because it lodges itself in our very being (Pyke and Johnson 2003; Tappan 2006). In his article, "Healing the Hidden Wounds of Racial Trauma," Kenneth V. Hardy defines racial oppression as "a traumatic form of interpersonal violence which can lacerate the spirit, scar the soul, and puncture the psyche" (2013, 25). One result of that oppression is a powerful "internal devaluation," of one's own racial group and a glorification of whiteness (Hardy 2013, 25). Members of marginalized groups have heard the negative messages of the dominant culture so often that we take them into our very sense of self. This results, Hardy argues, is an "assaulted sense of self," which occurs when one's very self-definition gets formed in the midst of this oppressive barrage. As Audre Lorde so powerfully wrote, "if I didn't define myself for myself, I would be crunched into other people's fantasies for me and eaten alive" (1984, 137). But for members of marginalized groups, forming one's own self-definition can be tricky, because most of us do not recognize how deeply this devaluation of self has gone. Often, our very notions of who we should be and how to define our identity are infused by internalized oppression (Pyke and Johnson 2003). Moreover, even if we do notice the negative taint on our being, we may not have the language to describe it or the support network to help counter those dominant ideologies and build a more empowering counter-narrative.

Social justice courses can provide a powerful antidote to the wounds of internalized oppression. But, as Hardy (2013) notes, it can still be hard to counter the harmful effects when many marginalized groups also internalize a sense of voicelessness and powerlessness. For some, any action one takes may feel dangerous. Hardy tells the story of a young Latino man who was racially profiled on a subway. This young man knew he was being discriminated against and could feel it further erode his sense of self but did not feel he had many options. As Hardy notes,

> His options are severely limited . . . he either speaks up and risks appearing to be threatening or remains silent and has his sense of self further assaulted.
> (2013, 26)

Not surprisingly, rage or a further devaluation of self are common ways to respond to this sense of powerlessness. While this example details the effects of racial oppression, both external and internal, similar processes occur for other marginalized groups.

This form of oppression is present in our students and, most likely in ourselves, in a variety of ways and degrees. Let us look at a couple scenarios about how it might appear in our classrooms. As with all the scenarios in this book, these are hypothetical composites of different students with whom I have worked over the years.

Scenario One

Lauren is a middle-class, heterosexual, White woman from a small town in the Midwestern United States. She chose to attend the four-year, state institution in a larger city because she wanted to get away from a place where everyone knew her and instead experience new possibilities. She is both excited and terrified at that prospect, as there are so many people at this university that she feels a bit lost. She took a course called "U.S. Race Relations" to fulfill a general requirement but did not really know what to expect and was not fully prepared for the opinions people express in class discussions. The ideas are so different than she heard from her family and friends back home. She came to college thinking she was strong and even cosmopolitan because she went a couple hours away from home, when many of her friends chose to stay at the local community college. But she feels so inadequate here. She is already gaining the notorious "freshman

(Continued)

fifteen" and feels awful about her body. She has always been kind of shy, and when she feels she does not look good, she is even less likely to be outgoing. How can she, when the inner self-talk is so critical of everything she does? She feels awfully intimidated to speak out in class—others will surely see how inadequate she is. When she does finally garner up the courage to contribute to class discussion, she prefaces her statements with "I don't know" and ends all of them with upward inflections that, unbeknown to her, makes her sentences sound like questions. When her professor challenges her to think more deeply about the concept, she hears that as confirmation that she has nothing really worthwhile to say. She gets smaller in her chair, quieter in class, lets her hair fall over her eyes and her shoulders round forward. After class, she goes to the dining hall and gets a large ice cream sundae but then feels even worse about herself for the rest of the day. She doesn't speak up in class discussion again, because, after all, she has nothing worthwhile to contribute, does she?

Scenario Two

José is a Chicano city kid who finds the Midwestern state school he attended far too suburban and White for his tastes. He misses the barrio, his buddies, and decent Mexican food. He notices that some of his classmates stare at all his tattoos, and he puts more and more walls up between him and his classmates. Everyone at home had them; it was a sign of manhood and belonging. Here it just makes him feel increasingly isolated. He finds himself getting gruffer and more defensive as the semester goes on, finding comfort in the displays of manhood so common amongst his buddies back home, so out of place in his current world. This display comforts him, even as it seems to alienate those around him. Without even realizing it, he is turning up the volume on his displays of masculinity because he is finding himself attracted to other men. Those feelings are not possible, he says to himself. He does not like "fags" he tells everyone any chance he gets, calling everything he does not like "gay." He makes sure that nothing he says or does could be read as effeminate and keeps his distance from the gay men on his floor. Part of him longs for their confidence in who they are, longs to ask them questions, but he will not give that part of himself any attention. They are "abnormal," he tells himself, (though secretly, they look happy and free in a way he longs to be); they are "freaks" and he wishes they would stop "flaunting" their new loves. He sleeps with numerous women to prove how manly and straight he is, though each experience leaves him disliking himself more. He cannot admit that, so he again finds comfort in the façade of heterosexual masculinity he is getting so good at. It is empty but it is safe and familiar.

Both of these scenarios illustrate different manifestations of internalized oppression. In the first one, Lauren has internalized the sense that she is not good enough and has little of value to contribute. The inner messages she tells herself are very gendered, as are the behaviors she exhibits. The upward vocal inflections and the ways she undermines her statements are common behaviors for women who have internalized the message that they have less value than those around them. Those messages are so strong that she tries to numb them with behaviors that only intensify them. Instead of seeing the statement from her professor as a way to grow and develop her thinking, she hears it as confirmation that she is worthless, and her voice becomes even more diminished.

José's experience is also deeply gendered, fueled by heteronormative, patriarchal, and racialized messages about what it means to be a man. He initially finds comfort in a certain display of masculinity because it reminds him of home and belonging; it becomes a kind of safety net when he feels racially Othered at his school. But as he begins to feel attracted to other men, he uses that heternormative, patriarchal masculine performance to bury those questions. He has learned a narrow formula for manhood that at times provides protection but at other times becomes a prison. He hides in that display and escalates public displays of homophobia and heterosexual libido to reassure himself and others that he is not gay. To explore those questions would mean revising his notion of manhood and unlearning all the deeply ingrained negative messages about gayness. Instead, he just keeps perfecting his performance of hypermasculinity, all the while feeling increasingly confused and empty.

As these scenarios illustrate, internalized oppression can result in a kind of self-fulfilling prophecy that ultimately supports the system of oppression because it gets the member of the marginalized group to "participate" in perpetuating our own limitations. In the scenarios above, Lauren believed she was inadequate in a way that continued to silence her, while José took refuge in a narrative of masculinity that made it impossible for him to explore his sexuality. When we believe the harmful messages about ourselves that society repeatedly reinforces, we begin to live into those limited realities instead of our full potential. For instance, perhaps an African American woman gets the message that she is not smart or capable enough to go to graduate school, so she never sees herself there. Because it seems out of reach, she either does not apply to graduate school or she does apply but fails because she does not believe she can do it. This subconscious self-sabotage compounds the external oppression she faces from institutionalized sexism and racism. If she fails, she may blame herself rather than institutionalized racism, which allows the latter to continue unchecked and makes it even less likely that she will ever try again, thus perpetuating her own marginalization. This pattern is *not* the same as blaming the victim. In these cases the individual is coerced into participating in his/her/zir oppression that is actually created and compounded by systems of marginalization and then to blame themselves in ways that keep those systems hidden and unchallenged.

As these examples illustrate, internalized oppression often takes the form of a brutal inner voice that does not speak our inner wisdom but instead reinforces the harmful narratives of the dominant culture.

I have learned over my years of teaching not to assume what such outer displays by students mean. A students' silence in class, for instance, might be a sign of deep listening or resistance. Students' outward performances usually conceal much more complex storylines than we might initially assume; more complex than even the students might recognize. Without unpacking those storylines, we will never get to the heart of authentic dialogues about oppression.

This insidious operation of internalized oppression is one of the most effective tools of systems of oppression because they erode a person from within but often operate invisibly (Heldman 2013). Moreover, it can be passed from generation to generation, which means that it becomes normalized in our communities and, therefore, is even harder to unearth. As E.J.R. David and Annie O. Derthick write in their article, "What Is Internalized Oppression, and So What?" this belief may become "conceptualized as a set of self-defeating cognitions, attitudes, and behaviors that were developed as one consistently experiences an oppressive environment" (David and Derthick 2013, 14). These messages can become embedded in both an individual and a community's very "cultural knowledge systems" to such an extent that "stimuli related to one's own group may automatically be associated with inferiority" (David and Derthick 2013, 14).

Internalized oppression results in self-hatred, depression, and violence toward oneself and others in one's group. David and Derthick (2013) assert that modern forms of racism are often more subtle than the more blatant attacks in the past, so that the individual doubts their own experiences. When the source of violence is not immediately evident, the resulting anger and pain often turns inward on oneself (David and Derthick 2013).

It is important not to blame the member of the marginalized group here. Rather, I am invoking Sandra Bartky's (1998) reworking of Michel Foucault to explain how we police ourselves. Power systems have infiltrated our psyches to such an extent that we conform without necessarily realizing we are doing so and without recognizing the deeply damaging effects that conformity has on our very sense of being. The system is so much more effective when we police ourselves because then we do the dirty work of institutionalized oppression but do not see its workings. Instead, we turn inward and do violence to ourselves.

One of the insidious effects of this process is that it can lead to intergroup fragmentation, which prevents people in marginalized groups from connecting to one another, thereby intensifying alienation. Individuals may try to emulate the oppressor because that is what is valued in society, which may result in conflict and accusations of assimilation within one's marginalized group. All of this ruptures the sense of community that is essential for combating the effects of internalized oppression. We need our community to resist these harmful messages, but when this support network is fractured by internalized oppression, we have fewer resources to draw on for resistance and resilience. Internalized oppression can also lead to intragroup violence, which prevents alliances between marginalized groups. Rather than bonding together against harmful systems, we turn on each other in a deeply effective divide and conquer strategy. This form of oppression remains unchecked if it is seen as the result of external factors rather than a process that has manifested internally. As people turn on themselves and each other they have no time or energy to dismantle the system of oppression itself.

Internalized Oppression as Trauma

While anti-oppression courses often address the harmful effects of internalized oppression, they rarely go so far as to consider it a trauma. I argue that precisely because of how it is embodied, we have to both recognize it as a trauma and use mindfulness as a way to heal it. This section will address the first point; later sections will address the second point.

Because it oppresses from the inside out, internalized oppression should be characterized as a kind of trauma, the intensity of which will vary from person to person. In this section, I will discuss this idea in terms of race-based trauma, with the understanding that it can operate in similar ways around sexual identity, gender identity, disability issues, and so on. The effects of everyday racism, both big and "small" are cumulative. They build up, often go unnamed, and can result in a hypervigilance that is very similar to that experienced by survivors of other kinds of trauma. Some call it "race-based trauma," and compare it to PTSD. Research suggests that this race-based trauma takes different forms in different communities of color. African Americans, for instance, are more likely to suffer from a kind of PTSD, while Latinos might be more likely to suffer from depression ("What Is the Psychological Impact of Racism" 2013). There are similar experiences for other marginalized groups. Because these experiences are often silenced, the individual often wonders if she/he/ze is imagining it. She/he/ze wonders if it is only happening to her/him/zir. If she/he/ze mentions the experience to a member of the dominant group, who likely has not experienced the series of microaggressions, that person will likely discount the experience. Rather than seeing the incident as a part of a larger pattern of oppression, it might be dismissed as someone just being rude or the person telling the story might be accused of overreacting. This silencing and invalidation are *part* of race-based trauma.

Moreover, because it happens so often, it becomes a part of the norm for the member of the marginalized group. Dr. Chris Emdin, Professor of Science Education at Columbia University, talks of this experience, "Because you've experienced this for so long, you're . . . experiencing life through this lens of what people are gonna do or not do, and that is the outcome of PTSD" ("What Is the

Psychological Impact of Racism" 2013). Like many traumas, these reactions are perpetuated and silenced by a sense of shame.

One very notable way that race-based trauma differs from the PTSD suffered by many soldiers is that unlike combat situations, in which a soldier serves on the front lines and then comes home with PTSD, racism is a system that most people of color cannot escape. There is no coming home from the front lines, except for, perhaps, surrounding oneself with one's own community from time to time. Some call this situation "racial battle fatigue" because it is present not just in the moment of discrimination itself but as an ever-present state of being, "navigating life in a world where you're always having the threat of being assaulted by racism" ("What Is the Psychological Impact of Racism" 2013).

Moreover, one's coping mechanism for internalized oppression may itself be racialized. For instance, Emdin tells the story of experiencing a shootout in his neighborhood when he was thirteen years old. When he went to school the next day, he jumped under the table when someone slammed a locker door. Instead of his action being understood as his natural aftershock from the shootout, his behavior was read as disruptive. Even if he could have told his teacher, "Hey, I heard gunshots last night and so I hit the floor reflexively," though his teacher might have accepted his explanation, the situation would likely still not have been situated with its larger context of daily, structural racism ("What Is the Psychological Impact of Racism" 2013).

If we think about this in terms of race-based trauma, then we can better understand how internalized oppression becomes embodied. Peter Levine, who works with somatic experiences and chronic stress, describes the difference between a healthy immune system and an unhealthy one. In the latter, a person is experiencing chronic trauma but has no outlets to release that traumatic stress. That person might be "stuck" in either a perpetual "on" or "off" state. The "on" state is characterized by hyper-vigilance and arousal, anxiety, panic, hostility, rage, emotional flooding, and digestive problems. The "off" state is characterized by depression, chronic fatigue, disorientation, disassociation, and poor digestion (Levine 2014). Trauma can result from an instance of acute stress or as an accumulation of ongoing, chronic stresses. It develops not only from the traumatic event itself but also from our inabilities to process, heal, and regulate those experiences (Levine 2014). What differentiates people suffering from PTSD from those who do not is that the former cannot integrate the experience into a coherent story; years later, they remain stuck on the same vivid, fragmented memories of the trauma and their story does not transform (van der Kolk 2014). In his work with the Somatic Experiencing Trauma Institute, Levine notes that animals who experience "fight or flight" moments of survival have mechanisms for releasing that stress, such as shaking trembling, or panting. Humans, however, may not have those releases. Levine writes that humans, have the problematic ability to neo-cortically override the natural discharge of excess survival energy. Through rationalizations, judgments, shame, enculturation, and fear of our bodily sensations, we may disrupt our innate capacity to self-regulate, functionally "recycling" disabling terror and helplessness.

(Levine 2015)

Levine (2014) offers a model of somatic experience to help clients recover, not by reexperiencing the trauma itself, but by coming back to their bodies and gently restoring a sense of peace and safety. His model seeks to provide the body with "corrective experiences" that counter the sense of powerlessness so prevalent in traumatic events. While I focus primarily on yoga, meditation, and other contemplative practices in this book, I do want to underscore a couple key points from Levine's work. Fully healing the trauma of internalized oppression is beyond the scope of academic classrooms, but we can nevertheless learn something from Levine's work.

First, he emphasizes the need to compassionately reconnect with our embodied experience in a way that is safe and appropriate for the individual. This will, of course, be based on the nature and timing of the trauma. For some students, coming back to their bodies in a classroom might not be a safe or healthy option. As Teo Drake, a social justice activist and a self-identified White queer man writes in one of his blog entries,

> There's the practice that calls me home to my body . . . as someone who has an immense amount of physical trauma, whose body wasn't quite the way I would have chosen, and who has been living with AIDS for eighteen years, coming home physically is not an easy task.
>
> (Drake 2013)

Not everyone has a positive relationship with their bodies. A combination of external trauma and internalized oppression, itself a trauma, can put some of us at war with our bodies. Contemplative practices that invite us to reconnect with our embodied experiences can be fraught for some students, and teachers need to be prepared for those complexities. See Chapter 6 for a further discussion of these tricky situations. But as a general rule, if internalized oppression is embodied, than the unlearning and healing process also needs to be embodied. Even if one does not believe the classroom's purpose is to heal, students are never going to really understand internalized oppression if they remain on a purely intellectual level, because it does not work exclusively on that level.

Internalized oppression is something we embody, often with a series of damaging effects well below the surface of our cognitive recognition. While diversity classes usually teach about this process conceptually and might even uncover the surface layers of its effects, students often do not learn how to recognize and dismantle its deeper roots. The first step, of course, is learning what internalized oppression is and how it operates. Students often get this layer on at least an intellectual level. They might, for instance, catch themselves judging their weight when they look in the mirror. Or they might notice that they believe that lighter skin people of color more attractive than darker skin people. Once they notice this, they can then unpack the sexist and racist history of those messages and see the detrimental effects those ideologies have on their communities. In many feminist classrooms, students have learned that "the personal is political," so they begin to understand that personal stories matter and that lived experiences are shaped by political power dynamics. These are all critical steps in disrupting the process and countering the consequences of internalized oppression. If we are really to understand and unearth these harmful consequences, however, we need to go even deeper. We need to help students understand how internalized oppression *manifests* in their bodies, psyches, and emotions. We need to help them recognize when those around them are caught in the throes of an internalized attack. And we need to provide them with tools they can use to meet those attacks with empowering, compassionate alternatives.

The second point to take from Levine's work is the critical need to feel an *empowered embodiment*. Levine (2014) talks about providing a corrective experience to counter the helplessness that accompanies traumatic incidents. Both the individual and the community need to feel that they have the power to create change in their life circumstances, what social justice advocates call agency. Mindfulness offers us practical tools that can be used in the moment to reframe our embodied reactions. When combined with social justice education that present empowering narratives about marginalized groups and helps subordinated individuals come to voice, we can better offer students *ways to claim* their agency.

Internalized Oppression and Identity Development Models

It is important to note that not every member of a marginalized group experiences internalized oppression or experiences it in the same way. Some people are proud of their culture and, if they have been surrounded by many positive counter-narratives, might have avoided imbibing many of the poisonous messages about themselves and their communities. We should not assume that all people of a marginalized groups have the same experiences. There is a fine line between recognizing patterns of oppression while also treating people as individuals with their own unique experiences.

Moreover, people are often at various stages in the process of unlearning internalized oppression, just as they might be at different stages of political awareness. Different messages may be more powerful for some individuals than others, a process that becomes even more complex when we consider intersectional identities. Our race, gender, class, ability, sexual, and national identity weave together to position us in complex ways in power dynamics and in relation to one another. An Asian American woman will experience her racialization differently than an Asian American man, which becomes even more nuanced if we consider their lived experiences as a Hmong American woman and Japanese American man, for instance. While a gay man and a lesbian woman might both have internalized homophobia, the latter's experience will be greatly shaped by the social messages that women receive, which she may or may not fit. Many masculine-performing queer women express alienation from the beauty messages and assumptions about women that position them as outsiders, which then compounds their internalized homophobia.

These multi-layered identities are present in most classrooms and they will shape people's experiences of internalized oppression, of each other, and of class discussions (Reynolds and Pope 1991). When students are discussing matters of power and oppression, their perceptions, responses, and understanding of class material will be shaped by their positionalities.

To complicate matters further, students will likely be at varying stages of their own identity development. Students will be coming to the material at different levels of self-awareness. There are many stages of identity development models, including ones that vary by type of identity (LGBTQ, racial identity, and so on). None of these models are neatly linear. A person can loop back through various stages or remain at one stage for a long period of time. Moreover, they may be at different stages with different aspects of their identity, so that they might be more integrated in their sense of gender identity but less so about their ethnic identity. Most students are not aware of these models and so are not yet able to see them at work in themselves or their classmates.

A full discussion of the different models are beyond the scope of this project. But it would be helpful to take a look at some of the common stages to better understand the impact it could have on a class discussion when students are coming to a topic such as homophobia or racism from very different places in their development. For members of subordinate groups, most of the models begin with a step before one has any experience or familiarity with marginalized identity, then move to the initial encounter stage, which is usually characterized by some denial, dismay, or dawning awareness. They often then deeply immerse themselves in the culture of the marginalized group, deeming it "better than" and "separate from" the dominant group. Eventually, there is usually a stage of integration, in which the marginalized identity becomes one aspect of a more holistic participation in a complex world. Members of dominant groups tend to follow a parallel path, which begins with a preencounter lack of familiarity with communities of color, for instance, and their own White racial identity (Helms 1993). Then, once the encounter happens, there tends to be a dismantling of all that they once knew, which usually produces an attempt to regain some solid ground by moving into a denial stage. Eventually, they, too, can reach a more holistic integration of understanding and identity. Beverly Tatum, for instance, denotes a common pattern for people of color as they come to a sense of racial identity as involving the following stages: Preencounter, Encounter, Immersion/Emmersion, Internalization, and Internalization/Commitment. Whites, she notes, also go through a parallel identity development trajectory, including Contact, Disintegration, Reintegration, Pseudo-Independent, Immersion/Emmersion, and Autonomy (Tatum 2014). Some models describe movement through stages (some for Whites, some for people of color, and some for both) of Conformity, Acceptance, Dissonance, Immersion, Resistance, Retreat, Emersion, Internalization, Emergence, and Integrative Awareness (Rabow 2014).

For our purposes here, the important point to note is that in any given classroom, students are likely to be at very different stages of their identity development. Moreover, they might be at different stages for different aspects of their identity. For instance, a student might be at an Integrative Awareness stage for their racial identity but may be in the process of coming out and so at a very different stage with his/her/zir queer identity. While these models are not definitive and should not be used to "categorize" or "rank" students, I do find them to be a helpful way of making sense of why some class discussions about oppression go the way they do.

For instance, if a White student is at the Resistant stage of identity development, he might be denying that racism exists or that he has any part in it. Think about how that response would be received by, say, a Chicano student in the Immersion stage, in which s/he/ze were passionately learning about and highly valuing all aspects of his/her/zir Chicano culture. Similarly, a bisexual student in the Immersion stage of LGBTQ identity might feel particularly frustrated if the focus of the class discussion is on race at the (perceived) exclusion of sexual identity issues. All of these different responses might be in the room, and the teacher's job is to help facilitate these differences in productive and compassionate ways.

Moreover, it is not just students who are on this identity development path or who are susceptible to internalized oppression. Teachers also need to engage in this process, because we are, inevitably, in our own processes of identity development, which can shape how we respond to students. Feminism has long recognized that change agents have to do our own work; we cannot expect society to change if we are not also examining and interrupting our own power and privilege, wherever we may find it. The same is true of internalized oppression. Most of us have imbibed detrimental cultural messages. They will vary based on cultural context, historical moments, and how we are positioned in power dynamics, but few of us are immune from those messages. Teachers need to be mindful of the ways our own identity development and internalized messages might be shaping how we respond to events in the classroom.

I will speak more to this challenge elsewhere. Here, I want to focus on the idea that when people are at different stages of processing their identities and their internalized oppression, those differences are going to be evident in class discussions. Mindfulness is a critical way of helping students learn to come to terms with their own sociopolitical locations and the ways it shapes their responses to others.

When Internalized Oppression Strikes

In order to explore some of the complexities of how internalized oppression might manifest in a classroom and how mindfulness might help us work with these situations in productive ways, let us explore an extended example. This happened recently when I was teaching an upper-division Heterosexism and Homophobia class at a Midwestern, four-year state university.

Shortly into the semester, some bantering between the Lesbian, Gay, Bisexual, Transgender, Queer, and Allied (LGBTQA) students and myself occurred—the kind of bantering that is fairly common in queer communities as a way of building community. The LGBTQ students in the class were predominantly gay men (some White, some Asian American), with at least one bisexual woman and several feminist LGBTQ allies (at least that is what I know from their comments in class; there may have been other LGBTQ students who did not come out).

Late that night I woke up unable to sleep (something that often happens when I teach night classes because my mind is still caught up in the teaching mode). Despite the late hour, I checked my work e-mail. There was a message from a male student of color with whom I had worked in several classes. The e-mail was a thoughtful and lengthy note about how uncomfortable he felt in class that night. He talked about how much he wanted to support LGBTQ people and people of color on campus but how White-centered he felt the discussion in class was that evening. It was a critique of institutionalized racism throughout his university career that centered the perspectives of whiteness while erasing and/or marginalized those of communities of color. He wrote of his deep sadness, his lack of a sense of safety, his feelings of inadequacy in fighting the system, his doubts in his own reactions, and his hope that, despite all these reactions, he could still, somehow make a difference.

Reading his note months later, I see it as a deep and painful realization of how institutionalized racism shaped his educational experience. But in my initial reading of the note, my body went into panic mode. My heart started to beat rapidly and the negative shame messages kicked in, reverberating for the rest of the night so that I hardly slept. It is a sign of how stressed and depleted I was at that point in my career that I checked my work e-mail at that hour, which I no longer do, as I think it is critical to a mindful and healthy well-being to have healthy boundaries between work and play. But I did not have healthy work boundaries that year. As I read the message, I felt waves of shame wash over me, accompanied by the soundtrack that I am an awful teacher and a horrible anti-racist educator/activist.

I never want any student to feel that way in my class; I felt like his note made glaringly clear that I just reinforced racism precisely when I was trying to work to undo both it and its intersections with heteronormativity/queer issues.

Fortunately, I had enough presence of mind to know that I did not want the student or my colleagues of color to bear witness to my reaction. It is not their job to take care of me. As a White, queer, feminist, anti-racist educator who grew up in a Midwestern suburb, I know that I will spend the rest of my life unlearning racism. Some days, I do that better than others, and whenever I make a mistake, I know that I need to process it and do my work of dismantling my power and privilege.

So in the morning, I wrote him a message that thanked him for sharing his feelings with me. I told him that classes like this one push all of us in different ways and part of what we need to do in our classroom and as marginalized communities is to make space for all the complex identities and experiences that are in the room. I said I wanted to be accountable for when I did and did not do that as a teacher. I invited him to keep talking with me throughout the semester about his reactions to the class. As the semester went on, he shared with me how he was working on his own internalized homophobia. We had several thoughtful discussions in class about intersections of identities—how race, ethnicity, sexuality, class, gender identity, and national identity interact in complex ways. Ultimately, I think they were productive discussions.

I have thought long and hard about this incident. It has been the combination of my feminist politics, my feminist pedagogy, and my yoga practice that have allowed me to make sense of it. I obviously know more about my own internal reactions than I know about his. For the latter, I can only reflect on his actions, his statements, and his e-mails. But I have carefully mined my own and here is how I am currently making sense of them.

The "gay bonding" bantering occurred partly because there are notably FEW spaces on campus where such things can happen, especially outside of student organizations and informal social gathering. The student who wrote me was also taking another class that semester that focused on communities of color—also a rarity on our campus. For both LGBTQ and students of color at our university, community can be found through student organization and in small, informal groupings, but it is rare in the institutionalized space of the classroom. In addition, though several of the students in my class were students of color, it was nevertheless a predominantly White class, as are many of the classes at this university. A feeling of outsiderness can be a common experience for students of marginalized groups.

This student's place in his identity development would also be a factor, as, I would add, was mine. If, for instance, he was in the immersion stage of his racial identity, that would affect his reaction; if I was at anything other than integration, that would also have been a factor. Moreover, few marginalized communities have done a very good job of addressing intersectionality and inclusion. Study any ethnic, racial, sexual, or gender identity group and there will be stories of people who felt excluded because of part of their identity. The queer community is no different. We have not done always done a good job of being inclusive, and so while the course readings represented a variety of different queer perspectives, there were still issues of inclusion. In fact, that was one of the discussions we had at length in the class.

One way of understanding this situation is to see the internalized oppression and privilege kick in for both of us. He described his ongoing sense of being an outsider on campus (and in society) that was triggered in our classroom. In addition, he noted that he was working through his own learned homophobia. My response reflected my own layers of internalized homophobia and my ongoing unlearning of racism and White privilege. I should add here that this all happened when there were intense academic curriculum fights over anti-racism curriculum on campus, which I was a part of both as an anti-racist ally on campus and because I was, at the time, chair of the department that offered the majority of those courses. At the same time, the faculty union had once again voluntarily taken domestic partnership benefits off the negotiating table for the current contract, and there had been little mention of queer issues in my department. So part of my reaction was also my frustration at the barriers to anti-racist work and some internal resentment about when queer issues were going to get some attention.

How do I know this was internalized oppression? For two reasons. One, that resentment I just mentioned is completely counter to my feminist politics. I do NOT believe that oppressed groups need to be pitted against each other or that queer issues and anti-racist issues are mutually exclusive. I believe they are all part of the same capitalist patriarchy that benefits when we see each other as separate, and I recognize that many people are located in multiple communities (such as queers of color) and, therefore, need all the issues addressed simultaneously. So, of course, I did not want to act on that internal resentment.

But I do not think it is helpful to pretend it was not there, because that, too, is learned behavior. And that leads me to the second way I knew it was internalized oppression: the intensity of the reaction was far out of proportion for the situation. I get e-mails from students processing things all the time. They do not all send me into a tailspin. Moreover, the volume of the shaming narratives that popped up ("You're a horrible person and an awful teacher. You will never be enough.") were all-too-familiar. As my partner said when I talked to her about the situation, the student did not say any of those things, and, in fact, probably would not have trusted me enough to share his feelings with me if he had thought them. This was more than the proverbial White guilt; it was the result of long-standing sexist and homophobic internalized oppression that simply took this opportunity to ramp up the volume.

The physical reaction was also evidence of that. If I were just working through something intellectually, I would not have had the physical symptoms that come with emotional distress. They were familiar narratives that I am more susceptible to when I am depleted and exhausted—which I was after nine years of a heavy teaching and administrative load. I had taken on this course as an overload because as a feminist queer woman, I firmly believe that it needed to be taught. In hindsight, I see what a mistake that was. As the famous slogan goes, "don't get too tired, angry, lonely, or hungry." We are more susceptible to the power of internalized oppression when our personal resources are low. Judging from the e-mail the student sent, he had a similar level of intense reaction.

I chose this example to illustrate that internalized oppression is in social justice classrooms (indeed, in every classroom) in a myriad of ways. Both students and teachers can experience it, albeit in different ways and for different reasons (internalized homophobia, internalized racism, internalized sexism, and so on) and at different stages of our identity development. All of these factors will affect how internalized oppression manifests in any given classroom.

While most social justice classrooms address the idea conceptually, few go so deep as to plumb this complexity. But if we do not get to the layer of embodiment, then the gut responses to these manifestations do not do them a service and, in fact, may perpetuate the problem. As one of my yogini friends says, she learned the difference between insight and anxiety by realizing that anxiety screams, and what it has to say is usually nonsense. Similarly, I have come to learn the different between a constructive critique of my teaching and a shaming condemnation of my very worth as a teacher and a person; the former is useful and has a basis in reality; the latter does not. What allowed me to process my reaction in some sort of productive way was my mindfulness, informed by my feminism. Either component alone would not have been enough. My mindfulness allowed me to recognize the disproportionate reaction I had and move it into a more intentional space, where I could make a better pedagogical choice. My feminism informed the choice I made about how to handle the situation. It allowed me to hold the space for the student to have whatever reaction he was having, without repercussion or judgment, which I hope allowed him to walk through it in his own way. It also helped me do my own internal work of reflecting upon and challenging my own internalized oppression and White privilege.

I believe that some version of these complex responses are happening in every classroom about social justice, which is one of the reasons the discussions are so intense and hard. While hard can be productive, we have to offer the tools with which to make them rich and compassionate learning experiences rather than merely fraught battlegrounds. Mindfulness can create the space in which to notice our reaction, allow it to be, and reroute it to a space in which we can make an intentional choice about how we react. This process is critical to unlearning internalized oppression. With its seeds in compassion for self and others, mindfulness is also a necessary tool for healing the consequences of internalized oppression. The wounds it leaves are deep, so we need to cultivate kindness, compassion, and resilience to recover from them. The remainder of this chapter will unpack some of the key steps of mindful unlearning.

Mindful Unlearning

The process of disrupting internalized oppression is not a linear one that leads directly to "progress." Instead, it loops back as it gets triggered, sometimes staying in one place, other times moving forward. Some messages are more easily unlearned than others. Internalized oppression works at the level of the subconscious, so often we are not aware of how deeply embedded the messages are. One of the most critical steps in the unlearning process is critical awareness or what feminist and anti-oppression pedagogy calls self-reflection. Mindful education takes this idea to an even deeper, *embodied* level.

Let us revisit Langer's definition of mindful learning; it involves "the continuous creation of new categories, openness to new information, and implicit awareness of more than one perspective" (1997, 4). She distinguishes this type of education from mindless learning, which is "characterizes by an entrapment in old categories; by automatic behavior that precludes attending to new signals; and by action that operates from a single perspective" (1997, 4). Unlike typical ways of understanding intelligence, Langer argues that mindfulness involves both:

> a stepping back from both perceived problems and perceived solutions to view situations as novel . . . [and is] developed from an actor's ability to experience personal control by shifting perspectives.
>
> (1997, 110)

This emphasis on empowerment and agency is critical to counter internalized oppression, which is demoralizing because it operates by making us think that the negative messages are "Truth," instead of a set of ideologies constructed by oppressive systems. Once we can step back and see them for what they are, we can begin to see we also have options. Because mindful learning helps us see things from different perspectives, we can begin to understand the function that those messages serve in upholding systems of oppression, how they manipulate us into participating in our own oppression, and the wounding effect they have on our very being.

Cultivating the Witness

A critical mindfulness skill for unlearning internalized oppression is the cultivation of the Witness, which means the ability to observe what is happening.

Rather than drowning in our experiences, the Witness lets us be bigger than our emotions. It is the ability to be present with what is happening without being consumed by it. We learn to see our experiences clearly and without judgment, but we also recognize that they are like clouds in the sky—there is a constant element to our self that is bigger than the momentary experiences, which we eventually recognize will pass.

I have already established that internalized oppression operates physically as well as emotionally. When triggered, it can feel similar to panic attacks; it often overwhelms the person and either immobilizes him/her/zir or compels him/her/zir to act out, often in unhealthy ways. A crucial step to unlearning it, then, it to become very familiar with how it operated in us (Ehrenhault 2014). We can more easily discern that when we realize that we are not our experiences: they are part of us, but they are not ALL of us. We can then get big enough to be able to witness the experiences, learning their texture, their shape, their tenor, and our own individual triggers. People experience internalized oppression differently and have usually developed different coping mechanisms for them. So part of the process of unlearning internalized oppression is to become very familiar with how it works for each of us as individuals and then to learn to see it at play in communities.

Internalized oppression regularly appears in our class discussions. When the subject matter hits close to home, students can become emotional and vulnerable. It is not uncommon, for instance, for a student in my courses to identify themselves as a survivor of sexual assault in the unit about violence against women. Students of color regularly share their experiences of racism, while LGBTQ students often share their processes of coming out. As teachers, we value these contributions because they help the students—both those who are speaking and those who are listening—apply the concepts we study to their everyday lives. These contributions deepen the learning process by having students participate directly in it. When examples come from the students themselves and not just the readings or the teacher, the overall learning process deepens for everyone.

But the pedagogy could go much deeper if we brought it to an embodied level. We hold our life experiences in our bodies and in our psyches. "Being able to tolerate visceral experience is indispensable in being able to change one's fundamental approach to life . . . change depends on the capacity to experience emotions directly and deeply. If our access to core experience is blocked or distorted, we are unable to deal with our most vital psychological processes" (Emerson and Hopper 2011, xxiv). They will then manifest in hidden, often harmful or unproductive ways. Of course, it is not our job as teachers to play the role of therapist. However, we will be able to much more productively facilitate discussions in which internalized oppression arises if we can teach students to recognize it for what it is and provide them with some tools for handling it more effectively.

Nonjudgmental Awareness

So the first step is to Witness what is happening. As we begin to observe what our reactions are in any given moment, it is imperative that we cultivate nonjudgmental compassion for what we are experiencing. When we judge or fight against our internal reactions, we perpetuate the violence done by external systems of oppression. Our internalized ideologies are inevitable byproducts of institutionalized oppression, so rather than condemn our own reactions, we can begin to see them as the system working exactly the way it is designed to work. We certainly want to unravel these ideologies, but, paradoxically, they actually get stronger when we fight against them. Moreover, since the ideologies are usually deeply embedded in our sense of self, when we meet them with aggression, we actually do more violence to ourselves, which then strengthens rather than undermines the systems of oppression. It is counterintuitive, but far more effective, to meet our responses with nonjudgmental compassion. Let me reiterate my assertion that greeting our reactions with compassion is not the same thing as accepting oppression itself. Instead, in a system that does violence to marginalized groups in a myriad of ways, filling ourselves with acceptance and compassion is a radical act of self-preservation. It can heal us in ways that lets us dismantle those negative messages and, as a result, lets us more powerfully fight oppression in the outer world.

When we become very familiar with how internalized oppression manifests in ourselves, we can also learn to have compassion for how it shows up in others. We can see it at work in our classmates, our friends, our coworkers, and we can have compassion for them as well. Sometimes, when a person lashes out at us, it is coming from a place of internalized oppression. José's public displays of homophobia, for instance, were symptoms of his own internal struggle with his sexuality. Audre Lorde describes something similar when she talks of the anger between Black women as being a manifestation of their own, learned, self-denigration (1984). Trujillo describes how Chicano lesbians have to learn to overcome the patriarchal hatred of women to love themselves and other women (2006). Each of these examples of internalized oppression produce outward behaviors that will only escalate if others in the room simply react to them. Instead, we could learn be allies and support network as we all strive to unlearn internalized oppression, which goes a long way in counteracting the Othering process so fundamental to oppression. Instead, we can learn new, more compassionate ways of relating to ourselves and others.

Choosing Which Storylines to Feed

If, as I argue, internalized oppression reflects learned and deeply ingrained ideologies, then this next step in mindfulness is a critical part of the unlearning process. After we discern and accept what we are experiencing, mindfulness practice teaches us to see the storylines we attach to the visceral experiences. The storyline is the narrative meaning we give to what are really physiological or psychological responses. Most of the time, our reactions are both prolonged and made worse by the storylines we attach to them. When we are upset about something days after the exchange occurred, that is a storyline. When we interpret a comment to mean that we are not good enough and then berate ourselves for all the times when we have not been good enough, that is a storyline. When we continue to get upset because we second guess ourselves, that is a storyline. While most mindfulness teachers, from a variety of traditions, talk of letting go of the storyline, I want to emphasize that the storyline itself is informed by oppressive ideologies. Notice that many of the storylines that cause us the most harm are negative ones that undermine our sense of self. These storylines do not come out of nowhere, nor are they accidental. They are learned ideologies that serve the purposes of systems of oppression. Let us think back to Lauren in Scenario One from earlier in this chapter. The actual event was an exchange with her professor. The lasting effect, though, was caused by how she interpreted that exchange through the lens of patriarchal assumptions about her inadequacy. The painful experience of listening to that constant internal barrage of gendered self-condemnation made her turn inward on herself even further, thereby creating a self-fulfilling prophecy. Similarly, José was unable to openly explore his sexuality and create his own definition of masculinity because of the homophobic and patriarchal storylines he internalized. Rather than blaming Lauren or José for these reactions, we can begin see how storylines as shaped by systems of oppression.

So the first step in this stage is to recognize the storylines as part of oppression and find ways to dismantle them. Often, what happens is that we react, and then we are well into the storyline before we realize it. Mindfulness teaches us to Witness that storyline and choose not to indulge it. We can refrain from being pushed by the momentum of the storyline and instead stay with our present reaction. When we do that, we can create a pause that allows us to more mindfully—rather than habitually—respond to any given situation.

How does this process work? Let us think back to our discussion about trauma and consider how our limbic system works. When we experience sensory stimuli, such as loud noises, our limbic system receives and processes the emotional stimuli. Sometimes that is done automatically throughout autonomic nervous system, which is good in a situation of survival. When we need to react quickly with fight or flight responses, this sympathetic nervous system response is useful. But if it happens consistently or in non-emergency situations, then it may no longer be serving us. It may be perpetuating gut reactions that are not helpful or relevant in the current situation.

Contemplative practices such as yoga and meditation help us create a pause that moves the stimuli from our limbic system to our frontal cerebral cortex, the area of our brain that is responsible for making rational decisions. Research on

MRIs have shown that meditation does indeed allow us to reroute our responses from an automatic, gut response in the limbic system to the prefrontal cortex, where we can make a decision about how to react. We may still choose to react in the same old way, but at least we can make a more informed decision. Yoga teacher Sara Martin (2014) calls this "creating the holy pause"—making space to determine mindfully what is actually happening. For instance, if we go back to the example given by Professor Emdin, his gut response during a shootout in his neighborhood was to hit the ground—probably a productive safety choice in that moment. The next day, when he heard a locker door slam, a "holy pause" might have allowed him to rationally realize that the situation was not one of life and death. He may have decided not to hit the ground.

It would be unreasonable to expect a different response immediately after a traumatic event, but if we are reacting in the same way for years, we may find that those reactions no longer serve us. Being in a state of hypervigilance and arousal takes its toll physically, emotionally, and psychologically. At some point in the healing process, it may be useful to learn to discern the difference between an emergency situation and an everyday one. We can learn to create that "holy pause" through mindfulness. I should emphasize here that I do not mean to reinforce the Cartesian patriarchal privileging of the rational (often associated with the masculine) over the emotional (often associated with the feminine). Rather, I mean to distinguish between a *reactive* action and an *intentional* one. Mindfulness creates the space that allows us to discern a better perspective on the situation and make an intentional choice.

Once we familiarize ourselves with how internalized oppression manifests in us as individuals, we also need to learn what our gut reactions tend to be. Those automatic responses will vary from person to person, just as the physiological responses may vary. Maybe we verbally lash out at the person who triggered the wave of internalized oppression. Maybe we physically shrink to take up as little space as possible in an attempt to disappear. Maybe we make ourselves busy to try to control the situation. Maybe we try to numb with nicotine, alcohol, or eating. For many of us, our automatic response to internalized oppression are probably survival mechanisms that we have developed over time. They may or may not serve us at this point in our learning process. We can all be more effective when we can intentionally respond after discerning what reactions are best in different situations.

Contemplative practices help us cultivate that discernment. By developing our Witness, mindfulness can help us create a space between what we experience and how we react. In that pause, we can gather ourselves and make an intentional decision about how we wish to respond. Most of us cannot be intentional when we are overwhelmed by the experience itself. The degree to which we can create that pause will, of course, depend on the nature of the internalized oppression, how many layers of our history it triggers, and our familiarity with mindfulness practice.

Just as the storylines of internalized oppression become stronger when they are fed, so too will our healthier sense of self. Anti-oppression pedagogy is not just about critiquing the injustice of what is; it is also about creating more empowered alternatives. Whatever we nourish becomes more powerful and resilient. So we not only choose to interrupt the oppressive ideologies, but we also choose to feed healthier ones. This, again, is where compassion comes in, alongside the pro-active and progressive contributions of feminist and other social justice praxis. We do not have to recreate the wheel; other social change agents have gone before us with wisdom from which we can learn.

Thus, when we notice internalized oppression arising, we can practice our skills of being with the present and letting go of the storyline. We can learn to meet ourselves with compassion and send loving energy to a more empowering vision of ourselves and our world. Doing so will not only divest systems of oppression of one of their most powerful tools; it will also make us healthier and happier.

Seven Steps to Mindfully Unlearning Internalized Oppression

Here are some practical tools to use in the moment of an internalized oppression attack. Like all mindfulness awareness, it takes time and regular practice to become adept at them.

1. Become Familiar with How It Works in Each Individual.

The first step to unlearning internalized oppression is to become deeply aware of how it manifests in each of us as individuals. There will be many commonalities between how different women, for instance, experience the objectification of women they have learned and how Asian Americans experience internalized racism. But there will also be very important differences because each person's lived experience will produce particular reactions to it. In diversity classrooms, we often teach students how to recognize dominant cultural messages, such as the pressure to remain thin or the feeling of not being beautiful enough. But how does that actually manifest in our bodies? That is where embodied mindfulness comes in.

When we are in the throes of an internalized oppression attack, we might feel waves of shame wash over us. Our face might flush, we might break into a sweat, our body might tense, we might be flooded with rage or sadness as our internal voice starts repeating messages of inadequacy. We have physiological and emotional responses to internalized oppression. In order to learn to recognize that, we have to learn to be present with what is. We need to help students learn to meet their experience with curiosity and nonjudgmental awareness.

But the first step cannot be to intellectualize the experience, because that can get in the way of understanding what is happening before the intellect kicks in, the first several layers of Levine's SIBAM model. For many of us, internalized oppression has insinuated itself into the very cells of our beings, and so we need to learn to sit with that in order to recognize it. As with most skills of this nature, we should be practicing mindful awareness everyday so that it is available to us in stressful situations; we cannot expect for the reflection to accurately kick in if we only practice the skill in high-intensity moments. Adopting a regular contemplative practice is critical.

2. Breathe into It. Accept It. Befriend It.

Mindfulness practices should help students find their centers and learn to trust and validate their own experiences. They can learn to understand their experience but also see it from different perspectives. The key to mindfulness is to allow the present to be as it is without judgment. This does not mean that we just acquiesce to oppression but rather that we accept that our reaction to it, in that moment, is what it is. Rather than fighting or condemning our reactions, we can witness our responses as the consequences of being a member of a marginalized group in an inequitable society. While it is not surprising that we have internalized some of the negative messages that saturate the society in which we live, we will not unlearn them if we harden against them—at least in relation to ourselves.

Counter to what our gut might tell us, the best way to dismantle the effects of internalized oppression is to soften, breathe, and befriend our experience. This is a process that occurs in relation to ourselves—it may make sense to keep barriers up to protect us from the people around us, particularly if we are in unsafe environments. But if we place those barriers on our relationship with our own experience, they will become stronger. The more we can meet our internal experience with compassion and acceptance, the quicker it will dissipate. Mindfully breathing and creating that holy pause will help it to pass without getting a foothold.

3. Use It as a Point of Connection with Others Rather Than an Alienation from Others.

Internalized oppression can result in intense feelings of both isolation and alienation. In his interview with the *Huffington Post*'s "What Is the Psychological Impact of Racism," Emdin argues that when it has affected an African American person psychologically, not only would she/he/ze be unlikely to talk with White people about the experience, for fear it would be misunderstood or invalidated, but she/he/ze would also be unlikely to talk with other African Americans about it. This isolation can intensify the effect of the internalized oppression and our own alienation. One way to heal from that would be to use it as a point of connection with others, at least when we feel safe enough to do so.

A common way to survive oppression is to harden ourselves to others, particularly those different from oneself, especially if one sees that person as an "oppressor." Admittedly, there are situations in which we need to keep our guard up. But mindfulness helps us learn how to use those moments of pain to connect with others rather than to separate ourselves. When we see internalized oppression as inevitable by products of living in an inequitable society, we can learn to connect to others who have experienced similar pain. Opening a space for connection rather than division lets us feel part of a greater whole.

4. Develop a Set of Tools to Meet the Wave of Internalized Oppression in the Moment.

Some contemplative practices, such as yoga and meditation, are not goals so much as ways of being. They offer a range of tools that students can learn to help them meet various life challenges. Different *pranayama* (breathing) and meditation practices serve different energetic and psychological functions. As we teach students mindfulness practices in the classroom, we can also teach them when such practices can be useful in handling their experiences of internalized oppression. Some practices will work more effectively for different people than others. Helping students experience a variety of practices and determine which are useful for them under which circumstances helps them build a rich and versatile tool belt. Learning which tools work for ourselves is part of the discernment that is critical for unlearning internalized oppression.

5. Develop a Process of Reflection.

Mindfulness is inherently a process of reflection and inquiry. If students are given a regular opportunity to cultivate this process, they can become adept at it. It is most effective when they can explore their reactions with curiosity on a regular basis in everyday situations, so that the skills are available to them when they are under a stressful situation. We cannot expect to access them under stress if we are not already familiar with them. Self-reflection is a process, so each time we engage in it, we have another opportunity to go deeper and become more nuanced in our understanding of ourselves and others.

6. Then Intellectualize It.

After these first five steps in the process, *then* it will be useful to intellectualize the matter. The kinds of discussions and analysis that already occur in most anti-oppression classrooms are invaluable, but they become more useful after students learn to unpack their embodied responses and see them as part of the process of oppression. Any attempt to analyze prior to this self-reflection will likely be distorted by the lenses of our own reactions. Once they understand what their reactions are, why they occur, and how they shape their perceptions, then the intellectual analysis serves more use.

7. Confide in Trusted Friends and Loved Ones.

Students can let their close community members know how internalized oppression manifests, how they tend to respond, and how they would like to respond, so that their community can help in the process. We will not immediately become adept at creating the "holy pause" to act intentionally. It will likely take some time to unlearn internalized oppression, and we will probably fall into old patterns many times. Letting our support network understand what that looks like in us and how we would prefer to respond can keep us on the right track. If our friends and loved ones can recognize that a particular reaction is an old pattern that we are trying to unlearn, they can, perhaps, choose not to react to our response but rather help us make different choices.

Unlearning oppression is not a linear or quick process. It took a lifetime to learn it, and it will take quite some time to unlearn it. We have to first learn to recognize the process, then accept and befriend it, then reflect upon and analyze it. Only then can we transform it. Teaching students a range of mindfulness practices in the classroom lets them cultivate a rich tool belt; teaching them to understand what is happening lets them make more mindful choices. Once they realize they have choices, they can feel more empowered to unlearn internalized oppression and to compassionately recognize that process in others. Many of these same skills are useful in another deeply powerful tool of oppression: privilege. The next chapter will explore how to build on the mindfulness skills outlined here to interrupt privilege held by members of dominant groups.

Mindfulness Practices

Tonglen

This practice comes from Buddhist traditions but can be practiced in a secular way. The point of this practice is to use the experience of suffering to connect with others rather than to separate. Often, we have to start with our own suffering.

To practice Tonglen, we breathe in the pain, confusion, and fear of those around us, and breathe out compassion, relief, and healing. Do this several times. The idea is to recognize that many people in the world feel overwhelmed by particular kinds of suffering and that we can use that knowledge to relate to one another.

Inhale: acknowledging the suffering so many people feel from oppression.

Exhale: relief and connections to everyone who suffers in that particular way.

As we breathe in, we take it in for ourselves and for everyone around us who feels that suffering. As we breathe out we send all of us relief, healing and loving-kindness.

Often, when we try to practice Tonglen for others, we get caught up in our own experiences of pain. In that case, we can do the practice by connecting to the raw emotions in our own body, just sitting with them even if we can't name it.

Tonglen can be done anytime we feel a sense of suffering as a way to diminish the isolation that oppression fosters and instead recognize our interconnectedness.

References

Bartky, Sandra Lee. "Foucault, Feminization, and the Modernization of Patriarchal Power." In *The Politics of Women's Bodies: Sexuality, Appearance, and Behavior*, edited by Rose Weitz, 25–45. New York: Oxford University Press, 1998.

David, E.J.R. and Annie O. Derthick. "What Is Internalized Oppression, and So What?" In *Internalized Oppression: The Psychology of Marginalized Groups*, edited by E.J.R. David, 1–30. New York: Springer, 2013.

Drake, Teo. "Walking Faith." *Roots Grow the Tree*. October 21, 2013. Accessed January 25, 2014, http://rootsgrowthetree.com/2013/10/23/walking-faith.

Ehrenhault, Jey. "How Mindfulness Supports Social Change. *Decolonizing Yoga*. Accessed December 21, 2014, www.decolonizingyoga.com/how-qmindfulness-supports-social-change/.

Emerson, David and Elizabeth Hopper. *Overcoming Trauma through Yoga*. Berkeley, CA: North Atlantic Books, 2011.

Hardy, Kenneth V. "Healing the Hidden Wounds of Racial Trauma." *Reclaiming Children and Youth* 22, no. 1 (Spring 2013): 24–28. www.reclaimingjournal.com.

Heldman, Caroline. "The Sexy Lie." *TED*. TED x Youth @ San Diego. January 22, 2013. Accessed December 21, 2014, http://tedxtalks.ted.com/video/The-Sexy-Lie-Caroline-Heldman-a.

Helms, Janet E. "Toward a Model of White Racial Identity Development." In *Black and White Racial Identity*, edited by J. E. Helms, 49–66. New York: Greenwood/Praeger, 1993.

Hipolito-Delgado, Carlos P., Stephany Gallegos Payan, and Teresa I. Baca. "Self-Hatred, Self-Doubt, and Assimilation in Latina/o Communities: *Las Consecuencias de Colonización v Opresión*." In *Internalized Oppression: The Psychology of Marginalized Groups*, edited by E.J.R. David, 109–136. New York: Springer, 2013.

Langer, Ellen J. *The Power of Mindful Learning*. Boston, MA: Da Capo Press/Perseus Books, 1997.

Levine, Peter. "Somatic Experiencing Overview." Accessed June 14, 2014, www.trauma healing.com/somatic-experiencing/index.html.

Levine, Peter. "What is SE." Accessed May 7, 2015, www.traumahealing.org/about-se.php.

Lorde, Audre. *Sister Outsider: Essays and Speeches*. Berkeley, CA: Crossing Press, 1984.

Martin, Sara. Yoga Teacher Training Workshop. Minneapolis, MN, February 26, 2014.

Pyke, Karen D. and Denise L. Johnson. "Asian American Women and Racialized Femininities: 'Doing' Gender Across Cultural Worlds." *Gender & Society* 17, no. 1 (February 2003): 33–53.

Rabow, Jerome. "Models of Racial Identity." Accessed June 14, 2014, www.diversity celebration.com/models-of-racial-identity/.

Reynolds, Amy L. and Raechele L. Pope. "The Complexities of Diversity: Exploring Multiple Oppressions." *Journal of Counseling & Development* 70, no. 1 (September/October 1991): 174–180.

Szymanski, Dawn M., Susan Kushubeck-West, and Jill Meyer. "Internalized Heterosexism: A Historical and Theoretical Overview." *The Counseling Psychologist* 36, no. 4 (July 2008): 510–524.

Tappan, Mark. "Reframing Internalized Oppression and Internalized Domination: From the Psychological to the Sociocultural." *Teachers College Record* 108, no. 10 (2006): 2115–2144.

Tatum, Beverly Daniel. "Racial Identity Development." Mercer County Community College. Accessed December 17, 2014, www.mccc.edu/pdf/cmn214/Class%203/Racial%20identity%20development.pdf.

———. "Defining Racism: 'Can We Talk?'" In *Women: Images and Realities, A Multicultural Anthology*, 4th ed., edited by Amy Kesselman, Lily D. McNair, and Nancy Schniedewind, 386–390. New York: McGraw-Hill, 2006.

Trujillo, Carla. "Chicana Lesbians: Fear and Loathing in the Chicano Community." In *Women Images and Realities: A Multicultural Anthology*, 4th ed., edited by Amy Keselman, Linda D. McNair, and Nancy Schniedewind, 429–432. New York: McGraw-Hill, 2006.

Van der Kolk, Bessel. *The Body Keeps Score: Brain, Mind, and Body in the Healing of Trauma.* New York: Viking Penguin, 2014.

"What Is the Psychological Impact of Racism?" (2013, May 21). *HuffPostLive*. Accessed May 7, 2015, http://live.huffingtonpost.com/r/segment/can-racism-cause-ptsd/519d084c2b8c2a4ebc00010d.

4

DISMANTLING PRIVILEGE WITH MINDFUL LISTENING

If we are interested in building a movement that will not constantly be subverted by internal differences, then we must build from the inside out, not the other way around. Coming to terms with the suffering of others has never meant looking away from our own.

—Cherríe Moraga (1983)

While internalized oppression is a powerful force in diversity classrooms, so too is another key factor shaping student responses: privilege. While some of our students will be uncovering socialized negative self-definitions as they learn about oppression, others will be realizing the extent and depth of the benefits they receive in society, not because of who they are as individuals, but because of their membership in a group that has been granted power in society. For these privileged students, this realization can evoke denial, despair, grief, and confusion. Moreover, many of our students will find that they struggle with both internalized oppression and privilege with regard to different aspects of their identities. In this chapter, I will first define privilege and discuss how it can manifest in our classrooms, then outline how mindful listening can offer critical ways to understand and dismantle privilege.

Defined perhaps most famously by Peggy McIntosh, privilege refers to the unearned benefits granted to members of dominant groups and denied members of marginalized groups. It is an "invisible knapsack" of advantages that make the life of privileged groups easier while typically remaining invisible to those who receive them. Indeed, privileged identities are the norms of society against which every other identity is defined as "abnormal" (Wildeman and Davis 2005). This normalization means that those identities often remain invisible. Whiteness tends to go unnamed as a racial identity, while people of color are marked as "raced"; heterosexual identity becomes the norm against which LGBTQ/queer folk have to "come out." These identities are set up in a binary and are defined against one another, with one half of the binary receiving power as the norm (Dalton 2005). Each form of oppression has its flip side of privilege: male privilege, heterosexual privilege, able-bodied privilege, class privilege (for the wealthy), and race privilege (which in the United States means White privilege). Moreover, though these identities are historically and culturally specific and have been constructed over time, that context is erased, so that society simply accepts the current construction of that dominant identity (Barrett and Roediger 2005; Omi and Winant 2014; "Race the Power of Illusion" 2003).

Privilege works hand-in-hand with discrimination to create both systems of disadvantage for members of marginalized groups and systems of advantage for privileged groups (Tatum 2006; Case, Iuzzini, and Hopkins 2012). In effect, privilege describes the ways that systems of oppression have been built to advance the lives of dominant groups while placing numerous barriers in the way of members of marginalized groups. Those barriers can be small but powerfully cumulative, such as the ability to easily purchase makeup that matches one's skin color, or large, such as the right to marry who one loves. Either way, they accumulate into a set of deeply inscribed advantages. People who receive them come to see them as entitlements, which means they often blame the victim for not succeeding because they fail to see the benefits they receive that others are denied. This deep entitlement and fear of losing their privileges is often hidden in another privilege: the "privilege of obliviousness," which means not having to be aware of one's privileged identity or systems of oppression in general because one is never the target of them (Wise and Case 2013, 23). This obliviousness characterizes all forms of privilege, including male, heterosexual, able-bodied, gender-conforming, and class privilege. It brings with it another key aspect of privilege: the ability to choose whether to fight against privilege or simply remain silent and allow it to proceed (Wildeman and Davis 2005).

Systems of oppression use privilege as one way to keep themselves working smoothly. When they work properly, the people who receive privilege remain oblivious to the benefits they receive and the fact that marginalized groups do not receive them. This allows people in power to blame the marginalized groups for not getting ahead, because they do not see the ways that life is made harder and resources scarcer for marginalized groups. Once we start revealing privilege, the system starts to hit bumps in the road. But it is an adaptable system, so it has a back-up plan that involves built-in, learned reactions that will come flooding in to protect the system of privilege, usually in the form of defensive, so-called resistant reactions. If it works properly, those reactions will keep the individual neatly participating in the system. While she/he/ze may no longer be completely oblivious to the concept of privilege, this "back-up buffer" prevents him/her/zir from really questioning the privilege and neatly reroutes them back into upholding the system.

I reframe reactions to privilege in this way because it helps us see this "resistance" as byproducts of the system rather than merely the fault of stubborn and unwilling students, an idea that I will discuss more fully in the next chapter. One problem with this framing, of course, is that it speaks of the system as disembodied and removes individual agency from the process. I have just described a system working on the individual but not the individual actions, choices, and responsibilities that occur when individuals engage with the system. The good news is that systems of oppression prefer that individuals not realize they have agency. They work much more smoothly if dominant groups do not realize that they can work against their privilege, unlearn the ideologies that support it, and ensure that the privileges that are currently granted to only a few become rights extended to all.

Many scholars argue that in order to truly dismantle systems of oppression, we need to not only focus on the discrimination faced by marginalized groups but also on the invisible, systematic benefits consistently granted to members of dominant groups. In her book *Deconstructing Privilege: Teaching and Learning as Allies in the Classroom*, Kim A. Case (2013) argues that social justice courses need to examine power and privilege, encourage student and teacher reflections about where and how they might receive privilege, and place a great deal of value on the voices and experiences of marginalized groups. This last point refers to the dangers of holding all perspectives in diversity discussions as equal; while it is indeed important to hear from and validate the experiences of all students, "privileged voices and experiences [cannot be] used to deny the existence of oppression and privilege" (Case 2013, 4). So while teachers in anti-oppression courses need to challenge students to uncover and dismantle their privilege, we cannot do so in a way that re-centers the experiences of the privileged while continuing to marginalize members of oppressed groups.

At the same time, I have seen this caution interpreted as rendering unimportant the experiences of privileged students. Some teachers err too far on the side of this caution in that they do not give any space to the deeply unsettling process of taking accountability for one's privilege. I have made this mistake myself, and I have come to see it as not only lacking compassion but also deeply pedagogically ineffective. When people begin to truly see the extent of their privilege, they often feel overwhelming guilt and shame, stemming, in part, from the conflict between their growing recognition of their privilege in systems of power and their desire to believe that they are good people (Wise and Case 2013, 19). While we do not need to "take care of" these feelings in a way that re-centers privileged stories, we do need to honor that they exist and help students cultivate the skills for processing through those emotions. Without these skills—which include the ability to see why those reactions are arising—students will never effectively be able to dismantle their privilege. Before I delve into some mindfulness practices that can help students develop those skills, let me make one more key point about why such skills are so necessary in anti-oppression pedagogy.

We All Have Work to Do

Feminist intersectionality theory tells us that many people receive privilege in some ways while being oppressed in others. While some of us fit neatly in the category of "oppressed" or "oppressor," many more of us straddle both of those categories at different moments in our lives. Much of the scholarship on privilege focuses on White privilege, but there are several different types of privilege: male privilege, White privilege, heterosexual privilege, Western privilege, class privilege, able-bodied privilege, and so on (Case 2013; Rothenberg 2008; Wise 2011; Cole et al. 2012; Coston and Kimmel 2012; Sanders and Mahalingam 2012). When viewed through an intersectional feminist lens, many of our students will receive privilege in some ways while being denied it in others. Some people are marginalized in so many ways that they do not receive any privileges (such as a poor, gay, woman of color living with a disability), but many people receive *some* privileges. That means that we *all* have some work to do in undoing systems of power and privilege (even those who do not receive any privileges likely have work to do around internalized oppression). This is an important bridge of common purpose to which I will return later in the chapter. Students need to be able to bring their full selves to the process of unlearning oppression, and for that to happen, they need to recognize where they are oppressed and where they are privileged. They also need to learn to have compassion for how we are *all* caught in systems of oppression, albeit in different ways.

There has been some discussion about the importance of strategically focusing on one aspect of privilege. Rachel E. Luft and others make important points about how an intersectional approach can be used to deflect conversations about privilege. This avoidance tactic occurs when people with privilege shift the focus onto the part of their identity that is marginalized rather than doing the hard work of confronting and taking responsibility for their privilege (Luft 2009; Keating 2007; Wise and Case 2013). This is a very real concern, and there are times and places when a strategic focus on one aspect of identity or one form of privilege is useful. When this mono-issue approach is taken, teachers should make students aware of the strategic reasons for that focus.

However, there are also limits to this strategy. As Abby L. Ferber and Andrea O'Reilly Herrera (2013) point out, this single-focus approach continues to fragment both people's identities and our understanding of how power, privilege, and oppression work. Instead, they argue that foregrounding the multiple forms of privilege that exist and noting that most people are privileged in some ways and marginalized in others helps to preempt several common tendencies to deflect difficult discussions of privilege (Wise and Case 2013). First, it helps avoid the guilt and blame that so often subsumes discussions about privilege, because students become aware that most people get some privilege of some kind. Not only does everyone have some work to do, but they can more effectively understand how the process works when they reflect on their experiences on both sides of the equation. Students are less likely to get defensive and avoid facing their own privilege when they realize what it is like to be denied privilege that their classmates receive. Second, it better illustrates the complexity of how power, privilege, and marginalization happens and demands a contextualization of those dynamics. This book takes the position that we need to utilize an intersectional analysis in order to both fully understand the complexities of power, privilege, and oppression work and to enable all students to bring their full selves to the unlearning process.

The other critical component of this intersectional matrix model, from the perspective of contemplative pedagogy, is that it "advocates a connectionist, non-divisive approach, which is relational and begins by focusing on something that ties students together" (Ferber and O'Reilly Herrera 2013, 89). While institutional power dynamics obviously pit us against each other in some ways, they also thrive by maintaining those "us" and "them" binaries. If we can forge connections between students and build communities in our classrooms, we have a much better chance of not only unlearning oppression but also learning important critical reflection and mindfulness skills that will continue to transform our communities in the broader society.

Common Student Responses in Discussions about Oppression

Much of the pedagogical discussion around privilege revolves around common student responses that emerge when they are challenged to confront their privilege.

For instance, Watt (2007) describes several tactics students often use to avoid dealing with their privilege. In her Privileged Identity Exploration (PIE) model, she states that fear and entitlement provide the foundation for most of the defensive mechanisms that are so common in diversity discussions. One critical point to make about entitlement here is that students' defensive mechanisms often arise because they view challenges to their privilege as "optional," which is part and parcel of privilege itself. People who are oppressed do not have the option of not dealing with oppression. The fact that privileged individuals can choose not to face it or dismantle it is part of their privilege.

According to Watt, different defensive strategies tend to be used depending on how individuals are asked to consider their privilege. When students are asked to "recognize their privileged identity," they often resort to denial, deflection, or rationalization. These tactics allow them to avoid noticing the privileges they receive because of their membership in a dominant group. When students are asked to "contemplate privileged identity," they often resort to "intellectualization, principium, or false envy." So, rather than critically reflecting on the nature of their systematic advantages, they fall back on principium, which occurs when individuals use a religious or personal principle as an excuse for facing their privilege. Or they invoke false envy, which occurs when the individual expresses affection for someone as a way of avoiding the complex power dynamics in the situation. When challenged to "address privileged identity," the defense mechanisms tend to take the form of "benevolence or minimization" (Watt 2007, 119–120). The former occurs when an individual expresses an overly sensitive attitude that is more about charity or patronizing than it is about truly wanting to dismantle power relations; the latter trivializes the situation.

Watt's point that intellectualizing can be a tactic that is used to avoid taking account of one's privilege is important to note here, because too often in social justice classrooms, we keep discussions of privilege on a conceptual level. Watt's theory suggests that such intellectualizing may actually prevent us from deeply dismantling privilege. Clearly the intensity of discussions about this topic indicates that a great deal is happening on the emotional and psychological levels. Students often become deeply upset on the one hand or immersed in avoidance techniques, on the other, when they are challenged to face the effects of their privilege. The tension in both these reactions indicates that we need to unpack privilege on a much deeper, embodied level, in addition to analyzing it on an intellectual one.

In their article "Deconstructing Privilege When Students Resist," Kim A. Case and Elizabeth R. Cole describe several key patterns than emerged in their interviews with teachers about how their students have "resisted" content about diversity. While I will discuss the issue of resistance in greater depth in Chapter 6, here I want to note that the first theme from their research is "worldview protection," meaning that students "resist" learning new material that deeply unsettles the paradigms through which they make sense of the world. When their ideologies, like the myth of meritocracy or their sense of who they are as a person, are deeply unsettled, students will often fall back on various defense mechanisms to try to maintain order. Often, this process happens subconsciously in an embodied way.

Psychologist Kristin Neff (2015), who is best known for her work on self-compassion, describes the way our body reacts to perceived threats to our well-being. Neff says that when we feel threatened, our bodies close off as we feel the rush of adrenaline and cortisol and prepare for fight or flight responses. In ancient times, this biological reaction was designed to protect us from physical bodily harm. Today, especially in the college classrooms that are the context for this discussion, bodily harm is not as likely as the harm to one's self-concept. Neff

(2015) suggests that when our self-concept is threatened, stress hormones will often kick in and our fight/flight response will serve to separate us from others. According to this theory, then, it really should be no surprise that students use defense mechanisms to avoid confronting privilege. Indeed, this theory suggests that their reactions are deeply embodied, which means that our pedagogical practices need to address these deeper levels if they are to be effective.

I find that informing students of the common patterns people use to avoid facing privilege is a helpful way of robbing these tactics of some of their power. I also find it is helpful to present some versions of the identity development models I discussed in Chapter 3. When students can see that there are common patterns that people move through as they become more aware of power systems and how they are positioned in them, they can become less defensive and more mindful to their own reactions and those of others. They can learn to have more patience and compassion with their classmates, their friends, their relatives, and even themselves, because they can see the various stages people are in that are shaping their responses (Ferber and O'Reilly Herrera 2013).

In addition, laying the foundation of feminist intersectionality early in the semester provides something to return to again and again. If many of us are both privileged and oppressed through different aspects of our identity, then we can learn to see our experiences of each with discernment and compassion. When we remember how painful it is to experience oppression, we can be more present with a classmate as she/he/ze describes their experiences of marginalization. When we recognize how challenging it is to try to dismantle privilege and the dismay we felt when we first became aware of our own privilege (whatever it may be), we can learn to have more compassion for our classmates when we see them having similar responses to their own privilege. For instance, I consider my anti-racist work to be, in part, a lifelong journey in dismantling my White privilege, and I recognize that I will make many mistakes along the way. I try to be humble and accountable in the moments when I do make a mistake, doubling down my efforts. My awareness of that fraught process makes me more willing to have compassion for people around me who are trying to unlearn their heterosexual privilege. When they make a mistake, I remember what it is like for me, and I try to value their commitment to the journey (if they have such a commitment) enough to continue to work with them in their unlearning process. We both have rocky journeys, and we will both make mistakes. Our commitment to one another and to a better world is what encourages me to keep an open heart.

Such patience is not always possible. People do not always have the capacity to keep an open heart, particularly in the face of unskillful or even willful denials of privilege. Those reactions also need space in the classroom—if for no other reason than that they are present in our discussions, whether we like it or not. Again, helping students understand and have empathy for where those reactions are coming from—in themselves and in their classmates—can go a long way to productively navigating those conversations and sustaining a sense of community.

One of my yoga teachers, Rod Stryker, notes that "each of us is both being and becoming" (qtd. in McGonigal 2013). We can have more patience and compassion for ourselves and others when we realize that it is a complicated journey for all of us, regardless of the exact nature of our individual work. This perspective allows for the "both/and" possibility for which Patricia Hill Collins (2000) and others call. "It asks students to examine both an oppressed identity and also requires White students to examine their White Privilege" or some other aspect of their identity in which they might receive privilege (Ferber and O'Reilly Herrera 2013, 94). Creating space for both elements of this process will enable more productive discussions in the classroom and beyond. Wise tells the story of a class exercise in which participants were asked to rate their privilege index in a variety of ways. Though Wise was not impressed with the instrument and expected Whites in the room to use it to avoid accounting for White privilege, he was surprised to see that most of them did not. By "being allowed to 'mark their pain,' . . . rather than being shut down as if to say that white privilege trumps all other systems of oppression . . . they had been able to relax, open up, and acknowledge the power of Whiteness in their lives without shame or guilt" (Wise and Case 2013, 25). This happened, in part, because everyone in the classroom was asked to account for the ways in which they received privilege and the ways in which they were marginalized. This both/and approach allows all participants to being their full selves to the table and, therefore, takes us further toward unlearning oppression.

How Privilege Harms

This relational, intersectional matrix framework also reveals how we are all harmed by these inequalities. Privilege, as Wise tells us, comes with a price. This is not to say that those who are privileged are harmed in the same ways or to the same degree as those who are oppressed, but it is to say that systems of oppression impede the full expression of our humanity for all of us. We, therefore, all have incentive to dismantle the systems, even if we receive some benefits from them. Wise and Case outline some of the costs of privilege for dominant groups, including: 1) a loss of connection to one's ethnicity and cultural heritage; 2) deep racial biases even when one does not want to have them; 3) a sense of expectation and entitlement that can result in despair when it is not granted; 4) isolation from community; and 5) a participation in power dynamics that produce vast inequalities (Wise and Case 2013). All of these costs create psychological stressors. This is NOT to conflate the pain felt by people who are privileged with the suffering of the oppressed. It is, however, to say that we all have a stake in dismantling systems of oppression because they hurt virtually all of us, despite the promised benefits.

These "costs" of privilege are worth discussing a bit further, since they explain why people with privilege would/should be motivated to dismantle privilege. One might wonder, if people receive so many benefits from the system, why they would want to deconstruct it. While it is true that those in the dominant groups accrue a great many advantages from the current system and that some people will want to cling to those privileges, there is also a price to pay. Wise defines this cost in a profound way:

> Racism, even if it is not your own, but merely circulates in the air, *changes you*, allows you to think things and feel things that make you less than you were meant to be. It steals that part of our humanity that is the most precious: the part that allows us to see . . . the goodness of creation in all humankind. And our unwillingness to see that, and more than to see it, to really feel it, deep in the marrow of our bones, is what allows us, and even sometimes compels us, to slaughter one another.
>
> (2005, 159, emphasis in original)

The cost to our humanity far outweighs the advantages we receive from our various privileges. To live our privileges means internalizing a dehumanizing sense of others and a false superiority for our own groups that rings hollow over time. Wise discusses what happens when people who are promised entitlements are suddenly faced with disappointment and conflict for which they have never been prepared. The result is often harmful for the privileged individual but also for the broader society, as that person sometimes lashes out in problematic ways.

Privilege signals belonging in a dominant group, but, paradoxically, it also disconnects us from one another and from a holistic identity. We receive privilege not as individuals but as members of a dominant group, but we are never fully in control of whether we are defined as "belonging" to that group. Think, for instance, of a person who identifies as heterosexual but who is "read" as gay; that person will be denied heteronormative privileges even if he is not gay (Johnson 2005). The power of self-definition is not entirely in the individual's hands. Thus, privilege is, as Allan Johnson (2005) notes, a paradox. Part of the paradox is that the price of "belonging" to a dominant group means forfeiting a sense of ethnic or cultural identity, because by definition, the privileged group usually remains undefined. Wise tells the story of being in a workshop in which participants were asked to describe what they liked or valued about being part of their racial group. All the people of color easily listed attributes about their communities that they felt strengthened them, but all the White people were at a loss to describe any of that. What they listed instead were White privileges, which rang hollow when the two lists were compared. While the people of color in the group described valuing the strength of their families and the camaraderie of their community, for instance, Whites listed things like not being followed in a store under suspicion of shoplifting. Wise notes that,

> none of what we liked about being white had anything to do with us. *None* of it had to do with internal qualities of character or fortitude. Rather, every response had to do less with what we liked about being white than what we liked about *not being a person of color.* We were defining ourselves by a negative, providing ourselves with an identity rooted in the external—rooted in the relative oppression of others, without which we would have had *nothing to say.*
>
> (2011, 170, emphasis in original)

While this cost is not the same as the deeply harmful effects of oppression, it is another price the system extracts: the full expression of our belonging as a cultural group. Ethnic heritage that was once marked as distinct becomes homogenized into whiteness, seemingly devoid of characteristics except for how it is not something defined as "undesirable." As Wise (2011) notes, many Whites come from ethnic groups that have rich histories and cultures—often even histories of resistance to oppressive systems—but all of that has to be erased as the price of admission to whiteness. Similar points can be made about membership in other dominant groups. All things considered, I do not think the benefits of privilege even come close to outweighing these costs.

Let me reiterate again that I am not in any way suggesting that people who are privileged suffer in the same way or to the same degree as people who are oppressed. But we cannot expect people who are privileged to automatically give up those privileges out of altruism. To recognize the wounds of the privileged does not need to mean supplanting the suffering of the oppressed nor does it have to mean shifting the spotlight from one to another. The framework that says there is only room in a discussion for the suffering of the most wounded creates a poverty of humanity. It also makes it impossible for everyone in the room to fully show up and do their work of unlearning oppression. Most of the great mindfulness teachers have taught this lesson. The renowned Buddhist monk and scholar Pema Chödrön notes that "injustice, by definition, is harming everybody involved" (2007, 24). This realization is a powerful incentive to deconstruct privilege.

Moreover, the rewards of privilege are not entirely granted to every member of the dominant group. I am not talking here of "exceptions" to the pattern, the atypical examples students will often cite to try to invalidate the larger cultural patterns. Instead, I am referring to the failed promises of privilege that leave a deep mark on many people, wounds that do not have names and that are often obscured by the myth of meritocracy. Many people do not receive the full benefits that are promised by systems of oppression, and the myth of meritocracy leaves them blaming themselves instead of seeing the deep flaws in the system. The next section outlines one such case for a student in one of my Women's Studies classes.

The Broken Promises of Privilege

The most common reactions I hear my colleagues describe as "resistance" (an idea which I will discuss in greater detail in the next chapter) comes from members of dominant groups who presumably do not want to acknowledge their privilege. Over the years, I have come to realize that often a great deal is going on underneath the surface of those outward reactions. For instance, one of my students wrote a paper for a Women's Studies class that illustrates some of the complexity of what might be going on for such a student. I will spend some time on this extended example here in order to illustrate how students need space to work through the dissonance that appears as students begin to unlearn oppression and deconstruct their privilege.

This White male student, whom I will call Jim, was a nontraditional-aged college student probably in his late twenties or early thirties. He did not speak much in class, though his first comment helped break the ice in our class discussions by making it "real." He had made a statement that expressed a different opinion than my own and then acknowledged with some surprise how vulnerable he felt doing so. This comment revealed a layer of self-consciousness that we often do not see when talking about White male privilege. During the first part of class, he explained that he had been injured on the job and was now living with a disability.

About a third of the way into the semester, he wrote a paper for me on masculinity. He had mentioned that he was searching for a new form of masculinity because he realized that the one he had been taught no longer included him. The story he told and the uncertainties he explored in the paper illustrated to me a complex process of unraveling privilege and a search for a new way of being. It also revealed the tensions and dissonance that are usually a messy but integral part of the process.

His paper described growing up in an abusive home, in which his father regularly beat him and his mother. He described feeling powerless to stop his father hurting his mother, noting that in the town in which he lived, cops did not arrest other cops. At one point in his teens, he fought with another young man (on the advice of his father) and ended up in the criminal justice system with a record.

Eventually, Jim decided to join the military to get away from the small town—an interesting choice, given how hurt he had already been by systems of hypermasculinity. But he was a working class young man, and joining the military offered options where few were available. While in the military, he described being passed over for promotion. The position, he wrote, was given to a Black person "because of affirmative action." Of course, this false interpretation of how affirmative action works reflects White privilege and institutionalized racism. It is also one of the ways the system pits working class Whites against people of color. But there is more to the story.

When he left the military, he decided to be a police officer so that he can help people—another interesting choice since law enforcement and criminal justice agencies had not necessarily served him well thus far. Jim mentioned in the paper how angry he became in our class discussions in which he felt people "bashed" cops for racial profiling. He acknowledged that some officers abuse their power but argued that many are good guys and that only someone who serves on the streets everyday knows what it is like working with the worst elements of society day in and day out. Other police officers have echoed his comments, noting that it is tricky to avoid becoming hardened when one is working with such awful situations day in and day out, usually in a state of hypervigilance. The toll that takes on a person's ability to remain open and compassionate is significant and speaks to a flaw in the system of law enforcement itself (Maples 2015).

This student went on in his paper to describe the incident in which he was injured in the line of duty. He tried to intervene in a domestic dispute, even though his backup had not yet arrived, and ended up being assaulted by two men. The event put him on disability but also caught him in a system of having to fight for benefits because he had not "followed protocol." The student noted how deeply he felt his masculinity is regularly challenged because his disability is not one that is "visible," so people question why he cannot work. He said he feels like less of a man because he cannot support his family.

What struck me when reading this paper is the dissonance he felt as he struggled with the ways he received privilege and the ways that promise of privilege failed him. On the one hand, this student repeatedly noted how the constructions of masculinity have failed him and are no longer available to him. I see them as the broken promises of whiteness and masculinity. He had been handed a script, but the system repeatedly denied him the promised benefits of that script and ultimately made it impossible for him to play that role. Simultaneously, however, he repeatedly strives to play the part: joining the military, becoming a cop. The choice to go into a dangerous system alone, in violation of protocol, on the one hand illustrates a kind of cowboy mentality that is common of our Western male heroes. On the other hand, in his description of it, it seemed to come from a deep childhood wound and it dramatically backfired. The paper described his repeated attempts to perform the cultural scripts of White masculinity. He keeps being attracted to its promises, at the same time that he is able to say quite clearly how it has failed him. He is having to unearth the deep roots of this paradigm even while trying to find or create a new script, which results in stark contradictions and deep dissonance.

Of course, even with the broken promises of White masculinity, he has still benefited from privilege. Had he been a working class Black man living some of those experiences, he would likely be in jail or killed. Black men do not get the breaks he got. But recognizing that inequality does not have to mean minimizing his experience, and I think we teachers impede transformational learning if we suggest that it does. His hurt and disillusionment need to be acknowledged before he will be able to see the ways he is privileged. The system hurts many people, not just the ones who are most deeply oppressed, and rather than continuing to pit the different groups against each other, we would be more effective if we can help our students see that. As a teacher reading this paper, I felt I needed to give the student the space to be in the confusing uncertainty of his soft edge. Had he stated the affirmative action comment aloud in a class discussion, I would have challenged it more explicitly, so as not to seem to condone it. But because he wrote it in a paper to me, and because I knew I still had the rest of the semester with him, I challenged it less directly, choosing to give him the space for his complex reaction. If I had simply framed his response as the "resistance" of a White guy to seeing his racism, I believe I would have missed the deep complexity of what was happening. And, I think, I would have shut down his transformational learning process rather than helping to facilitate it. In the next section, I outline the mindfulness skills that can help both students and faculty effectively dismantle privilege.

Mindfully Interrupting Privilege

The question becomes, then, how to more effectively allow for this complex unlearning process in the classroom without reinforcing or perpetuating privilege, a challenge that becomes even more complex when we realize that oppression, internalized oppression, and privilege will show up for different students at different times and in different ways.

In her article "Blazing the Trail: Teaching the Privileged about Privilege," Lisa F. Platt offers three basic tips for addressing privilege in the classroom: 1) "make it personal; 2) make it relevant; and 3) manage emotional responses" (2013, 207). While all three tenets are, I agree, critical to helping students unlearn their privilege, they will be of limited effectiveness if we utilize them only at the cognitive level. Even Platt's point about "managing emotions" is revealing, since it is mostly framed as teachers managing students' outwardly expressed anger, guilt, fear, and other defensive reactions. This approach sends the message that such reactions are "problems" to be "handled." A more effective approach, I suggest, is to help students understand that privilege—and the defensive reactions that emerge to keep it in place—are the inevitable byproducts of living in an inequitable society. If students get clear on the deep costs of privilege, for themselves and for those who are oppressed by it, they will be far more motivated to dismantle it.

The first step, as always, is to see clearly what is happening, without reacting, without judging—just clear awareness. We need to teach students how to listen to their own inward responses with clear awareness. Rather than "managing" emotions, I prefer to strive for a kind of emotional intelligence that allows students themselves to learn to discern what is happening for them and why. Only then, I argue, will we begin to dismantle the safety mechanisms that keep privilege intact. This skill needs to be modeled by the teacher (an idea that I will discuss in a moment), but it ultimately needs to be learned by the students so that they learn to sit with and understand their own internal reactions, which, in turn, will actually have the effect of "managing" external displays of defensive emotions. Helping students learn to hear their own complex reactions will help achieve Platt's outlined pedagogical goals of "(a) increasing awareness and knowledge of awareness; (b) increase empathy and compassion for those who do not possess privilege; and (c) promote action for initiating societal change in the future" (2013, 208).

In order to cultivate this awareness, students need to practice cultivating the Witness that we discussed in the previous chapter. After gaining some experience with merely observing and disidentifying from the emotions and physiological responses, we can bring another layer into the mindful unlearning process: deep, contemplative listening. Let me be clear that ALL students need to practice the skills of the Witness and deep listening; I am not saying that only those with internalized oppression need to Witness or only those with privilege need to learn to listen more profoundly. All these steps are necessary for the unlearning of oppression, but they need to be developed incrementally. Students usually need to become familiar with one or two parts of the process at a time and then develop it further, or they become overwhelmed. Critical for each step of the process is the meta-level. As teachers who are implementing this process, we need to explain why we are integrating mindfulness into social justice courses and how it works. Students will be far more likely to sit with the process if they understand how and why it works, particularly in the context of oppression.

So why is listening so important to dismantling privilege? Because many of the defensive tools that I have already described that emerge to keep privilege intact and invisible occur at an intense and usually precognitive level. They provoke strong emotions that most people do not know what to do with, especially early in their journey of learning about oppression. Even for those who have been on a social justice path for years, the subtlety of the reactions require increasingly refined emotional intelligence to unpack. Layered upon those gut reactions are the storylines used to keep privilege intact: ideologies such as the myth of meritocracy, blaming the victim, or entitlement that explain away the critiques of privilege. Those of us who teach social justice classes have likely seen these reactions emerge intensely in class discussions about privilege. These are the reactions that shift discussions of oppression from marginalized experiences to those of the dominant groups. The inability to see how deeply privilege manifests usually produces intense frustration, pain, and anger from those who are marginalized, which, when expressed, often causes those with privilege to dig their heels in and/or shut down. What is needed in these moments are mindfulness skills that allow us to listen more fully to ourselves and others.

It may seem counterintuitive, but the first step in learning how to effectively and authentically listen to others is to learn how to listen to ourselves. If we expect students to be able to truly listen to the perspectives of their classmates and to interrupt their privilege, then they need to become very adept at listening to their own defense mechanisms that arise to keep privilege in place. Those defenses are very loud, usually preventing an individual from hearing what else is happening. Contemplative listening can help a person Witness what is arising for him/her/zir without overidentifying with it. Instead, the student can learn to listen deeply and with curiosity to the embodied responses and the accompanying ideological storylines. This process can help students resist initial outward reactions and help them feel more empowered to dismantle the socially constructed narratives that, as we have already seen, are limiting their humanity.

Many academic scholars and psychologists talk about active listening, which involves empathy, attention, caring, receptivity (Brady 2003). But the form of contemplative listening I am invoking here goes deeper. This form of listening starts from a place of self-awareness. We cannot be truly open to others' perspectives if we are not attuned to what arises for us that may block that openness. Particularly in hard conversations, those barriers are likely to arise, and we need to be aware of them so that we do not feed them. Deep listening comes from a place of receptivity that is open, attentive, and calm (Rome and Martin, n.d.). It involves a radical openness—both in terms of receptivity and in terms of an open heart. It is a skill that students can learn that, when practiced, becomes an "attentive rather than a reactive listening" (Barbezat and Bush 2014, 138). It requires that we learn to sit in a place of uncertainty, that we learn to be in the process of learning which, paradoxically, means accepting the state of not knowing. This form of listening comes from a place of inquiry rather than certainty. When we are listening deeply, we approach the conversation from a place of belief that the other person is communicating something important to them. "Trust here does not imply agreement, but the trust that whatever others say, regardless of how well or poorly it is said, comes from something true in their experience" (Rome and Martin 2014).

David Rome and Hope Martin (2014) distinguish between poor listeners and deep listeners. The former, they write, are generally preoccupied with how the conversation affects them. They tend to spend their time awaiting their turn to speak and planning what they will say, rather than truly focusing on the speaker (Rome and Martin 2014). Because they are preoccupied with how the narrative affects them (though they are often unaware that this is their focus), they typically respond by either restating already formed opinions or debating the person to whom they are supposed to be listening (Rome and Martin 2014). Those of us who teach in social justice classrooms have seen both of these modes at work in class discussions.

Effective listening, on the other hand, means being receptive to new perspectives and truly focused on trying to hear what someone else is trying to say, both on the surface level of content and on the deeper level of intention (Rome and Martin 2014). This receptivity is much closer to what we strive for in social justice classrooms because it draws on the "radical openness" that hooks describes. Rome and Martin's model of Embodied Listening includes three central components: mindfulness to cultivate self-awareness; the Alexander Technique, to ease tension and cultivate an embodied awareness; and mindful focusing, which lets you access the "felt sense" or "intuitive wisdom of the body"(Rome and Martin 2014). Whether deep listening uses this particular model, the embodied nature of listening is critical for discerning when ideologies of privilege motivate our actions and for tapping into a deeper wisdom, beneath those storylines.

Though it draws on a different tradition and uses different language, the mindful focusing in the Embodied Listening model is akin to the yogic traditions of the *koshas*. *Koshas* are the layers of the subtle body, though most of us only access the outer, grosser or more material levels (Johnsen 2014). The most accessible *kosha* is the physical body, called the *annamaya kosha*. This is the one accessed through physical yoga practice, but the purpose of doing so is to be able to connect with the increasingly subtle layers beneath it. The next *kosha*, or "shealth," is the *pranamaya kosha*, which refers to the breath. This is why so many yogic practices involve breath work, because *prana* is considered the life force energy. Our third layer of the body is the *manomaya kosha* or the thought body. This is thinking mind, but it is also the entire nervous system. The last two *koshas* are far more subtle and, therefore, require regular practice to access. *Vijnanamaya kosha* refers to the higher mind, including conscience and will. It is the discerning, higher, best self that is in every one of us. This is the level of connection we can ultimately strive to connect through if we are to truly create a socially just society. Most of the time, we operate on the layer of *manomaya kosha*, but the thinking mind is informed by the ideologies of the culture in which we are embedded. The *vijnanamaya kosha* is a more authentic self. The final, deepest, *kosha* is the *anandamaya kosha*, which refers to the bliss body (Johnsen 2014; Judelle personal communication, November 29, 2013; Devanadi Yoga Teacher Training 2014). Each of these sheaths exist within the other one, like Russian nesting dolls. We have all of them all the time, but we are most aware of the most material ones, the ones closest to the surface. If we can learn to access our higher, discerning self, we would, ideally, bring our "best selves" to anti-oppression work.

Few students will come into our classes knowing how to listen in this deep way. It is a skill that they will need to learn and that is, fundamentally, a radical act. Norman Fisher describes the act of listening in the following way:

> to listen is to be willing to be simply present with what you hear without trying to figure it out or control it. . . . Because truly listening requires that you do this, listening is dangerous. It might cause you to hear something you don't like, to consider its validity, and therefore to think something you

never thought before.... This is the risk of listening, and this is what it is automatic for us to not want to listen.

(qtd. in Barbezat and Bush 2014, 137)

It is dangerous to listen not only because we might consider new ideas but also because we might begin to question our very self-concepts and realize how infused they often are with systems of oppression. We might be motivated, then, to dismantle them. Rather than immediately shoring up our self-concepts when they are challenged, this mindful practice allows us to sit with the uncertainty and discomfort that arises in that moment and learn to probe, explore, and question what is happening for us, what function those defensive mechanisms serve, how they manifest in our body, and whether they let us open up or close down.

It may seem counterintuitive to listen without trying to figure it out or control it. After all, we want students to interrupt their privilege, right, so what is with this nonjudgmentalness? This step in deep listening works much the same way accepting our reactions to internalized oppression works: we have to first truly listen, without laying any interpretive storylines atop them, if we are to discern what is happening. When we listen deeply, "we let go of our inner clamoring and our usual assumptions and listen with respect for precisely what is being said" (Barbezat and Bush 2014, 137). As soon as we start to "spin" it, we move into our thinking mind, which is already shaped by systems of oppression. The conceptual frameworks through which we make sense of the world are learned, which means they are likely shaped by oppressive ideologies. Moreover, moving into the intellectual mind too quickly usually takes us out of our embodied experience—that disconnect between mind/body/heart is also a learned fragmentation that supports systems of oppression. We disconnect from our own entirely human experience and, therefore, it becomes easier to dehumanize others. In order to interrupt that fragmenting process, we need to first learn to just stay present with whatever is happening, listen and reflect, and accept. Once we do those steps, *then* we can intellectualize, analyze, and politicize. We can then determine which responses are in line with our vision of how we want the world to be. But first, we just listen, with our whole bodies and hearts. As the yoga teacher Tara Judelle points out, "we can't listen if we aren't present" (personal communication, November 29, 2013).

Contemplative Listening as a Way of Building Compassionate Classroom Communities

I can already hear some critics arguing that this mindfulness skill puts the focus back on the privileged person thereby perpetuating the marginalization of the oppressed. This is a valid concern that needs to be monitored and the focus cannot stay there. But learning to really hear and discern how ideologies of privilege manifest within ourselves (for any of us who hold any form of privilege) is important for several reasons. First, as teachers, we expect students to challenge their own privilege and often condemn them if they do not, so it is only ethical to give them the tools they need to dismantle their privilege. Second, the reactions that keep privilege entrenched emerge in our classrooms whether we effectively address them or not. They will continue to exist long after our class ends, since unlearning privilege is a life-long journey. So it makes sense to offer students the tools with which to recognize and interrupt these deeply entrenched ideologies so that they can continue to do this work even after the conclusion of the semester. Third, listening inwardly is the first of several steps in deep listening. It lays the foundation to listen outwardly. While we commonly address the outer layers of voice and listening, social justice class discussions would become far more authentic and effective if we can practice *all* these layers.

Deep listening occurs on multiple levels: first, at the intrapersonal level, which means learning to Witness, be present, and listen to what is happening internally ("Deep Listening" 2014). This is a crucial step in unlearning privilege because we first need to recognize how the narratives of entitlement and fear are embedded into our sense of self. What do they sound like for each of us? When do they arise? What do they urge us to do in order to preserve this privilege? What do they feel like in our bodies? Many of the responses teachers describe in discussions about privilege emerge, I believe, from gut reactions to these internalized narratives of privilege or oppression. So the first step in interrupting them is to listen deeply, with curiosity not judgment, to discern how exactly they show up for ourselves.

The next layers of deep listening are interpersonal and group levels, in which an individual is listening to another person or several individuals are listening to others. The idea here is to withhold judgment or a planning of our own statements and instead give our full attention and awareness to the person who is speaking. This listening is informed by three central principles: "listening to learn; listening for understanding rather than agreement; and ask[ing] powerful questions" ("Deep Listening" 2014). This form of listening enables a much more authentic presence with one another that can build the trust essential for sustainable communities that can dismantle systems of oppression. Because so much of oppression happens in the ways we relate to one another—ways that are learned behaviors—truly receiving one another while suspending our internalized assumptions enables new possibilities to arise ("Deep Listening" 2014).

When practiced at all three levels, deep listening enables a profound bearing witness—something that is vitally important in discussions about social justice. This form of listening is not the way most students understand participating in a discussion, which usually entails listening with one ear while forming one's own opinion, preparing what one is to say next, or waiting for a point of disagreement. None of these tactics can enable deep listening. Of course, discussion and debating have important roles, especially in a college classroom. But those discussions will become much more profound if students can first learn the skill of listening deeply to themselves and others with a compassionate presence and receptivity. In his book *Right Listening*, Mark Brady offers several characteristics of this kind of listening, including "listening without an agenda; listening without 'should'ing on people; 3) Establish support for speaking truth to power; . . . avoiding letting your story take over their story" (qtd in Barbezat and Bush 2014, 146–147). These skills bring us closer to what Kramer calls "insight dialogue" that helps us learn to bridge our inner and outer landscapes with the compassionate awareness that "much of our suffering tends to come into relief through our relationships with others" (Barbezat and Bush 2014, 146). It helps relieve the suffering of ourselves and the other person in the conversation, because the point is to listen with the purpose of helping the other person empty his/her/zir heart. This purpose is important, says the Vietnamese monk Thich Nhat Hanh, because then, even if the person says something hurtful that is full of wrong perception, we can continue to maintain an open and compassionate heart because we remember our purpose. It will be important to help him/her/zir "correct" the wrong perception, but that happens at a later time. In this moment, the point is to try to truly understand his/her/zir perspective and to relieve his/her/zir suffering by listening fully. He says, "the fear, the anger, and the despair is born on the ground of wrong perception. We have wrong perceptions concerning ourselves and the other person, and that is the foundation for conflict and war and violence" (Hanh 2014).

When I was first watching this short but profound video of Thich Nhat Hanh discussing deep compassionate listening, it seemed so clear to me that what so many of my students long for in the classroom is to speak and to be heard. Whether they are describing experiences of oppression or speaking from a place of privilege, they long to be understood—truly heard. What so often prevents that are the learned ideologues that construct an "us" and a "them," the inner narratives that keep our identities positioned against each other. A critical step in dismantling these power dynamics is to learn to profoundly listen to one another. That requires learning to witness when those narratives of privilege arise and learning to dial them down long enough to really try to understand what the other person is saying. Then we can discuss points of disagreement or debate. It is incumbent for everyone in the room to practice this skill, which means people who are oppressed also need to learn to listen deeply to people who are privileged—not to say that their perspectives count any more than their own, but to hear where they are coming from. This is a deeply difficult process for people on both side of that divide, but it is a critical mindful step in unlearning oppression.

A couple things can help with this process. The intersectionality framework can help students see where they are privileged and where they are oppressed. Since many of our students will hold identities in both of those categories, they can learn to have more patience and compassion for others. They will likely experience their own difficulty in disrupting the places where they are privileged, for instance, which may allow them to have more patience for their classmates when they struggle. Similarly, because they know how painful it is to be oppressed, they can form empathy for their classmates as they describe their own pain of marginalization. Even though it will not be the same experience—and certainly should not be conflated—it can become an entry point for empathy and connection.

Second, we can recognize that we will not always be able to remain open, patient, and compassionate. There are times when the oppression is so raw and cumulative that we cannot hold that space, and understanding where that comes from in someone else can help us not react as strongly if we are on the receiving end. This self-awareness is not the same thing as the poor listening described earlier, in which the listener is preoccupied with his/her/zir own retorts. Instead, self-awareness in this context means being deeply aware of how our own responses may be getting in our way of truly listening, combined with a consistent effort to bring our attention back to the speaker with an open heart. This is a skill that needs to be learned, particularly since it is fairly counter-cultural.

The Resistance of Privilege

Once we learn to both witness and listen to what is happening for us in the moment, we can more skillfully work with the "holy pause" I discussed in previous chapters. That pause between reacting and responding allows us to make more intentional choices about which responses we want to feed, remembering that whatever we feed gets stronger. Pema Chödrön teaches us that we can learn, in this pause, to not "bite the hook." In her book *Practicing Peace in Times of War*, Chödrön describes the force of *shenpa*, which in Buddhist traditions is the source of conflict, cruelty, and oppression. Even if we are not Buddhist and are adopting mindfulness in secular ways, Chödrön's explanation of *shenpa* and how to mindfully work with it is useful here. *Shenpa*, she writes, is the "charge" behind our negative gut reactions. Say someone criticizes you. What do you feel? She describes its common sensation:

> It has a familiar taste, a familiar smell . . . there's a tightening that rapidly spirals into mentally blaming this person, or wanting revenge or blaming yourself. Then you speak or act. The charge behind the tightening, behind the urge, behind the storyline or action is shenpa.
>
> (2007, 56)

The good news is that we can learn to work with this process by learning how to not bite the hook. Mindfulness teaches us to learn to sit with the raw energy underneath the storyline we attach. So, before interpreting, judging, or acting out, we simple learn to listen and sit with the uncomfortable feelings. This will likely be hard for students to learn (for everyone to learn really) because U.S. culture is flooded with attempts to distract us from discomfort. Sitting with it patiently and with curiosity is the last thing most of us want to do.

Moreover, one of the "benefits" of privilege means that the world is structured in such a way so (not to) protect privileged people from discomfort. Once again, though, this is a false promise. For many people from dominant groups (in fact, possibly for all but the literal 1%), that promise will fail to come through at some point in our lives. When that happens, the ground under us will be unsettled in small or large ways. Discomfort is a part of life and learning to sit with it an important component of resilience. Chödrön describes this discomfort as "the underlying insecurity of the human experience, the insecurity that is inherent in a changing, shifting world" (2007, 58). The urge to react from our gut is a quick fix attempt to run away from that discomfort. If we can practice contacting it, lightly, with curiosity and compassion, we have a better chance of breaking the cycle of oppression and violence that occurs when we "bite the hook."

For anyone new to mindfulness, this suggestion to listen to and explore the charge underneath our reactions will likely seem abstract and impossible. Even for those of us who are experienced with mindfulness practice, the ability to do this will vary by how deeply a particular comment or event triggers us. We may be able to engage this teaching in less fraught moments but likely will still have trouble with more intense ones. This is part of the process. Here, the meta-explanation is critical for anti-oppression pedagogy. In order for this practice to be effective, we need to explain why we are doing it, elucidate the various common reactions that arise for people, and give students regular opportunities to both practice deep listening and reflect on their experiences of the practice. Here again is a profound parallel between mindfulness and anti-oppression efforts: *what arises for us is the work.* The complex reactions are not things to get past in order to get to the "real" social justice work. The grief, anger, pain, confusion, horror, and denial that arise, along with the storylines we attach to try to avoid sitting with the intensity of those feelings, *is* the work. When we regularly reflect on what arises for us in discussions about oppression, along with our various attempts to examine them through various mindfulness practices, we will learn a great deal about our own role in oppressive systems and how to interrupt it. Only then can we imagine new possibilities into reality.

The majority of the privileged students I have encountered over the years want to believe themselves good people who do not hurt others. To the degree they have thought about it (which may have been very little), students of privilege want to believe that the atrocities of oppression are mostly in the past, or perhaps confined to certain egregious events, but not perpetuated by daily actions and ideologies in which we all participate. To the degree that it still exists, many of them want to believe that they work against injustice. As they start to learn how extensively they benefit from systematic oppression, whether or not they ever do anything explicitly oppressive, they often experience dismay, horror, grief, and confusion. They can become deeply unsettled as their entitled worldview is shattered. That paradigm includes their very sense of who they are, which then becomes deeply shaken by this process. Inevitable questions start to arise: "I thought I 'earned' those accolades because I was more talented than others. What if that's not why I got them?"

Moreover, unearthing privilege is not like lifting a veil to reveal it all at once. It will likely take years, even a lifetime, to excavate all the vestiges of privilege in various places in their lives, so when students see it in one place, that awareness is weighted by all the other entitlements throughout their lives that counter that awareness.

Naming the privilege is one tool. Analyzing how privilege works is another tool. These are the ones we usually do pretty well in diversity classrooms. But if we go back to Levine's SIBAM model from Chapter 2, these tools are the latter part of the process. The earlier part of the process is the more embodied part: what emerges emotionally, psychologically, and physiologically when we help students unearth privilege. In the next section, I outline six steps for unlearning privilege.

Tips for Learning to Deeply Listen and Dismantle Privilege

So how do we work with this energy? Chödrön suggests a model based on the four Rs:

1. *Recognize* the Shenpa.
2. *Refrain* from scratching.
3. *Relax* with the underlying urge to scratch.
4. *Resolve* to interrupt the momentum like this for the rest of our lives (2007, 63, emphasis in original).

This is an effective model for working with the intense charge to "react," but since most of our students will be unfamiliar with mindfulness practices, I find that a more context-specific model makes it more relatable and useful for them. In the remainder of this chapter, I will offer a model for students to learn to listen to their own privileged storylines, when they arise, and to sit with the raw energy behind them rather than acting out. I will then conclude with some tips for teachers as they facilitate this model in social justice classrooms.

How to Learn to Listen to the Workings of Privilege

1. Someone has just pointed out how you are privileged. Notice the waters of privilege getting churned. Do not respond verbally or move immediately to outward engagement. Instead, turn inward and listen to what is happening.
2. Pause. Ask for a moment while you listen to your response. Witness your response with curiosity, not judgment. This may only take a moment if the situation does

not allow you to take longer. But try to get a good snapshot of what those churning waters feel like so that you can reflect more deeply on them later.

(Note: This step gets more familiar the more you do it. That is not to say that it gets easier. The intensity of the experience of turning inward will depend on the depth of privilege being unearthed, the role in your own sense of identity that that piece of privilege has, and the amount of pain caused by the entitlement that is granted to you and denied others).

3. Listen to both yourself and to the person speaking. If you do not entirely understand what the person is saying, ask for clarification. Do it in the spirit of inquiry. This is not about asking members of marginalized groups to "educate" you about racism or sexism. It is about getting clear on what they are trying to say to you in the moment.

4. Turn inward. Get familiar with your internal landscape. What is arising for you at this moment? Anger? Defensiveness? Confusion? Grief? Where do you experience those emotions in your body? Do they have a texture? A color? How intense are they? Notice and feel.

5. Cultivate the Witness. Get bigger than the experience. So often, we get consumed by our thoughts and feelings. We think we ARE our thoughts and feelings. When we think that, we often cannot help but act on them. We become overwhelmed by them and so the reaction is immediate. The focus, then, is on the intensity of the emotion and our reactions, along with whatever ripple effects that reaction produces, both internally and externally.

When we can create a pause between our reaction and the acting on it, we can also learn to get bigger than the reaction. We can see the reaction as the inevitable churning that happens when our sense of self is challenged. We can also begin to see that what is getting churned is our *learned sense* of self, not our self itself. *Not our very being.* They are merely the layers of socialization and learned privileges that have been layered upon our being. We can begin to see that each time we peel away another layer of oppression, we can learn to have more choice in what messages we learn and what we choose to integrate into our sense of self. For many of us, the ideologies of privilege were internalized without our even knowing it. So unlearning them means we have more choice about the role we play in the world, how we relate to others, and how we understand ourselves. While the process of unlearning privilege can be deeply unsettling, the potential results are liberating, for marginalized groups and for ourselves.

Tips for Teachers as They Facilitate Deep Listening in Conversations about Privilege

1. Normalize the process. The complex range of emotions, and the difficulties sitting with them, are a natural part of the process. They are how privilege works and we can learn to sit with them.

2. Sitting with the negative charge of sensation when privilege is unsettled is challenging, but we can learn to do it. When we sit with it rather than "biting the hook," the tenor of the raw energy changes and sometimes dissipates. It is a skill that can be learned. Remind students that reacting in habitual ways to privileged narratives is also uncomfortable and comes with deep costs to the humanity of privileged groups and oppressed groups, despite the promised benefits.

3. Model our own process of unlearning privilege, in whatever areas of our identity we might have privilege. Share the mistakes, the denials, and the successes. It can be very helpful to students who are new to this process to learn from the journeys of those us who have been at this work for quite some time. Being honest and humble about when we do it well and when we "fail" can give permission to students to continue their work even as they stumble along the way. Indeed, normalizing that iterative journey can give them the courage to stay on the path even when it becomes rocky.

4. Help students connect with how deeply they want to be heard. Remind them that all of their classmates also want to be heard that deeply, whatever their experience. This realization gives students an opportunity to empathize with one another, and that empathy goes a long way toward helping them stay in the conversations about oppression even when it is hard.

5. Make very clear distinctions between when we want students to practice deep listening and when we want them to engage in more normative college discussions. Eventually, we can learn to merge the two skills, but in the beginning, it will be important for them to understand when they are supposed to listen from a place of receptivity, inquiry, and with the goal of relieving the suffering of others by really hearing them, and when they are expected to contribute their own thoughts, perspectives, and experiences. Without these clear parameters, students will be unclear about what is expected of them, particularly since deep listening is countercultural in much of academia. Murky boundaries between the two forms of listening, in the beginning when students are learning how to deeply listen, will likely impede the formation of an honest and connected community in the classroom. For instance, one student might take the risk of baring their feelings and experiences, expecting to be deeply heard, when another student responds with opinions rather than listening; the result may cause more conflict and prevent the first student from being that open in future discussions. Clear parameters for when to practice which skill will help prevent that confusion. Students will also become more adept at choosing when to use which skill, which is another important life skill that will serve them long after the completion of the course.

6. When things get messy, model how to navigate the fraught nature of the conversations with compassionate reflection. Remind students (and ourselves) that what comes up for each of us *is the work*. Dismantling privilege

is not easy, or we would have done it by now. When we make mistakes, get upset, feel silenced or frustrated (whether we are privileged or oppressed), we have opportunities to learn from rich moments that are key to the process. The tensions and difficulties are not something to be brushed over; they are something to be compassionately examined and learned from. The stronger the community in the classroom, the more effectively that can be accomplished.

7. Remember that this is a lifelong journey. We are learning about deeply entrenched systems of oppression and becoming familiar with deep listening techniques that we can continue to practice long after the end of our classes, indeed, long after students graduate from college. It takes patience and courage to do this work, but it can also be reassuring to recognize that it is a journey that will take quite some time. Accepting that reality makes it far less likely that students will give up when the going gets tough, particularly if we teach them how to meet themselves and their classmates with compassion, wherever they are in their journey.

Parker Palmer writes that, "when we learn how to listen more deeply to others, we can listen more deeply to ourselves" (2004, 121). I believe the reverse is also true.

The mindfulness skill of deep listening allows us to better understand and interrupt our own privilege by preventing many of the defensive reactions that keep privilege intact. In turn, we then learn how to more authentically be present with others. This skill will prove in valuable when we have difficult dialogues and conflict in the classroom. In the next chapter, I will discuss how to reframe student "resistance" in ways that help us more productively unpack what actually happens. The result, I hope, can be more authentic and transformative dialogues, both in our classrooms and in our communities beyond.

Mindfulness Practices

Contemplative Listening

An Hour of Silence

Go someplace where you can sit, undistracted, for an hour. Your phone should be off (except, perhaps, for an alarm set to signal the end of the hour). For one hour, just sit quietly and pay attention to what is happening around you. Listen to the sounds, feel the wind (if you are outside), smell whatever scents float by. Do not interact with anyone: just notice. When you find your attention wandering, gently invite it back to your breath and to the present moment. At the end of the hour, journal for ten minutes about what you noticed and what your experience was. Notice whether it was difficult for you to be with silence. Notice what thoughts flooded your mind as distractions.

Contemplative Listening with Community Members

For five minutes, listen to someone else with the full intention of just being present with her/him/zir. Take a few deep, grounding breaths and then turn your full attention to your classmate as she/he/ze tells you about his/her/zir perspective. This is not about what you think about the issue, this is about fully listening to him/her/zir. You will have your chance to speak. For now, as your classmates speaks, do your best to be fully present to hear that perspective. Make eye contact, focus on their words and their body language, breathe deeply and evenly. If you notice yourself reacting to what is being said, just take mental note of what is happening for you but keep your focus on her/his/zir perspective. You are bearing witness to them, not engaging in a debate. At the end of five minutes, both of you can pause, close your eyes, and breathe deeply for five slow breaths. Then switch.

After both of you have gone and have taken the five deep breaths, talk about your experience of the activity. Focus on what it felt like to be heard in this way, not on the content of the speech. Reflect on what it felt like to listen in this way. Once both of those reflections have been discussed, then the two participants can discuss the content of what was said, paying particular attention to whether that discussion has a different tenor than most because of the contemplative listening that has occurred. (Note: this last step can be done as a large group as well.)

Like many mindfulness practices, this one will likely work best if students become familiar with it in low-risk situations first. We cannot expect them to be able to practice deep contemplative listening about a loaded topic if they have never practiced it before. But if we start early in the semester with topics such as what our day is like or what we hope to achieve in college, then this practice will be more available and effective later in the semester around more loaded topics.

References

Barbezat, Daniel P. and Mirabai Bush. *Contemplative Practices in Higher Education: Powerful Methods to Transform Teaching and Learning.* New York: Jossey-Bass, 2014.

Barrett, James E. and David Roediger. "How White People Became White." In *White Privilege: Essential Readings on the Other Side of Racism,* 2nd ed., edited by Paula S. Rothenberg, 35–40. New York: Worth, 2005.

Brady, Mark, ed. *The Wisdom of Listening.* Boston: Wisdom, 2003.

Case, Kim A. "Beyond Diversity and Whiteness: Developing a Transformative and Intersectional Model of Privilege Studies Pedagogy." In *Deconstructing Privilege: Teaching and Learning as Allies in the Classroom,* edited by Kim A. Case, 1–14. New York: Routledge, 2013.

———, J. Iuzzini and M. Hopkins. "Systems of Privilege: Intersections, Awareness, and Applications. *Journal of Social Issues* 68, no. 1 (2012): 1–10.

Chödrön, Pema. *Practicing Peace in Times of War.* Boston, MA: Shambala, 2007.

Cole, E.R., L.R. Avery, C. Dodson, and K.D. Goodman. "Against Nature: How Arguments about the Naturalness of Marriage Privilege Heterosexuality." *Journal of Social Issues* 68, no. 1 (2012): 46–62.

Collins, Patricia Hill. *Black Feminist Thought: Knowledge, Consciousness, and the Politics of Empowerment*, 2nd ed. New York: Routledge, 2000.

Coston, B.M. and Michael Kimmel. "Seeing Privilege Where It Isn't: Marginalized Masculinities and the Intersectionality of Privilege." *Journal of Social Issues* 68, no. 1 (2012): 97–111.

Dalton, Harlon. "Failing to See." *White Privilege: Essential Readings on the Other Side of Racism*, 2nd ed., edited by Paula S. Rothenberg, 15–18. New York: Worth, 2005.

"Deep Listening." University of Minnesota Center for Spirituality and Healing. Accessed December 31, 2014, www.csh.umn.edu/wsh/Leadership/DeepListening/.

Devanadi Yoga Teacher Training. Minneapolis, MN, August 2013–September 2014.

Ferber, Abby L. and Andrea O'Reilly Herrera. "Teaching Privilege Through an Intersectional Lens." In *Deconstructing Privilege: Teaching and Learning as Allies in the Classroom*, edited by Kim A. Case, 83–101. New York: Routledge, 2013.

Hanh, Thich Nhat. "Deep Listening." Accessed December 31, 2014, www.youtube.com/watch?v=EjyF1ARV5AM.

Keating, A. *Teaching Transformation: Transcultural Classroom Dialogues*. New York: Palgrave Macmillan, 2007.

Johnsen, Linda. "The Koshas: Five Layers of Being." *Yoga International*. July 8, 2014. Accessed January 5, 2015, https://yogainternational.com/article/view/the-koshas-5-layers-of-being.

Johnson, Allan. "Privilege as Paradox." In *White Privilege: Essential Readings on the Other Side of Racism*, 2nd ed., edited by Paula S. Rothenberg, 103–108. New York: Worth, 2005.

Luft, Rachel E. "Intersectionality and the Risk of Flattening Difference: Gender and Race Logics, and the Strategic Use of Antiracist Strategy." In *The Intersectional Approach: Transforming the Academy Through Race, Class, and Gender*, edited by M. Berger and K. Guidroz, 100–117. Chapel Hill: University of North Carolina Press, 2009.

Maples, Cheri, Thich Nhat Hanh, and Larry Ward. "Mindfulness, Suffering, and Engaged Buddhism." *On Being* with Krista Tippett, American Public Media. January 22, 2015. Accessed June 8, 2015. http://onbeing.org/program/thich-nhat-hanh-mindfulness-suffering-and-engaged-buddhism/74.

McGonigal, Kelly. "How to Create a Sankalpa." *Yoga International*. June 12, 2013. Accessed January 2, 2015, https://yogainternational.com/article/view/how-to-create-a-sankalpa.

Moraga, Cherríe. "Refugees of a World on Fire, Foreword to the Second Edition." *This Bridge Called My Back: Writings by Radical Women of Color*, 2nd ed., edited by Cherríe Moraga and Gloria Anzaldúa, i–iii. New York: Kitchen Table Women of Color Press, 1983.

Neff, Kristin. "The Space Between Self Esteem and Self-Compassion." TEDx Talk. Accessed January 2, 2015, www.self-compassion.org.

Omi, Michael and Howard Winant. *Racial Formations in the United States*, 3rd ed. New York: Routledge, 2014.

Palmer, Parker. *A Hidden Wholeness: The Journey Toward an Undivided Life*. San Francisco, CA: Jossey-Bass, 2004.

Platt, Lisa F. "Blazing the Trail: Teaching the Privileged about Privilege." In *Deconstructing Privilege: Teaching and Learning as Allies in the Classroom*, edited by Kim A. Case, 207–222. New York: Routledge, 2013.

"Race the Power of Illusion: The House We Live In." Part III. California Newsreel, 2003.

Rome, David and Hope Martin. "Deep Listening." *Mindful*. Accessed December 29, 2014, www.mindful.org/in-love-and-relationships/relating-to-others/deep-listening.

————. "Embodied Listening." Accessed January 5, 2015, http://embodied-listening .com/about-embodied-listening/.

Rothenberg, P. S. *White Privilege: Essential Readings on the Other Side of Racism*, 2nd ed. New York: Worth, 2008.

Sanders, M. R. and R. Mahalingham. "Under the Radar: The Role of Invisible Discourse in Understanding Class-Based Privilege." *Journal of Social Issues* 68, no. 1 (2012): 112–127.

Tatum, Beverly. "Defining Racism: 'Can We Talk?'" In *Women: Images and Realities, A Multicultural Anthology*, 4th ed., edited by Amy Kesselman, Lily D. McNair, and Nancy Schniedewind, 386–390. New York: McGraw-Hill, 2006.

Watt, Sherry K. "Difficult Dialogues, Privilege, and Social Justice: Uses of the Privileged Identity Exploration (PIE) Model in Student Affairs Practice." *Colleges Student Affairs Journal Spring* (2007) 26(2), 114–125. Accessed May 7, 2015, http://files.eric.ed.gov/fulltext/EJ899385.pdf.

Wildeman, Stephanie M. and Adrienne D. Davis. "Making Systems of Privilege Visible." In *White Privilege: Essential Readings on the Other Side of Racism*, 2nd ed., edited by Paula S. Rothenberg, 95–102. New York: Worth, 2005.

Wise, Timothy. *White Like Me: Reflections on Race from a Privileged Son*. New York: Softskull Press, 2011.

———— and Kim A. Case. "Pedagogy for the Privileged: Addressing Inequality and Injustice Without Shame or Blame." In *Deconstructing Privilege: Teaching and Learning as Allies in the Classroom*, edited by Kim A. Case, 34–48. New York: Routledge, 2013.

5

REFRAMING STUDENT RESISTANCE AS MINDFUL DISSONANCE

Teaching about oppression, power, privilege, and social transformation is an exciting and fraught process. The issues we cover in diversity classes are often counter-cultural, so it should come as no surprise that many students have not learned much about these issues prior to college. Even those have encountered multiple perspectives regarding issues of oppression or had their own experiences with oppression may have not yet learned the analytical framework of anti-oppression pedagogy that helps deconstruct the systems. Students often find this new knowledge disturbing. Much work has been done on the various aspects of student resistance to critical, feminist, queer, and anti-racist pedagogy (Bell, Morrow, and Tastsoglou 1999; Kumashiro 2002; Deal and Hyde 2004; Rodriguez 2008; Haddad and Lieberman 2002; Lewis 1992).

These "disturbances" can take many forms, including defensiveness, counter-critique, emotional outbursts (anger, sadness, frustration, fear), numbness, shutting down, and absenteeism. Over the years, I have heard many of these student reactions characterized as "resistance." "Students are resistant to learning about these issues," some teachers will say. "They are unwilling to let go of their privilege," others will say. "They refuse to see that oppression still exists because they have bought into the myth of individualism," faculty might say about a member of a marginalized group who appears "resistant" to this content.

Resistance, then, becomes the catchall phrase for people who do not immediately respond in desired ways. Moreover, the assumption is that students intentionally resist; words like "refuse," "unwilling," and "bought into" position students in a willfully antagonistic relationship with the material. In this framing, teacher and student are pitted against each other. The former's task, then, is to "overcome" or "break down" student resistance. This framing of the situation does not put us all on the same side of the learning process but rather positions us in opposition with one another. While some students certainly do fit this characterization, far more students, I suggest, are not willfully resistant so much as they are deeply unsettled by the new awareness and lacking of the necessary tools to productively understand and unpack their responses.

This chapter focuses on reframing student resistance in order to better help students work through their discomfort. One of the biggest problem with characterizing these student reactions as "resistance" is that it is far too simple an explanation for the complexity of what is actually happening. We need to nuance our discussion of student reactions much more than we often do if we are to really take account of what is happening in our classrooms. Just as importantly, we need to help students learn to nuance their own reactions and those of their classmates, so that we can teach them the skills of mindfully processing through those complexities that will be of use to them long after the completion of our semester. While the outward manifestation of different reactions may take similar forms (anger, for instance), what is underneath those expressions is often far more complicated. Two students may express anger coming from very different places. As Moore notes, "the roots of their resistances may arise from a wide range of social positions, not just from privilege, not just from identity rebellion, not just from entrenched cognitive stages of development" (Moore 2007, 36). I will first trace out some of the different reactions that I see surfacing in Women's Studies classrooms, then discuss why we need to reframe these responses as dissonance rather than "resistance." Finally, I will offer mindfulness tools for more effectively meeting the resulting discomfort in the classroom.

Types of Student Resistance

Having taught Women's Studies courses for more than fifteen years, I am well-acquainted with the perception that students are "resistant" to learning about oppression. Whether it is men who "refuse" to examine their male privilege, White people who become defensive when challenged on their racism, heterosexuals who are fine with gay people as long as they do not "flaunt it," or wealthy people who nestle down in their class privilege while demanding that poor people just "get a job," members of dominant groups are often framed as actively refusing to see the institutionalized systems of oppression that grant some groups resources, power, and privileges that are denied other groups. Other reactions by members of the dominant group are also lumped into the term "resistance." Shame, guilt, tears, shock, and concern are commonly seen as ways that privileged groups shift the focus back to themselves, get others to "take care" of them, and thus avoid doing the hard work of unpacking their own roles in systems of oppression.

While this awareness is developing for privileged students, members of marginalized groups in the classroom often experience frustration at what might be perceived as deflecting the attention back to the dominant group. Some might even feel an element of "well, you should suffer. My people certainly have." Both of these responses are coming from a place of deep hurt. Marginalized students have not been taken care of or nurtured in their experiences of oppression, at least not in most institutionalized spaces. Their suffering has not been acknowledged or heard. This pain and grief needs to be understood and contextualized, not just by the teacher, but by the other students in the room. While I have seen variations of all of these reactions in my students, I have also learned that underneath the surface responses is often a great deal more complexity.

Members of marginalized groups also have reactions that are sometimes labeled as "resistance." Students of color, for instance, might be called complicit with racist systems if they too happily embrace myths of individualism and the "pull yourself up by your bootstraps" ideology. Women who strive for a certain unattainable beauty standard in their never-ending search for heterosexual male validation as a marker of their worth are perceived to be "buying into" patri-archy. I have already discussed how internalized oppression is often at work in our classrooms, producing these reactions and others. It is important, I think, to recognize that there is not one "correct" way of working toward social justice; our class discussions get unproductively circumscribed when we presume that "our way is the only way" and label other perspectives "resistance." At the same time, there are degrees of complicity with the system that are reflected in many student responses. These responses, however, are not "resistances" that need to be shot down but rather rich opportunities for modeling how to unlearn oppression in our communities.

If we think back to the identity development model I cited in Chapter 3, dif-ferent reactions often characterize different stages. In the Disintegration phase, for instance, Whites may feel shame and anger as they begin to realize the advan-tages they have been given as members of the dominant/privileged group in the United States. In the racial identity development model she presents, Tatum says that in this stage, "attempts to reduce the discomfort may include denial or attempts to change significant others' attitudes towards people of color" (2014). In this phase, then, reactions such as shame, guilt, and anger are not only common, but are to be expected when White students begin to face, maybe for the first time, their positionality as Whites in society. While those reactions might be frustrating for those of us who have been doing this work for many years and for students who are denied these privileges on a daily basis, our task is to find an effective way of moving students through those responses.

In any given classroom, students will likely be at a variety of stages in their identity development and likely positioned in complex ways in relation to one another. Some students may be in the Immersion phase, while others may be in the Denial stage, which is one reason why class discussions about oppression go the way they do. As students move beyond the Denial stage and begin to recognize the role they and other members of their group have played in oppressing others, they often encounter feelings of grief, remorse, guilt, and shame. These reactions are manifestations (albeit unskillful ones) of students' attempts to wade through the horror that comes with beginning to more fully see oppression and begin to recognize one's own role in it.

In addition to being at different stages of identity development, many students are likely accessing privilege in some ways while being denied privilege in other ways. So when they are "accused" of being privileged (and some students experience it as being accused), they might feel confusion and resentment that people are not acknowledging how they are oppressed in other ways. In fact, chances are they are much more aware of how they are denied privilege than they are of how they receive it—again, not necessarily because of willful ignorance but because that is how the system works. This is one of the deep challenges of doing intersectional work: most of us have hard work to do and have experienced the deep pain of oppression. Paradoxically, this "beyond duality" perspective also opens the door for deep empathy, compassion, and community-building. Mindfulness provides a powerful bridge to take us there.

Reframing as Dissonance

In any given classroom, student reactions are likely coming from a variety of these places. While they might manifest outwardly in similar ways, what is behind them is very different. Think of it like this: each student's identity and experience is like a different combination of metals, and we as teachers do not necessarily know the exact composite. When we teach about power and privilege, the teachings act like a gong. When the gong of privilege is rung, the reverberations echo outward into the classroom. For a less privileged student, the gong might be a gong of oppression which, when rung, also reverberates outward. When the two sound waves meet each other, they affect one another and then flow back to the original students, who then have another, different wave of gong reverberations (Amy Boland, personal communication, November 2014). And this goes on, creating a complex cacophony of reactions in the classroom.

Rather than see these reverberations as "resistance," I argue that we need to reframe them as the dissonance that inevitably occurs whenever we deeply challenge students' worldviews. Cognitive dissonance, according to the psychologist Festinger (1957), occurs when an individual tries to hold two contradictory ideas simultaneously. The result is disequilibrium, and the human tendency is to work to restore equilibrium.

It should come as no surprise, then, that students react with shock and disturbance when they are thrust into disequilibrium. Social psychologists tell us it is the natural human tendency to try to restore equilibrium, and there are several common tactics used to do so, including changing some of the contradictory ideas to make them more consistent with one another, gathering more information that supports their current ideas, and minimizing the apparent contradictions (Walton 2011, 5). Most of these responses are spontaneous, gut responses, not intentional ones. These strategies, not accidentally, look quite similar to the "resistant" reactions I have previously described. They are symptoms of a student trying to restore comfort and equilibrium. Students who have their sense of selves challenged, for instance, may try to "recast themselves in a positive light" in order to reaffirm their pre-existing sense of self. Rather than these gut responses being interpreted as students "supporting" oppression, teachers would be more effective if we understand that, from a social psychology perspective, this is natural human behavior. According to Walton, for "dominant culture students, *pedagogical resistance may result when conflicting value judgments and practices generate deep uncertainties about a seemingly certain social world*" (Walton 2011, 6, emphasis added).

The dissonance that arises from learning about oppression is more than a cognitive one. It is also an emotional and psychological one, because the ideas we are challenging are often embedded in the students' very sense of selves. These are not merely facts we are challenging but also worldviews that have long structured their worlds. Students and faculty alike have been socialized, often learning ideologies that uphold social inequalities, regardless of the cultural framework of that socialization. Dominant group identity, for instance, has been constructed with an invisible sense of entitlement already embedded into its very definition, so to challenge it inevitably creates fundamental dissonance. When privileged students have a hard time seeing their privilege or do not immediately warm up to the idea, they are not necessarily being stubborn or willfully clinging to their privilege because they want to oppress others. The initial reactions of defensiveness or denial of responsibility do not necessarily mean that they are unwilling to dismantle their privilege. The reactions may mean that students' very sense of self is being shaken, and students are grasping at ways to maintain some sense of stability when the ground is pulled out from under them.

These learning experiences can create a great deal of tension and discomfort for students. Deconstructing these ideologies also means deconstructing the self, our relations to others, and our ways of understanding the world (Walton 2011). When we understand it in this way, we should be surprised if students do not exhibit some dissonance, rather than get frustrated when they do. Mindfulness teaches us how to sit with the discomfort that arises in this process. When we learn to be fully present in the moment with whatever we are feeling, then we can ask ourselves, "What is my feeling of discomfort trying to tell me, about myself, about my social locations in the society?" (Wong 2004). But asking the question without first learning how to recognize, sit with, and understand the discomfort misses a large portion of the journey and is, therefore, of limited use. As teachers, we need to offer students helpful tools for mindfully processing through these emotions.

Moreover, these gut "resistant" responses are produced by the very systems of oppression we are trying to dismantle. They are the result of socialization processes that embed ideologies of superiority into dominant identities and subordination into marginalized ones. So these "resistances" are a kind of "safety mechanisms" that systems of oppression have in place to prevent individuals from dismantling it. By trying to restore equilibrium, individuals are redirected away from deconstructing the system and moved comfortably back into reinscribing it. Rather than blaming students or assuming ill will for these reactions, we should see them as ways that the system hurts both members of dominant groups and members of marginalized ones, albeit in different ways.

This resulting dissonance—and even the initial attempts to bring themselves back to equilibrium—is both a natural and inevitable part of the process of unlearning oppression. In fact, truly transformational learning *requires* that students go through some level of this dissonance. The trick to being pedagogically effective is not to attack the "resistance" but also not to allow the "resistance" to prevent further learning by enabling the student to quickly restore equilibrium before truly grappling with the implications of the conflicting beliefs. It also means teaching students the tools with which to effectively recognize and work through their dissonance and that of others.

Discernment and Meta-Dissonance

Just as social justice courses offer language and cognitive tools to make sense of social events, cultivating discernment through the Witness helps students see what is happening to them through a broader lens while still remaining in their embodied experience. Preparing students ahead of time for the kind of dissonance that can occur as they are exposed to multiple perspectives and alternative knowledge can go a long way toward disrupting the habitual patterns of reducing cognitive dissonance. Indeed, educating students about the typical tactics used to reduce cognitive dissonance can help them begin to recognize them in action and help students make more intentional choices about how to engage them. Several educators have suggested that helping students see that cognitive dissonance is part of the process develops what McFalls and Cobb-Roberts call a "meta-dissonance" (2001; Gorski 2009). In mindfulness language, this "meta-dissonance" is really the Witness. Once we provide the framework, we can then come back to it when we see dissonance happening in class discussions. Those moments can then be reframed as rich opportunities to model self-reflection in the moment of deep disequilibrium, which then helps students develop critical skills for unlearning oppression that will serve them long after the "content" of the class is completed.

I found myself arriving at this conclusion independently of my research when I listened to the struggles several students were having as they tried to make sense of the disturbing material we were covering. As a teacher, I see students go through these processes every semester, but for the student it is raw, real, and uncharted terrain. In order to help students see the myriad of ways cognitive dissonance might show up for them, I wrote the following scenarios and shared them with the class; like all the scenarios in this book, they are hypothetical composites of students with whom I have worked over the years. We then discussed whether and how they resonated with students' own experiences. The "distance" of hypothetical scenarios, combined with the relief of seeing their experiences reflected, provided an opening for self-reflection that not only created a powerful discussion in the moment but also gave us a framework to return to when dissonance appeared in later discussions.

Cognitive Dissonance Scenarios

Scenario #1

Miguel is a working class Chicano student who is taking a Diversity class to fulfill a requirement for college. He was looking forward to it because he is interested in issues of oppression and wants to learn more about women's issues. Each time he goes to class, he learns about so many things that his mind gets blown. He thought he knew about inequalities in the world, but the more he learns about systematic oppression, the more overwhelmed he gets. By the end of the hour-and-fifteen-minute class, he has so many thoughts and questions on his mind, but then the class ends, and he doesn't know where to go with them. Who does he talk with? His friends do not really know much about these issues nor do they really see it from his perspective. Miguel feels alone and isolated. He also feels committed to doing something to change things but does not know where to go with that energy. On the one hand, he believes that individuals can make a change and, in fact, have the responsibility to do so. On the other hand, the problems are so big, so deeply entrenched, and so interconnected that he wonders if they can be undone. What can one individual do? Where does he go with this energy, rage, and passion?

This scenario describes the overwhelming outrage and immobilization that many students experience when they begin to truly develop a systematic analysis and realize the extent of oppression. Every semester, I see students experience this combination of motivation to create change and a paralyzing disillusion that they are too small to make a difference. This form of dissonance entails learning to live with a very real contradiction: holding both the awareness of intractable systems that are far bigger than individuals *and* recognizing that change has to start with individuals, even if that transformation is a limited one. The dissonance that students like Miguel feel is almost palpable in a classroom: there is this itching need to DO SOMETHING and an outrage that they need to talk about and understand, combined with an immobilization that they often do not know what to do with. The confusion can make it even worse, especially if the student has nowhere to process the roller coaster of thoughts and feelings outside of the classroom. Later in this chapter, I will outline some mindfulness tools that can be critical in helping students do just that.

Scenario #2

Amy had grown up in a middle-class suburb of the Twin Cities. She knew she was White since diversity issues were covered in her high school and she spent lots of time with her best friend's family, who were from India. Many of her White classmates did not notice their race but she does. She goes to many educational programs on different cultures and races and does her best to work toward equality: she votes for progressive politicians and is treasurer in a student group committed to social justice.

So when she got to her required Diversity class in college, she was excited to learn about it. Amy wants to do her part to make the world a better place. But her teacher keeps saying that she has a lot of privileges because the very construction of whiteness is anchored in a system of oppression. Amy does not disagree with this claim, she is just trying to wrap her mind around what that means. How does she "get rid" of or "undo" her privilege? How does she redefine her whiteness? She truly wants to know, but when she asks the question, she feels attacked by both her teacher and some of her classmates. She thought she was a good person, but now she is beginning to see that she may be a part of the problem. That awareness is really upsetting to her, but she does not know where to go with those feelings. Who does she talk with? What can she do?

This student is experiencing a dissonance that is fairly common for those who are privileged. While some students do not want to confront their privilege because they want to maintain it and believe they deserve it, I have found that far more students are in Amy's situation: they are beginning to see it and want to work toward a more just world, but they are not sure how to go about doing so. They cannot step out of their White skin or their male privilege, for instance, so how can they work to dismantle the effects of that privilege. Students in this position might express their confusion with various degrees of skillfulness, but they sometimes find that their responses are interpreted as resistance to letting go of their privilege. Those judgments typically just confuse them further, since they do not know where else to go with their questions and may either continue floundering or shut down. Dissonance can also occur for students such as Amy when they work to dismantle their privilege in good faith but find themselves startled and even disturbed about what it means to truly let go of their privilege. That dissonance does not mean that the student does not want to let it go, but if the sense of entitlement is as deeply embedded in our sense of self as I have suggested, then this will inevitably be a deeply unsettling process.

What is required here is an ability to hold contradictions with compassion, rather than creating a kind of moral dichotomy. A person can be deeply committed to undoing his/her/zir own privilege *and* be unsettled by the process. In fact, most of us probably are, especially early in our journey. Rather than condemning that, we can be more effective teachers if we help all of our students—both the students experiencing this particular dissonance and that students' classmates—understand that the disequilibrium is a part of the process with which we can learn to sit. I believe everyone in the room needs to understand this process for a couple reasons. First, we will have more compassion for our colleagues/classmates as they proceed along their journey when we more fully understand what is happening for them. Second, that discernment makes it less likely that we will react with a gut judgmentalness that will shut down the process. Third, we are likely to be in a similar place in our own journey at some point. Remember that in any given classroom, students are in a variety of places power and privilege, as well as a variety of stages of identity development, political awareness, and even capacity with mindfulness skills. Different issues will bring up different dissonances for all of us, so whereas one classmate might find themselves in Amy's situation around racial privilege, the student next to her might find herself/himself/zirself in that position around heterosexual privilege. If she/he/ze wants people to meet her/his/zir dissonance and struggle to grow with empathy and compassion, then she/he/ze needs to learn to meet hers/his/zir with the same openness. That capacity is what mindfulness can teach us. I will talk more about how it can do so after discussing the next scenarios.

Scenario #3

Miyumi is a Japanese American college student who is super excited to be in her Women's Studies class. She has not had very many out queer teachers, and since she just came out a couple years ago herself, she was excited to take a class with this particular queer teacher. Miyumi has gotten involved with a lot of the LGBTQ student groups on campus, gets excited to go to Pride every year, and is learning as much as she can about LGBTQ and women's issues. She feels more empowered than she ever has in her life. She has a group of friends, has a girlfriend she is head-over-heels in love with, and wears all kinds of rainbow colors. Sure, she doesn't like to look at her body. She still feels pretty uncomfortable in her own skin because she does not fit the standard model of beauty in society, but that is weird, because she does not want to fit it. She is proud to be butch, and she loves women, so why is she still so body conscious, she wonders? Of course, it probably does not help that her mom, who moved to Minnesota from Japan when she was a teenager, still wants her to get married (to a man) and start a family. Her Mom makes comments all the time about her hair being too short and her clothing to baggy and not attractive enough. She wants to please her Mom (her family is super important to her) but she also wants to be able to be who she is.

The dissonance that Miyumi is experiencing is also quite common in social justice classes. She is becoming empowered in some ways, but is also still caught in oppressive beliefs that undermine that empowerment. Her adamant queerness suggests that she is in the Immersion phase of identity development around her lesbian identity, but that does not mean that she is in that stage for other aspects of her identity. She has clearly internalized negative body issues as a woman and still struggles with that. It should be noted that she is experiencing that struggle *as a queer woman*; in other words, she has internalized all the shaming body messages that haunt most women in the United States, but her experience of those messages is further complicated by being a queer woman. In the queer community, there is often a greater acceptance of different body types and a broader definition of attractiveness for women, but our self-image is also often complicated by both internalized sexism and internalized homophobia. As Carla Trujillo writes, lesbian women who grow up in a misogynist culture have to overcome an internalized hatred of themselves and women in general in order to express their love of women (Trujillo 2006). Moreover, depending on her performance of queerness, Miyumi might also be gender policed for not "conforming" to society's definition of femininity and womanhood. All of these layers complicate her relationship to her body image.

So while Miyumi is super empowered in some ways, that liberation does not necessarily extend to all aspects of her identity or to all issues she faces in the world. Like many students, she will experience this dissonance as she lives out these contradictions. Moreover, she is also experiencing a longing for connection to her family—a connection that is deeply intertwined with her racial and cultural identity—but cannot conform to familial expectations without selling out part of herself. This burden also raises some painful dissonance that resonated with some of my students. One biracial student, who identified her parents as White and Filipina, said, with some pain in her voice, that the latter part of this scenario felt very familiar to her. Seeing the experience validated in the scenario gave this student a sense of support and offered a language with which students could talk with one another about the experience.

Scenario #4

Sam is a working class Black college student who worked hard to get to college. He is the only one in his family and one of the few kids from his high school who went to college. He is taking a Diversity class to fill a requirement, but to tell you the truth, he doesn't like it much. His teacher keeps talking about systems of oppression and acts like all students should be activists. Sam knows racism exists; he survives it every day. Moreover, his family struggled economically. His single mom had to work multiple jobs to try to put food on the table, and even then, there was not always enough. But that is why he worked so hard to get to college. He plans to graduate, get a good job, and live a better life. It is not that he does not care about oppression, it is just that he does not think it is his problem to solve. He has already suffered enough from inequalities and now just wants to keep his head down and do what he needs to do to succeed in college, so that he can have a successful career. Then he and his family will have enough. If his teacher wants to be an activist, great, but Sam does not. Two more months of this class to go.

This dissonance describes the experience of some students for whom oppression is a daily, lived experience, but who have chosen as their survival mechanism an attempt to rise above it rather than combat it directly through social change efforts. For some students, succeeding in daily matters, including getting to college given the economic and racial discrimination they face, is more than enough resistance. They do not want to be looked to as activists. Though they understand that these are real issues and have a much more direct relationship to them than do some of their classmates, they feel frustrated dissonance when they are expected to rally around social change. Sam, for instance, has chosen a form of individualist meritocracy as a survival mechanism, and though he recognizes the oppression that has put barriers in his way, his resistance strategy is to keep his eyes on the prize and succeed anyway. The expectation that he should want to be a social change agent stirs up some dissonance for him. Embedded in that dissonance may be the discomfort of a deeper recognition that the individualism he has embraced is not really within his power to choose, given that the system of racial and economic oppression can disempower him at any moment, but that is not for his teacher to say. That is his journey to determine, and at the moment, that is not his reality.

These scenarios describe some of the many ways I have seen students experience dissonance in my classrooms over the years. It is not only experienced by privileged students nor does it come in only one form. In any given classroom, a variety of these experiences are likely happening, often below the surface in ways that teachers may or may not know. These reactions are not something to be overcome so much as they are something to help the students *mindfully work through*. The first step in helping students learn to navigate through this dissonance is to explicitly name it as an essential part of the unlearning process. We need to take it to the "meta" level by teaching students what it is, why it occurs, and what tools are typically employed to stunt the dissonance rather than work through it. We can help students learn to recognize dissonance when it occurs in themselves and in others. This "meta" awareness lets them become more aware of their experience of learning. We can, for instance, prepare students ahead of time with a definition and an example similar to their own but removed from them, such as some of the scenarios I offer here. We then have the opportunity to understand why dissonance occurs, what it looks and feels like, and to offer some useful tools for working through the dissonance in ways that allows transformational learning to occur.

These scenarios illustrate the many ways that systems of oppression hurt everyone by denying us the full expression of our humanity and a truly profound connection with one another. We are not hurt in the same way or to the same degree, but we all have motivations to dismantle the systems in order to step into the fullest expression of ourselves. We will not be able to dismantle the systems, however, if the various types of dissonance that are produced by this process are not allowed space. This is where the teacher needs to be bigger than the moment so that she/he/ze can help students develop a meta-level of experiential awareness. Our role, then, is to help students learn to WITNESS what is happening and provide them the tools to more mindfully work through it.

Cultivating Our Capacity to Grow

There is a productive and transformative level of dissonance but there is also a counterproductive level of dissonance. Mark William and Danny Penman (2012) call this the "soft" and "hard" edge. The "soft edge" of dissonance is a dynamic place of transformation. It is a place of uncertainty and some discomfort, but it is also exciting and dynamic. When we are in our soft edge, we are not too far from our usual comfort zone, which means we can usually be in that place of radical openness. While college academics sometimes privilege mastery of content over exploration, truly transformational learning occurs in the place of the unknown. This "soft edge" is the place where we move beyond our comfort zone of what is familiar and into the discomfort of uncertainty. In this liminal space, there is a synergy of energy as old and new ideas come into contact with one another, new knowledge is generated, feelings arise and transform, and possibilities emerge and become manifest. This is a space that we need to be in if we are to truly have transformational learning—the alchemy does not occur on the other, safer, side of that edge. Artists and athletes know the liminal space, because that is where they create and excel. In the classroom, the space may be a little less accessible, so our job as anti-oppression teachers it to help students learn to navigate it.

However, if we go too far into deep dissonance, the student is likely to go past his/her/zir capacity to handle it. Williams and Penman (2012) call this the "hard edge," the place so far past their comfort zone that they cannot handle it; students will either shut down or lash out in this space. This hard edge is not a dynamic place of growth and learning; it is a place of avoidance, fear, anger, and defense mechanisms that are usually beyond the individual's capacity to sit with in that moment. I see these two edges at work in my yoga classes all the time: at the soft edge, students are listening to their experience and feeling into the subtlety of the pose. Their faces are usually soft, curious, and attentive. When they go to their hard edge, however, their bodies become hard, their shoulders scrunched, their breathing shallow and constricted, and their faces become a mask of endurance rather than of listening. This latter place is not a safe place for them to be; they are likely to injure themselves and disconnect from their embodied experience.

Similar processes can happen in the academic classroom. When students go to their hard edge, they are less willing and able to sit with the discomfort and engage in the inquiry that is necessary for transformative learning. This place can be so frightening that they lash out in ways that then get framed as resistance. What is really happening, however, is a defense mechanism in reaction to dissonance too powerful for them to handle. When we are caught in intense emotional and cognitive dissonance, we often "lose our sense of proportion and perspective" and we "lose sight of the likely impact of our actions on others" (Dalai Lama 1999, 31). It is critical for us, as social justice teachers, to remember that we cannot force people through this hard edge and hope for transformative learning, because that is a space *beyond their capacity at that moment.*

Imagine this: a student goes to her first yoga class. She is a bit scared because she is completely unfamiliar with yoga and has a lot of lower back pain and has learned many coping mechanisms to protect her back. The overly enthusiastic yoga teacher chooses this student to demonstrate how to do a dropback (dropping into a backbend from a standing position). Though the teacher is there assisting and encouraging, this pose is so far past the students' comfort zone and literal ability that her whole body and heart tenses up, making it that much more impossible for her to do the muscular nuances that are necessary to safely do the dropback. Even if she manages to get into the pose, she will likely have increased her negative reactivity so much that she may avoid not only the pose but yoga itself for quite some time after that.

Of course, no qualified yoga teacher worth her/his/zir salt would ever take a beginner into a dropback; it is far too advanced a pose. I am not sure I can accurately say the same of academic teachers. Those of us who teach social justice are usually so deeply committed to the issues we study that we sometimes want to move students along faster than they are ready to go. I include an earlier version of my own teaching in this category. The more seasoned we become as teachers, the less this overly enthusiastic approach is likely to occur. But just as that yoga student cannot go that far beyond her experience and ability that early in her yoga practice, neither can a student in a social justice classroom go beyond her/his/zir capacity to unlearn oppression. This is not willful ignorance or a stubborn refusal to account for privilege (though it may look like that on the surface). They literally may not be able to learn when they are in the hard edge space. It would be beyond their capacity. If we are to truly help students unlearn oppression, we need to meet students where they are. This is not about "coddling" students. It is about being both strategically effective and compassionate. They are not capable of doing the work of unlearning oppression once we get to the hard edge space.

The good (and complicated) news is that the edges are moving targets. A person's edges vary from day to day and from topic to topic. While we as teachers cannot know the nuances of each student's edge on any given day, we can *teach students to befriend and understand their own edges*, so that they can name where they are. This self-reflection integrates a level of mindfulness with the intellectual self-reflection many of us teach in social justice courses. It empowers the students to understand when they are in a space of dynamic learning and teaches them how to embrace that space of uncertainty. It will also help them recognize their own defensive mechanisms that emerge when they hit the hard edge, so that we can provide them with more productive options in that moment. Since transformative learning is a process, both students and teacher can better recognize that the line between the hard edge and soft edge will change over time. Students in upper division Women's Studies classes, for instance, are often able to sit with a deeper level of discomfort than are students in an introductory Diversity class because they have done the earlier work and moved the line of their soft edge farther along (not to mention the fact that they are older).

As professors who may only work with students for a semester, we need to offer students the tools that they can draw on as they continue this journey outside our classroom. Many of us see our job as planting the seeds; we know that we will not teach students how to unlearn oppression in a semester (or even in four years). So if we carry this idea further to realize that their "edge"—what degree of dissonance they are able to process—will likely continue to move long after they leave our class, then we need to provide them with the tools not only to analyze oppression but also to mindfully navigate through the embodied discomfort so that they are more empowered on their journey when they may not have a teacher or even a support network to help them on their travels.

Creating Space for Our Complex Identities

Students need to have space to process their emotions and they need to be taught how to do so in productive and compassionate ways. I get a certain layer of dissonance in my Introduction to Women's Studies courses, which, for some students, is the first time they are encountering feminist analysis. For those students who have had other courses about anti-oppression, the initial surprise is no longer there, but the deeper unlearning is still taking place. In my upper division Women's Studies courses, the dissonance appears on a different layer yet. Here, we have students who are deeply committed to a feminist cause and are usually quite well-informed about certain feminist issues (whichever ones interest them the most). They are usually committed to ending oppression, which they recognize means unlearning any privileges they have. But the process of dismantling that privilege still often stirs dissonance that takes the form of guilt, shame, and an initial "I didn't mean it like that" response that precedes the work of dismantling the privilege. This dissonance is also part of the work of unlearning privilege.

Even more complicated levels of dissonance occur when students (and faculty, for that matter), insist that the focus remain on one form of oppression (sexism or racism, for instance) but have difficulty addressing their participation in other forms of oppression (such as ableism or homophobia, for instance). This last form sometimes results in an unproductive and harmful "oppression olympics" that prevents us from seeing how we are all hurt by these systems, albeit in different ways. Sometimes, this insistence on multiple forms of oppression can be used to avoid facing one's role in another form of oppression. For instance, when a White woman in an anti-racist workshop is challenged to confront her White privilege, she can avoid doing that hard work by continually shifting the discussion to how she is also oppressed because of sexism. While it is likely true that she has experienced sexism, Rachel Luft (2010) argues that this is one way that intersectionality can be used to distract the discussion from power and privilege. Luft certainly values intersectionality but argues that it can be used to derail discussions about race. She argues instead for a *strategic* focus on a single issue. We can see this debate at work in the recent discussions of race relations in the United States. Many people insist that the #BlackLivesMatter movement keep the focus the experiences of Black communities. Others tried to change the phrase to #AllLivesMatter. Of course, all lives do matter, but the movement wants to strategically focus on the particular pattern of institutionalized racism that has been targeting Black men in the United States. The aim here was not to devalue the loss of other lives but to be able to analyze the specificity of a particular pattern. There are certainly times and places for this single-issue/single-identity strategy. As a teacher, I have found students of all backgrounds much more willing and able to discuss these nuances when the *strategic* rationale is fully explained to them and when they are assured that everyone's experiences of oppression count and will have a space in the classroom discussion at some point.

However, there is also a real feeling of marginalization to want one's own experience to be recognized. If an individual is truly trying to show up and do their work of unlearning their privilege, it can feel like a slap in the face to be told that their experience of oppression, albeit a different type of oppression, has no place in the discussion. A person cannot truly do the work of unlearning oppression if she/he/ze cannot bring her/his/zir full self to the table. It is indeed important for them to not use their experience of oppression to distract from their privilege or to conflate all experiences of oppression as the same, but it is also true that if they have experienced some pain of marginalization, then they have a point of entry into understanding the pain of others. Mindfulness can help us learn how to use our own pain as a point of connection and empathy, rather than a distraction from, the experiences of others.

In addition, we cannot so easily compartmentalize ourselves. Many feminists of color, for instance, have pointed out that they cannot extricate their experience of gender from their experience of race, so to understand one we have to understand the other. As a queer, White, middle-class, able-bodied Western woman, I cannot truly dismantle my White privilege by separating it from my Western privilege or from my marginalization as a queer woman, because its particular form is inflected by those other aspects of my identity. To compartmentalize is to fragment ourselves, which is actually a tool of oppression.

What would be more useful than always bracketing part of our identity is to cultivate the mindful quality of discernment. We discern when we can distinguish the fine nuances between the sources, substance, and effects of our responses. Discernment requires profound honesty with ourselves; it demands that we admit when we might be using "intersectionality" to avoid doing our work. Discernment sheds a clear light on our motivations and their effect in any given context, helping us begin to realize when our own walls of privilege might be keeping us from dismantling our learned oppression. But discernment is also courageous and fierce, giving us the ability to commit ourselves wholeheartedly to unlearning our own role in oppression and to simultaneously insist that our own experiences be seen.

Getting Bigger than the Reactions

Teachers need to get bigger than these reactions and to try to meet students where they are. Even if we feel personal frustration at some students' responses, it is our job to facilitate transformational learning. Judging or condemning student reactions generally accomplishes little except forcing the student to disengage. Moreover, as teachers, we see student after student go through these awareness trajectories, so it should be easier for us to get bigger in the moment and help the student put their responses in context. That ability, of course, will depend on our capacity in our own mindfulness and anti-oppression work and on whether or how our own pain is triggered by whatever has been said in the classroom. To the degree that it is possible, we can help students navigate through their dissonance when we can help them learn to embody the reactions without getting consumed by them.

When we get lost in our reactions and see them as "Truth," we tend to react in ways that often prove counterproductive to the unlearning process. Mindfulness helps us see these reactions as important and valid, but also helps us observe them through the Witness so that we don't get lost in them. When the veil of invisibility begins to lift, those students who have privilege experience intense reactions. Those that do not—or do not in certain aspects of their lives—may begin to see the depth of the oppression they have internalized. Both realizations produce deep dissonance that, in general, should not be characterized as flaws of the individual student or as evidence that they do not want to take account of their privilege. Instead, these reactions need to be understood as the *inevitable dissonance* that occurs when their very identity is called into question. When we, as teachers, begin to peel back the veil of subterfuge, we reveal how deeply engrained power and privilege is in the lives of dominant groups and how deeply internalized oppression shapes the self-identity of marginalized groups. This revelation begins to dismantle students' very identity, their very sense of who they are in the world. This process inevitably provokes some intense responses. We teachers might remember what it was like when we first had our privilege and/or self-identity challenged. (While some people in the world are not privileged in any way, many of us are privileged in some ways.) Chances are, the first time we were confronted with these issues, it was deeply unsettling. If we add to that memory the identity development issues that are typical for traditionally aged college student (ages 18–22), then we can begin to understand what our students are experiencing.

Our diversity classrooms will become much more effective to the degree that we can make compassionate and discerning space for the wide variety of dissonance I just described. Making space does not mean to allow it to run rampant; when that happens, the different forms of dissonance will clash with one another, creating event more entrenched divides between students. Instead, it means to understand that the range of reactions people feel are the inevitable byproducts of living in an inequitable society. It means helping students step back and understand where their responses—and those of other students in the room—are coming from and providing them the tools to more intentionally discern how they want to respond. According to the Upaya Zen Center, which draws on the work of renowned meditation teacher Sharon Salzburg, when we learn to mindfully sit with our emotions, we can learn to recognize a feeling just as it begins, not 15 consequential actions later. We can then go on to develop a more balanced relationship with it—neither letting it overwhelm us so we lash out rashly nor ignoring it because we're afraid or ashamed of it.

(Upaya Zen Center 2013)

The mindfulness tool of the Witness, combined with kindness, compassion, and non-judgmentalness, helps us get bigger than our thoughts and hopefully gives us more choices about how to respond.

Students will not always be able to get bigger than their reactions; neither will faculty. When a particularly raw wound is touched or a foundational belief in our own selves is challenged, we may not, in that moment, be able to create the meta-awareness that prevent us from being utterly consumed by it. That is where more compassion is the key: the rest of us in the room need to hear and acknowledge that response, but we do not always need to attack it. We might remember that we do not have all the answers and that we will not always handle difficult dialogues as skillfully as we might like.

Learning to Sit with Discomfort

People lash out with what looks like resistance when they do not know what to do with overwhelming reactions. For most of the students and colleagues I have encountered over the years, the dissonance that they expressed had more to do with not knowing how to process highly uncomfortable feelings than it does with being unwilling to dismantle oppressive systems. Even those people who fall into the latter category have aspects of their selves that can soften if they connect with people on a human, rather than an ideological level. In other words, we might fundamentally disagree about politics or ideologies, but my guess is there is a place where we could connect on the level of basic humanity. Once we do that, it becomes harder to "other" a person, which first depends on dehumanization. This is not an easy process nor is it always successful, but it is a start toward learning more compassionate ways to relate to one another.

So a key step in the process of working through our dissonance is to learn to sit with deep discomfort. Mindfulness offers us a plethora of tools to do so. Most meditation invites us to refrain from immediately acting when we feel discomfort. When we meditate, we often get the urge to scratch, fidget or move, and the instructions are usually to refrain from doing so and notice what happens. Usually, the distraction passes. Even if it does not pass, we can learn a great deal about ourselves when we see how much we try to avoid being uncomfortable. We cultivate the ability to tolerate increasing levels of it, particularly when the result is transformative. In other words, we know that powerful learning usually requires some degree of stepping out of our comfort zone. For those of us who live with oppression, states of discomfort are, unfortunately, very familiar to us. Mindfulness practices can enhance our resiliency to sit with it and offer us a broader range of responses.

Discomfort is not the same thing as pain. Most meditation leaders note that the urge to distract ourselves by fidgeting is something to sit with; literal knee pain is not. If we are feeling actual pain, the instruction is usually to address it and then come back to stillness. The same would be true for heart-felt pain around oppression. We cannot always just sit with the pain that comes up in the classroom; that will depend on the raw intensity of the pain, the sense of safety or lack thereof in the space of the classroom, and the individual's capacity to hold the experience. But to the degree that it is possible, the mindfulness practice of sitting with discomfort can prove invaluable to working through the dissonance of unlearning oppression. As Pema Chödrön notes,

> When things are shaky and nothing is working, we might realize that we are on the verge of something. We might realize that this is a very vulnerable and tender place, and that tenderness can go either way. We can shut down and feel resentful or we can touch in on that throbbing quality.
>
> (2000, 9)

When we gently lean into that tenderness, new possibilities for healing and intentional action arise. In addition to refraining from distraction, mindfulness instruction around discomfort invites us to lean into it *with a sense of curiosity*. What does the sensation feel like? What is its texture? Color? Where is it showing up in our bodies? What is our immediate tendency when it arises? What happens if we do not engage in that immediate reaction? What if we breathe deeply and direct our breath to the place where that discomfort arises? Can we invite ourselves to soften? These practices, of course, become harder based on the intensity of the discomfort. Like all mindfulness practices, they become more accessible to us in difficult moments if we practice them in less intense ones. We also need to have compassion for ourselves and others when we cannot take these steps. But to the degree that we can, meeting our discomfort with curiosity and a sense of inquiry offers an empowering alternative to the typical tendency to get lost in it.

The other important piece here is to use those experiences as opportunities to connect with ourselves and to one another with empathy and compassion. Too often, oppression causes us to separate from one another. We harden and create an "us" and "them," either as a survival mechanism or in a way that perpetuates oppression. In both cases, this separation is deeply limiting. Chödrön once again describes the effect profoundly, "When we protect ourselves so we won't feel pain, that protection becomes like armor, like armor that imprisons the softness of the heart" (2000, 89). Mindfulness offers us another approach: one that cultivates empathy and compassion for one another.

Compassion, according to Buddhist roshi Joan Halifax, is the ability "to see clearly into the nature of suffering" and to recognize that we are not separate from it (2010, n.p.). Recent research indicates that mindfulness practice enables practitioners to feel deeply and to connect to the suffering of ourselves and others, but it also lets us return to baseline much faster, which strengthens our resilience. Meditation, along with other forms of mindfulness, enhances neural integration, meaning it "hooks up all the parts of the brain" (Halifax 2010). In other words, it allows for a deeper integration and wholeness. Compassion also means that we are motivated to transform suffering, but, Halifax (2010) notes, we cannot be attached to outcome as we do so. This is tricky for those of us who devote our lives to social justice, since we typically are pretty attached to creating a more equitable and just world. But when it comes to compassion, Halifax, suggests, this attachment can get in the way of us being fully present with the suffering that is. Moreover, compassion has several near enemies, Halifax (2010) notes, including "pity, moral outrage, and fear," emotions that often arise in social justice classrooms but which can get in the way of truly transforming the conditions of the suffering. Halifax notes that all humans have the capacity for deep compassion, but we need to water the seeds and create the proper conditions for them to grow.

Inevitably, some people hear this call for compassion and think it means being weak or letting injustice slide. I would argue that it does quite the opposite and, in fact, that this fear is based on a misunderstanding of compassion. The quality of compassion enables us to deeply connect with the suffering in ourselves and others, and once we feel connected to it, we are far more motivated to work to transform it. Moreover, there is a type of compassion that some call fierce compassion, which meditation leader Sharon Salzberg defines as "redefining strength, deconstructing isolation and renewing a sense of community, practicing letting go of rigid us-vs.-them thinking—while cultivating power and clarity in response to difficult situations" (2012, n.p.). When the pain arises, we can breathe into our heart center, feel the pain, and use it to connect with others who have felt that pain. We can mourn the disastrous impacts of systematic oppression that robs all of us of our humanity, in different ways. Fierce compassion helps us connect with one another in a radical openness, offering us an alternative to hardening and cutting ourselves off.

Intersectional feminist and social justice work means that virtually all of us have work to do around power, privilege, and healing from oppression. While some of us are neatly in the category of the oppressed, many more of us are oppressed in some ways and privileged in others. Even if we are fully oppressed with no privilege, we still have deep unlearning of oppressive messages to unearth. The unlearning process is a painful and unsettling one. Recognizing that gives us points of empathy with one another that can help dissolve separations between us. Chödrön describes this process in the following way:

The ground of not causing harm is mindfulness, a sense of clear seeing with respect and compassion for what it is we see. . . . As we become more wholehearted in this journey of gentle honesty, it comes as quite a shock to realize how much we've blinded ourselves to some of the ways in which we cause harm. Our style is so ingrained that we can't hear when people try to tell us, either kindly or rudely, that maybe we're causing some harm by the way we are or the way we relate with others. We've become so used to the way we do things that somehow we think that others are used to it too. It's painful to face how we harm others, and it takes a while.

(2000, 32)

When we recognize how painful it is to experience oppression in our own lives, we can become even more committed to making sure we do not participate in oppressing someone else. When someone tries to tell us that they experience something as hurtful, remembering our own painful experiences of oppression can keep us tuned in with deep listening, instead of dismissing it as an "overreaction" (because we know how it feels when people dismiss our experiences of oppression). When someone calls us on our privilege, instead of getting defensive and shoring up our privilege, we can remember what it feels like to be denied privilege. Noticing how frustrating it is to try to point out someone else's privilege and have it dismissed can keep us from behaving in similar ways. As I mentioned elsewhere in this book, I see unlearning my privilege in the ways that I receive it as a lifelong journey, one in which I will make mistakes. But I also know how frustrating it is to try to point out someone's heterosexual privilege, for instance, and have them get defensive. When I remember that feeling, I try even harder to engage in some cultural humility when I am called on my privilege. While our experiences of power, privilege, and oppression cannot be collapsed into sameness, they can provide points of empathy to remain open to each other's perspectives. This openness, in turn, allows for a greater connection with one another, which is a powerful motivator to not only better understanding one another but also to dismantling systems of oppression.

One way to help forge this connection in our classrooms is through a mindfulness practice that helps students tap into their own pain of marginalization. When they get clear about what that feels like, we can then explore the conversation about whether they want to participate in making someone else feel that way, even inadvertently. This can be a hard conversation to have, particularly given the fact that the institutionalized space of the classroom is unsafe for many students. I often name that, so that it does not remain hidden. I also point out that the reality is that that pain is in our classroom whether we explicitly explore it or not. The more transparently we can discuss these matters at the "meta-level," the more students and teacher can become intentional about how to engage it. The other component of this process that helps build this empathy and compassion is forging a sense of community in the classroom, an idea I will further discuss in the conclusion of this book.

A Word about Safe Space

Social justice advocates often recognize the need for "safe space" to have truly honest and authentic discussions in the classroom. These initiatives are particularly popular in LGBTQ Centers, who often offer "Safe Space" training. The idea behind such language is usually to educate people on respecting others, avoiding stereotypes, and learning how to listen. It is a deeply helpful model and I believe we should continue to strive toward creating safe space in our classrooms and throughout college campus. We should practice all the principles central to safe spaces and make our campuses as safe as possible.

However, I do not actually believe that safe space exists. Or, more precisely, I believe that space can turn unsafe in a second, often unpredictably. So while we should do everything possible to work toward safe space, I also believe we need to recognize that colleges are institutionalized spaces that have not historically been safe for many marginalized groups, and that history does not simply disappear when one completes a training or puts a safe space sticker on the door. Moreover, in any given classroom, people in a transformative learning process will likely say or do something that turns a space "unsafe." This is to be expected if we are to have truly authentic difficult dialogues with one another. Think about the most intense social issues of our time—the moments in our broader communities when we need to have hard conversations. Those are not safe spaces. So it is yet another critical mindfulness skill to teach students how to have honest, compassionate, challenging dialogues in fraught moments in which they do not feel entirely safe, because that is how it happens in the "real world." I am not saying that we should completely abandon our quest for safe space. I am saying that we need to recognize that such safety is fragile and that it is possible—even necessary—to be honest and authentic in spaces that are not entirely safe.

What might be more useful is building something more akin to the "circle of trust" that Parker Palmer describes in his book *A Hidden Wholeness: The Journey Toward an Undivided Life*. The literal format of a circle of trust probably cannot transfer directly into the academic classroom, since those discussions serve a different purpose than the gatherings Palmer describes. But some of the principles behind them may be quite useful in building community in our classroom spaces. He writes that in a circle of trust,

> we neither evade the mystery of another's true self nor evade another's struggles. We stay present to each other without wavering, while stifling any impulse to fix each other up. We offer each other support in going where each needs to go, and learning what each needs to learn, at each one's pace and depth.

(2004, 64)

Of course, this is far easier said than done; it is a competency that needs to be developed, but it is one that foregrounds our relationship with one another. When we learn how to do so, we will recognize that people can make mistakes without necessarily jeopardizing the bonds of the community we are trying to build. This form of community means "never losing the awareness that we are connected to one another" (Palmer 2004, 55).

Tips for Helping Students Mindfully Process Dissonance

The meta-level of mindfulness combined with anti-oppression analysis can more effectively facilitate students' journey into and through this space of discomfort. A couple key steps need to guide our pedagogy here:

1. Help Students Cultivate the Mindfulness Skills to Sit with the Discomfort That Arises When They Start to Feel Dissonance.

Few of us enjoy sitting with discomfort nor do we usually know how to do so. Human nature often tries to immediately decrease discomfort and re-establish equilibrium. So students are not likely to want to sit with the discomfort unless they are taught how to do so and why it is important. The discomfort that is produced when deeply held paradigms are questioned is precisely the sort of discomfort we have to go through to have truly transformational learning. It is the soft edge of dynamic growth and learning. The discomfort is produced, in part, because our sense of ourselves are being unsettled. It is the safety mechanism for systems of oppression to keep themselves intact. More on that under number three below.

But students will not automatically know how to sit with their discomfort. We have to provide them with the guidance and the tools to do so, of which mindfulness offers an abundance. Helping students learn to pause, breathe, witness, and befriend their discomfort is a critical step in this process. Like all mindfulness, it is best to practice the skills regularly, for short periods of time, so that the skills are available in fraught situations. They will not be as available or effective if students only try them in intense situations: we need to develop our capacity in everyday situations so that that we are adept enough to draw on them in more intense ones.

2. Offer Students a Language to Name What Is Happening in That Moment of Dissonance. Normalize It.

Social justice classes provide a language and a framework of analysis that can explain people's experiences. I often hear students say they had certain feelings or perceptions throughout their life but did not know how to name or make sense of them until they came to a Women's Studies class. Those students bring their experiences into every other classroom on campus and they likely affect their presence and performance, but it is in social justice classes that they learn how to reflect upon and analyze those experiences.

As I have mentioned before, diversity classrooms do a great job of analyzing the power dynamics and making intellectual sense of their social locations (how their identities position them in society). But since oppression is also an embodied experience, as is the disequilibrium that comes from having our sense of self fundamentally challenged, we also need to help students learn the skills of witnessing their embodied reactions. Helping them make sense of these reactions *as part and parcel of an oppressive system* can go a long way in helping them dismantle the effects of oppression on their sense of selves. Merging mindfulness abilities with social justice analysis and activism enables what Dr. Kerrie Kauer calls a "personal transformation with a critical awareness"—the process of personal transformation informed by a social justice consciousness (2014).

While eradicating oppression obviously requires change at the systematic level, it begins with changes at the individual level. Without those personal transformations, attempts to change at the collective level will likely be impeded. Structural change requires groups of people to work together to produce them. Such coalitions will be more likely if we can learn to better understand each other and work together across differences. By teaching students how to sit with and work through their discomfort, we provide them with the possibility of making more intentional choices about how they react and relate to one another. We are planting the seeds for more compassionate and collaborative community building when we help students learn how to relate to one another across and through their differences.

3. The Process Is a Messy One. What Will Sustain Us Through That Messiness Is Our Commitment to Our Common Humanity and to a Larger Vision of a Socially Just World.

I find it helpful to just acknowledge that sitting with our dissonance is messy and rocky. It is not an easy or smooth journey. But it is one we all go through, though it will look different for each of us. I often share the missteps and discomfort of my own journey as a way of "giving permission" for students to accept the messiness of their own. This authorization can be important given the focus on "mastery" that often pervades academia. More importantly, it can be very discouraging to hit roadblocks in the journey toward unlearning oppression unless we understand that they are both normal and inevitable. Having a role model—the teacher and hopefully other students—share our own process with discomfort can provide students with helpful guidance through their own journey.

Ultimately, what motivates us to continue with the process even when it gets hard is our commitment to a more just world. It cannot be because the path is easy—because it is not. It cannot be because we know how to do it—because most of us do not. What sustains us when things get hard is our connection to one another and to a world that honors and values the humanity of every one of us. Making this explicit and creating space for conversations about this topic can help students cultivate their own resilience toolkit.

A Model for Mindfully Moving through Dissonance

Here is a model to use during difficult dialogues. Like all mindfulness practices, it needs to be practiced regularly during our everyday lives if it is to be available to us during our most intense feelings. With practice, we will likely become more skillful at it over time. Indeed, our ability to use it well will likely vary by issue; when we begin to dismantle the more intense blockages created by oppression, we will probably have a harder time smoothly practicing the model than we will with "easier" issues. Knowing this up front can help us better understand what is happening for us. I will first explain the model, then unpack some of its nuances.

BE AWARE

Be: Just Be. Breathe. Befriend.

Embody: Turn inward. Feel whatever is going on for you at that moment.

Aware: Notice what you are feeling. This is not the time to judge or react; this is the time to just become aware.

Witness: Get bigger than the feelings. Remember that you are not your thoughts or feelings. They are a part of you but not the WHOLE you. Observe what you are experiencing without drowning in it.

Accept: whatever you are feeling. No judgment, no aversion, no attachment, just an acceptance that this is what is happening for you in this moment.

Reflect: Consider your responses. Place them in the context of anti-oppression analysis. How are those responses shaped by power and privilege? How are they reflections of your own position in society? How do they—or don't they—align with your values and the kind of person you want to be?

Engage: Decide how you want to respond and act accordingly.

Regardless of what response arises for you in discussions about oppression, pause and just try to sit with your response. The first responses during intense unlearning processes are usually both raw emotions and our habitual reactions and defense mechanisms. Both need to be honored but neither need to necessarily be acted upon. We can rarely make a wise decision right in the moment of feeling these intense responses, at least not until we become more practiced.

These initial reactions can be overwhelming, so simply breathing while we experience them can allow them to move through us and dissipate. Mindfulness teaches us that emotions are impermanent, so when we breathe and let them be, we can usually watch all but the most intense emotions transform on their own, rather than diving into them and lashing out, or pushing them away and shutting down, both of which will make the responses get stronger. Simply pausing and breathing allows us to get a bit more perspective on the emotions, particularly when we meet them with kindness. Even when we dislike the emotions, we can lessen their hold over us when we befriend them and recognize that they are natural responses to the situation. (Remember there is a big difference between befriending our emotions and befriending or accepting oppression itself.)

As you begin to practice the BE AWARE process, please notice the following key elements:

1. The first four steps are completely inner practices. They are done quietly and inwardly. The more practiced one becomes, the more quickly one can move through these steps. Remember that it is acceptable to ask for a moment of silence to process one's responses.
2. The intellectual and political analysis does not appear until the Reflection step. Prior to that, we are practicing mindful awareness and just being with our internal experience. This part is important because intellectual analysis can be one way to avoid intense feelings (Watt 2007). So while we absolutely want to critically analyze the points made in discussions, we also want to actually face our emotional responses, rather than avoiding them or acting them out.
3. Action, if there is any, does not occur until the very last step.

The length of time it takes a person to process through these steps will vary, depending on the intensity of the reaction, the context, and the level of skillfulness with mindfulness. When we are new to mindfulness, or new to shining a light on our own oppression, power, or privilege, the process will likely be rockier and take longer. In intense situations, it will be harder to turn inward and sit with our reactions. But that is precisely the skill we need to develop so that when we do respond outwardly, we can do so in a way that furthers social justice rather than deepens the divide between us.

So part of what is necessary to BE AWARE is to provide students with the mindfulness skills to sit with discomfort when it arises and the social justice framework to understand where it is coming from. Mindfulness teaches us to move toward the discomfort with curiosity so that we can better understand it. Mindfulness is also, according to Dr. Kristen Neff, one of the three core components of self-compassion, which she defines as treating ourselves with kindness. Self-compassion, Neff (2013) says, is about embracing ourselves with kindness (the first core component), and recognizing our common humanity (the second core component). This common humanity of imperfection is the key to engaging difficult conversations mindfully. In any given classroom, we are likely positioned in different ways in sociopolitical power dynamics. But we are all human, and forging bridges of empathy and compassion based on that common humanity is the only way we will be able to engage in the hard conversations that are necessary—with ourselves and with each other—to unlearn oppression.

By calling for a compassionate connection based on our common humanity, I am not calling for sameness. Too often, social justice advocates have tried to embrace sameness at the erasure of difference. That will never work, because our differences are what make us who we are and what is used to position in differential power dynamics. For Neff (2013), this common humanity means a recognition that we are all imperfect. We all have work to do in dismantling systems of oppression. It will likely be different work, but none of us are immune from it. Moreover, transformation will inevitably stir up dissonance; I have never, in all of my years of teaching, encountered a student or a colleague who has not experienced some form of dissonance along their journey. The fact that we will all encounter it, and that we are all imperfect, is the point of connection, empathy, and compassion.

Mindfulness Practices

Loving Kindness

This practice comes from Buddhist traditions but can be practiced in secular ways. The ideas is to send love, friendship, and kindness to ourselves and people around us, starting with people for whom it is easy to wish well-being and ending with those we may have a very difficult time forgiving. Wishing the latter well does not mean we do not hold them accountable for the oppression they have enacted. Instead it is to both heal ourselves and to refuse to reproduce the tools of oppression by finding new ways of relating to one another. This practice is about softening and connecting to the part of ourselves that connects with others. It is not about how that person feels or what that person does; it is about how we relate to them and others, how we want to be in the world.

Loving kindness practice goes like this. Start by taking a good seat someplace quiet. Bring your attention to your heart center. Breathe in and out from your heart center.

Begin loving kindness for yourself. You can use these traditional phrases or some variations with which you feel more comfortable. Say them several times as you breathe in and out, noting any areas that cause self-judgment or harsh feelings as you do so. If any of those spaces arise, breathe into them.

May I be free from suffering.

May I be safe.

May I be happy.

May I be free to live fully as myself in this world.

Next, send loving kindness to a person for whom you feel unconditional love. That person might be a family member, a best friend, or a mentor—anyone for whom it is easy to feel love and respect. Repeat the phrases above, directing the energy toward that person. "May she be free from suffering. . . ."

After doing that several times, move to a neutral person for whom you do not have strong feelings. You might think of a classmate you barely know, the person who served you in the coffee shop this morning, or a person you do not know but pass in the hall regularly. Wish that person loving kindness.

Then shift your attention to someone you with whom you have difficulty—someone who has oppressed you or toward whom you have resentments. Send that person loving kindness. If you begin to feel ill will toward this person, pause, come back to your heart center, and try again. Recognize that this process may take months or even years to truly be able to send loving kindness to someone who has deeply hurt you.

Finally, send loving kindness to all beings.

After doing so several times, gently let the practice go, breathe into your heart center, and open your eyes.

Note: Many people find the hardest parts of this practice to be sending themselves loving kindness and sending it to the person who has oppressed or hurt them. This is quite normal. It may take years to fully be able to do so. Some people choose to focus on the first step for a long time, before they even move to the person they unconditionally love. However you need to engage the practice is fine.

References

Bell, Sandra, Marina Morrow and Evangelia Tastsogloul. "Teaching in Environments of Resistance: Toward a Critical, Feminist and Anti-Racist Pedagogy." In *Meeting the Challenge: Innovative Pedagogies in Action*, edited by Maralee Mayberry and Ellen Cronan Rose, 23–48. New York: Routledge, 1999.

Chödrön, Pema. *When Things Fall Apart: Heart Advice for Difficult Times*. Boston, MA: Shambala, 2000.

Dalai Lama. *Ethics for the New Millennium*. New York: Riverhead Books, 1999.

Deal, Kathleen Holtz and Cheryl A. Hyde. "Understanding MSW Student Anxiety and Resistance to Multicultural Learning: A Developmental Perspective." *Journal of Teaching in Social Work* 24, no. 102 (2004): 73–86.

Festinger, Leon. *A Theory of Cognitive Dissonance*. Stanford, CA: Stanford University Press, 1957.

Gorski, Paul C. "Cognitive Dissonance as a Strategy in Social Justice Teaching." *Multicultural Education* 17, no. 1 (Fall 2009): 54–57.

Haddad, Angela T. and Leonard Lieberman. "From Student Resistance to Embracing the Sociological Imagination: Unmasking Privilege, Social Conventions, and Racism." *Teaching Sociology* 30, no. 3 (July 2002): 328–341.

Halifax, Joan. "Compassion and the True Meaning of Empathy." TEDWomen, December 2010. Accessed February 15, 2015, www.ted.com/talks/joan_halifax?language=en# t-765191.

Kauer, Kerrie. "Yoga and Body Image Coalition Podcast." Personal communication.

Kumashiro, Kevin K. "Against Repetition: Addressing Resistance to Anti-Oppressive Change in the Practices of Learning Teaching, Supervising, and Researching." *Harvard Educational Review* 72, no. 1 (Spring 2002): 67–93.

Lewis, Magda. "Interrupting Patriarchy: Politics, Resistance, and Transformation in the Feminist Classroom." In *Feminisms and Critical Pedagogy*, edited by Carmen Luke and Jennifer Gore, 167–191. New York: Routledge, 1992.

Luft, Rachel E. "Intersectionality and the Risk of Flattening Difference: Gender and Race Logics, and the Strategic Use of Antiracist Singularity." In *The Intersectional Approach: Transforming the Academy Through Race, Class, and Gender*, edited by Michele Tracy Berger and Kathleen Guidroz, 100–117. Chapel Hill: University of North Carolina Press, 2010.

McFalls, Elizabeth L. and Dierdre Cobb-Roberts. "Reducing Resistance to Diversity Through Cognitive Dissonance Instruction: Implications for Teacher Education." *Journal of Teacher Education* 52, no. 2 (March/April 2001): 164–172. Accessed December 24, 2014, http://works.bepress.com/cgi/viewcontent.cgi?article=1018&context= deirdre_cobb-roberts.

Moore, Helen A. "Student Resistance in Sociology Classrooms: Tools for Learning and Teaching." University of Nebraska-Lincoln, Sociology Department, Faculty Publications, Paper 88 (2007). Accessed December 24, 2014, http://digitalcommons.unl.edu/ sociologyfacpub/88.

Neff, Kristin. "The Space Between Self-Esteem and Self-Compassion." TEDx Centennial Park Women. February 6, 2013. Accessed December 27, 2014, www.youtube.com/ watch?v=IvtZBUSplr4.

Palmer, Parker. *A Hidden Wholeness: The Journey Toward an Undivided Life*. San Francisco, CA: Jossey-Bass, 2004.

Rodriguez, Dalia. "The Usual Suspect: Negotiating White Student Resistance and Teacher Authority in a Predominantly White Classroom." *Cultural Studies ↔ Critical Methodologies* (2008). Accessed February 14, 2015, http://csc.sagepub.com/content/early/2008/ 08/08/1532708608321504.short.

Salzberg, Sharon. "Fierce Compassion." *Huffington Post*. August 14, 2012. Accessed February 15, 2015, www.huffingtonpost.com/sharon-salzberg/fierce-compassion_b_ 1775414.html.

Tatum, Beverly. "Racial Identity Development." Mercer County Community College. Accessed December 17, 2014, www.mccc.edu/pdf/cmn214/Class%203/Racial%20 Identity%20development.pdf.

Trujillo, Carla. "Chicana Lesbians: Fear and Loathing in the Chicano Community." In *Women Images and Realities: A Multicultural Anthology*, 4th ed., edited by Amy Keselman, Linda D. McNair, and Nancy Schniedewind, 429–432. New York: McGraw-Hill, 2006.

Upaya Zen Center. "Mindfulness and Difficult Emotions." November 4, 2013. Accessed December 27, 2014, www.upaya.org/2013/11/mindfulness-and-difficult-emotions/.

Walton, Justin D. "Dissonance in the Critical Classroom: The Role of Social Psychological Processes in Learner Resistance." *College Student Journal* 45, no. 4 (December 2011): 769–785.

Watt, Sherry K. "Difficult Dialogues, Privilege, and Social Justice: Uses of the Privileged Identity Exploration (PIE) Model in Student Affairs Practice." *College Student Affairs Journal* 26, no. 2 (Spring 2007): 113–126.

Williams, Mark and Danny Penman. *Mindfulness: An Eight-Week Plan for Finding Peace in a Frantic World.* New York: Rodale Books, 2012.

Wong, Yuk-Lin Renita. "Knowing Through Discomfort: A Mindfulness-based Critical Social Work Pedagogy." *Critical Social Work* 5, no. 1 (2004). Accessed June 9, 2015. www1.uwindsor.ca/criticalsocialwork/knowing-through-discomfort-a-mindfulness-based-critical-social-work-pedagogy.

6

CRITIQUES AND CHALLENGES OF MINDFUL ANTI-OPPRESSION PEDAGOGY

Thus far, I have made a strong case for how and why we need to bring contemplative practices into anti-oppression pedagogy. Many diversity educators urge us to directly examine our power and privileges. In her powerful TED talk "How to Overcome our Biases: Walk Boldly Toward Them," Vernā Myers (2014) urges us to let go of our denial, get real, and move into our discomfort. But HOW do we do that? Mindfulness practices offer us several skill sets with which to do so. Beyond providing us with powerful tools, mindfulness teaches us *how to engage the process*, which, when combined with anti-oppression pedagogy, can take us much further down the path of social justice than can either component on its own.

However, integrating contemplative pedagogy into higher education is not without its challenges. It is not a "quick fix" or a silver bullet. If one existed, we would have ended oppression a long time ago. Though I firmly believe this combination is powerful, it does raise some important concerns. This chapter will explore these potential pitfalls in depth. I will first outline some of the more prominent criticisms of using these practices and then argue for why these concerns, while valid, are particularly relevant for anti-oppression courses. The second part of the chapter will explore how different students may respond to these practices in unexpected and fraught ways, then conclude by offering several tips for addressing those responses.

Critique #1: Using These Practices Is a Form of Cultural Appropriation

One of the criticisms leveled against the popularity of yoga and other mindfulness practices when they are taken up in the West is that they are culturally coopted traditions that are taken out of context. Many of the practices included in contemplative pedagogy, including yoga, *pranayama*, Tai Chi, Qigong, and particular meditation practices, come from Eastern and Indian cultures. Their increasing popularity in the West has garnered accusations of cultural appropriation, particularly if these rich traditions are taken out of context, transplanted into different cultural contexts, and oversimplified. When practices become popularized in the West, they often lose much of their original meaning as certain components are "cherry picked" while others are left behind.

I will use the example of yoga to illustrate these concerns, but variations of them apply to other practices as well. Yoga culture in the United States, for instance, tends to be either removed from its rich and complex history and philosophy, on the one hand, or shallowly reduced to its window-dressings by non-Indian yoga teachers, on the other. If the former, the critique goes, then decades of philosophy, cultural context, and the science of why yoga actually works is erased, while the word "yoga" comes to mean hyper-thin White women in expensive yoga pants doing super-bendy poses (Horton 2012; Ahuja and Wiggins 2014; "Yoga Beyond Asana" 2014). The proliferation of yoga in the West means some practitioners strive to honor its traditional roots, while other variations emphasize exercise, weight loss, or material commodification. Since most people who practice yoga in the West do not have access to its centuries-old tradition, this repackaging of yoga often reduces its meaning and takes it out of context ("Yoga Beyond Asana" 2014). Given that the process of colonization usually involves divesting communities of their traditional practices, it can be deeply painful and problematic for a façade of a practice to be taken on by Westerners when some Indian communities may have been denied access to the practices in the colonization process (Ahuja 2014; Park 2014d; South Asian American Perspectives on Yoga in America, n.d.).

Of course, many yoga practitioners in the West highly value the scientific, philosophical, and spiritual roots of the tradition. Some Western yoga teachers align ourselves with a tradition and learn as much about that philosophy and history as we can. We resist the commodification of the practice and the reduction of it to "exercise." Instead, we note that the physical asanas were designed to help us more effectively access meditative states and align our energies. In some ways, this is an approach that aims for more integrity with the traditional context of yoga. But it is not accidental that so many yoga teachers in the West are middle-class White women or that many yoga studio spaces have fairly racially, culturally, and economically homogeneous participants. Recently, a plethora of public conversations have emerged that note the absence of people of color, LGBT/queer people, people living with disabilities, or other disenfranchised groups in many Western yoga studios (Park 2014a–d; Yoga & Body Image Coalition 2014; Decolonizing Yoga 2014). These discussions aim to make yoga more accessible to a variety of people (Park 2014a). As some groups are excluded or marginalized, some White yoga teachers may claim to be "experts" on a tradition that emerges from a cultural context and history very different from our own. Given the history of colonization, this phenomenon can clearly be understood as another example of cultural appropriation.

Both critiques have significant kernels of truth in them. Yoga is available in the West in part because of both globalization and colonization. Yoga was first brought to the West by pioneers such as Yogananda and B.K.S. Iyengar (*Awake* 2014; Syman 2011). Many people in the United States were attracted to its promise of peace and self-realization amidst the fast-paced, materialist, and much more secular culture of the West. But we cannot forget the history of power dynamics between Western and Indian nations. While many Westerners now see the benefits of yoga, when India was colonized, traditional spiritual practices were forbidden and denigrated. The result of that oppression still exists today, through what Tannis Neilson describes as denial, destruction, eradication, surface accommodation and tokenism (Ahuja 2014). Denial, according to Nisha Ahuja, occurs when Western yoga fails to acknowledge or understand its roots in a 5,000-year-old tradition. Instead it is often presented as though "Westerners" discovered its value, even though what they represent as yoga is often just the surface of a much more complex tradition. Some would argue that recent trends in scientific research in the value of meditation is replicating some of this denial, lending "credibility" to ancient practices only once it is "validated" by Western scientific knowledge, despite the centuries-old wisdom of Eastern yogis and mediation leaders.

Destruction, according to Ahuja, refers to the ways colonization disrupted the traditional ways yogic knowledge and practices were shared, resulting in a "severing between people, and culture, and spiritual practice" (Ahuja 2014). One of the key components of colonization is always to demonize traditional practices, labeling indigenous spirituality "heathenous," disparaging and even imprisoning spiritual leaders, and often outlawing the practices. While this happened more in some colonial contexts than with others, it is, nevertheless, a common and painful part of the colonization. This severing occurred through a process of violence, the history of which is often absent from yoga studios and schools in the West. The unsavoriness of this past is often erased in the glorification of qualities such as peace, compassion, and enlightenment.

These are all important critiques that also point out the complexity of transporting a phenomenon that emerged from deep roots in a particular historical and cultural context to a vastly different time and place. Yoga is something very different in the West than it was in ancient India. It also, in fact, is quite different in postcolonial India than it was prior to colonization. Yoga transformed as the world became more globalized, so to posit a "pure" or "authentic" yoga is a bit problematic as well (Horton 2012; Lindsay 2013). Given that yoga is a process of turning inward, it makes sense that it would take a different form in contemporary U.S. culture, because its participants have different experiences than ancient renunciate yogis. But it is also important to acknowledge its roots and the people who created and preserved it even in the face of colonization ("Yoga Beyond Asana" 2014).

While it may not be appropriate for an hour-long yoga class in the United States to delve into a lesson on the violence of colonization, it does need to be understood and acknowledged, something that does not happen when White Western yoga teachers, for instance, act like they "discovered" or "own" the practice. While many yoga teachers do try to acknowledge their teachers and the roots of the lineage they practice, the dominant image of yoga in mainstream media often does not. As Ahuja points out, when yoga is seen through a "white, skinny-bodied, cisgendered, man/woman, framing . . . [Indian people] are erased from the picture [as are] people who carry knowledge" (Ahuja 2014). When aspects of Indian culture, such as the use of Sanskrit, are used by non-Indian people, particularly when it is misused or mispronounced, it can be very painful to people whose relationship to that knowledge has been severed (Ahuja 2014; Park 2014d; South Asian American Perspectives on Yoga in America, n.d.). Moreover, because of institutionalized racism, people of Indian descent who do use Sanskrit are often received very differently in the West than are White people who use it. Ahuja, for instance, tells of being spit on, on the one hand, or tokenized on the other. White teachers do not experience either response because they are protected by their/our White privilege (I say "we" here to acknowledge my own positionality and privilege in this process as a White, Western yoga teacher).

Thus, while the forms of yoga in the West that try to preserve its tradition and lineage are, it seems to me, closer to the mark than the "butts and guts" style of exercise that is often labeled yoga, there is nevertheless a power dynamic that remains. The problem comes when these teachers presume to be experts without recognizing the complexity of stepping into this tradition from a different cultural context and a different historical moment, one with greater power and privilege (South Asian American Perspectives on Yoga in America, n.d.). One yogini of color, for instance, describes her frustration of seeing a White woman yoga teacher at a temple in India, mispronouncing Sanskrit and yet somehow seeming to have more access to the space than did the woman telling the story who was of Indian descent (Park 2014d).

Sometimes these "kernels of wisdom" are also used without awareness about how systems of oppression affect different people in the room (Dark 2014). For example, I was in an Ayurvedic training once with telling racial dynamics: the room was filled with White people—mostly women—and the one South Asian woman in the room was looked to by some participants as an "authentic" expert, though she pointed out that she was disconnected and unfamiliar with much of the material. She was tokenized by a "presumed" knowledge of the material. Recently, there has been an explosion of analysis of the ways institutionalized oppression appear in Western yoga spaces to make them unwelcoming for marginalized groups. Popular blogs such as *Decolonizing Yoga*, documentary videos such as the *Yoga and Diversity* series, and organizations such as the Yoga & Body Image Coalition seek to raise awareness of these issues and challenge Western yoga culture to live up to the philosophical and political ideals of yoga by dismantling these power dynamics. Nevertheless, it is important to be aware of these critiques as we integrate contemplative practices such as yoga into higher education in general and social justice courses in particular. Organizations such as the Contemplative Mind in Society and the Association for Mindfulness in Higher Education have provided strong leadership in grappling with issues of oppression and creating change through contemplative practices and pedagogy.

While these critiques have a great deal of validity, they do not mean that yoga should not be practiced. Rather, they speak to the complexity of cultural hybridity, globalization, colonization, and cultural appropriation. How can they be practiced in a way that does not reduce them or appropriate them? They also pose the question of identity politics: does a person of Indian descent automatically have more access to yoga than a White person who has studied with Swamis in India for decades? These are not easy questions, but they are precisely the sort of issues that diversity courses are uniquely prepared to discuss. Since we are teaching students how to ask those types of questions and analyze these issues, these are ripe areas for class discussion. We can teach students that complexities such as these do not mean we should never practice yoga in the West; they mean we should carefully consider the complexities and decide where we stand on the issues. That, it seems to me, is what we are trying to teach students to do in our classrooms. Bringing these practices into Western classrooms offers a prime opportunity to see these issues in action and teach students intentionality: how can they learn to adopt practices such as yoga that have deep physiological, emotional, and psychological benefits while grappling with the fraught nature of cultural hybridity and appropriation? In fact, this example offers students the opportunity to examine how their own positionality affects their use of any particular practice. Does it mean something different for a person from India to practice yoga than it means for a White Western woman to practice yoga? What about a person of South East Asian descent who was raised in the West and has never been to India? How do each of these identity positions complicate the question? Bringing these practices into the classroom allows students to garner the benefits of the practices while also examining their fraught nature and make their decision with intentionality.

Critique #2: Are These Religious or Secular Practices?

Another significant concern in bringing these practices into the classroom involves the religious or spiritual roots of many of them. Practices such as yoga, loving kindness meditation, and so on were and at times, still are, embedded in spiritual traditions. That history raises concerns about: 1) bringing them into secular institutions; and 2) asking students to practice them when the students' own religious beliefs (or lack thereof) might be very different.

In her book *Exploring Spirituality and Culture in Adult and Higher Education*, Elizabeth J. Tisdell differentiates between religion, which she defines as "an organized community of faith that has written doctrine and codes of regulatory behavior," and spirituality, which she defines as a "more personal belief and experience of a divine spirit or higher purpose, [and] about how we construct meaning" (2003, 29). The latter, she argues, includes several components, including an honoring of wholeness and interconnectedness, a guidance toward greater authenticity, and a focus on meaning-making and knowledge construction (Tisdell 2003, 28–29). Most of us have what Professor John A. Powell calls "a hunger for meaning in human life" (2012, xix).

Critics have raised concerns over whether mindfulness is a religious or spiritual practice. Many of the practices that fall under the umbrella of mindfulness do indeed come from different spiritual traditions. Yoga, in particular, has come under some fire recently from people of particular religions (Vitello 2010; Dreher 2013; Carless 2012; Kremer 2013; Ebrahimji 2013). However, as discussed in the previous section, these practices become somewhat different phenomena when they are transplanted to the West and taken up in a very different cultural context (Horton 2012; Lindsay 2013; Rajghatta 2013; Holpuch 2013; Schultz 2013; Karpel 2013). The original context of yoga, for instance, is in a cultural environment in which spirituality is the norm. When taken up in the religious pluralism of the United States, yoga is removed from much of its religious roots and is practiced by people from a variety of religious traditions and by atheists. One does not have to embrace any particular religion to practice turning inward and cultivating clarity, focus, and compassion. With its rise in popularity in the West, mindfulness has developed into a more secular set of practices (Barbezat and Bush 2014). While some of them did initially come from religious traditions, the practices have long since been revised to be practiced in a secular way by people from a variety of faith traditions and atheists (Barbezat and Bush 2014, 21–22). Thus, mindfulness in the West can be practiced without adhering to any particular religious tradition (Holpuch 2013).

It is certainly worth discussing the ethics of taken those practices out of their original contexts. Are they the same practices when they are removed from their Buddhist or Hindu contexts? Do we disrespect to those traditions by secularizing those practices? How do the practices resonate (or not resonate) with our individual belief systems, whatever those might be? Here again we have a rich opportunity for discussion that diversity classrooms are uniquely prepared to address.

Some critics have raised concerns about precisely this divorcing of the practices from their original religious traditions ("Yoga Beyond Asana" 2014; Drake 2013). These critics argue that doing so both dilutes the practices and appropriates them. These, too, are valid concerns that are worth discussing in social justice classrooms. Given that we live in a highly globalized world, we are likely making these kinds of decisions every day, but may not be aware that we are doing so. Bringing a level of self-reflection and critical analysis to choices that many of us do unconsciously is partly what we are trying to do in diversity classrooms. Contemplative practices offer another opportunity for these discussions. Much like the previous critique, I believe this debate offers fertile ground for discussion that diversity classrooms are uniquely situated to address. Having concerns about these issues does not mean one should not engage in the practices. Rather, it means that we engage in critical reflection and dialogue about these issues to determine where we stand. Modeling this process for our students offers rich material for social justice classrooms. Indeed, this point illustrates the challenge of living contradictions, which I argue is the reality for all of us. As we try to live our beliefs, we will have to continually consider which contradictions we can live with and which we cannot. Course material that raises such contradictions allows for us to weigh that balance in thoughtful ways with our students, so that they become practiced in that process.

It is important to distinguish here between religion and spirituality or what we might call a belief in something larger than ourselves. The former is often met with deep skepticism by social justice activists because of the role that organized religion has often played in colonization and other forms of oppression. But it is also important to remember that for some marginalized groups, religion has also been a source of strength and resilience (think the Black Church in the Civil Rights movement, for instance). Indeed, Powell (2012) argues that we have a great deal to learn from these interconnected spiritual and social movements.

Moreover, many social justice activists do, in fact, believe in something larger than themselves. Most of us are motivated by a commitment to equality, justice, humanity, and dignity for all. If we did not have a vision and a set of values, we would not be able to make the choices we make or sustain our work toward social justice in the face of setbacks. Indeed, Tisdell avers that "when people are invited into their own authenticity, they are invited to explore and reclaim aspects of their cultural identity," by which she means their racial, ethnic, or gendered identity (2003, 34). In other words, spirituality, defined in this way, means integrating into wholeness, which can be a radical political act for those who are marginalized in social institutions. I think it is important to use these practices in a secular way in university classrooms, but it is also important to talk with students about finding/refining their own set of values and their own vision of how they think the world should be. Contemplative practices can be used to get clear on what they believe—not to align with any particular religion, but to turn inward to themselves, engage in a process of inquiry, and gain clarity about what their value systems are. Students (and teachers) need this if we are to sustain our commitment to social justice, given the odds we face. Tisdell draws on the work of Rabbi Michael Lerner on emancipatory spirituality, which, she says, "highlights a sense of awe and wonder, the cultivation of mindfulness, and a love and care for the universe, but that is manifested in actively working for environmental sustainability and a focus on the transformation of the world" (2003, 41). By integrating contemplative practices into the classroom, we offer students tools they can continue to draw on long after the semester ends to sustain this clarity in their values and to maintain a connection with their better selves. We are all faced with hard choices along the path to social justice, and the answers are not always clear or easy; these practices offer tools that can be used in those moments of hard choices to become as clear as possible about which choice is consistent with our values (whatever those values may be). They also help cultivate resilience by maintaining our connection with something bigger than ourselves, which can help sustain us during the inevitable setbacks as we work toward social transformation. Call that spirituality or simply a vision of justice, but I believe we need it to do this hard work. Indeed, Powell (2012) argues that spirituality and spiritual traditions have a great deal to teach us about shared humanity, healing from deep wounds of oppression, and working toward a more just world. Tisdell notes that this form of spirituality is not about pushing a particular belief system but is, rather, about, "creating an environment and a space where people can bring their whole selves into the learning environment and acknowledge the powerful ways they create meaning through their cultural, symbolic, and spiritual experience, as well as through the cognitive" (2003, 42).

Of course, not every student in our diversity classrooms will want to work toward social justice. That has to be OK. If we are teaching students to challenge, to question, and to think for themselves, then we have to accept what they decide to think, even if it is completely counter to what we believe. We have to accept that as teachers, not as individuals; in other words, as a teacher, I do not believe that I can tell students what to think, though I can, as an individual, fundamentally disagree with what some students think. I believe that if we, as teachers of social justice, "require" students to agree with feminist politics (or other similar sets of politics), then some of them will simply "toe the party line" to get the grade but never fundamentally examine the implication of their own beliefs nor will they really believe us when we try to teach them to question authority (if we mean question everyone's but ours). Teaching students to think for themselves means we need to allow what they come up with, whether we personally agree with it or not. Contemplative practices can help teachers and students learn to sit with things they disagree with and still hold compassion for others. They also, though, require us to be accountable for the effects of our actions, which is critical in diversity classrooms. Even if students fundamentally disagree with some of the material read in class or some of the statements made by the professors or other students, how can they learn to express that disagreement without harming others? That is also a critical skill to learn that will serve our communities long after the close of the semester.

Critique #3: Are These Practices Exclusionary or Inaccessible for Some?

Another prominent and valid critique of some contemplative practices are issues of accessibility and exclusion. Again, I will use the case of yoga to illustrate the critiques, though it is not the only practice that is susceptible to them. The image of yoga that dominates U.S. media is that of an affluent, thin, conventionally beautiful White woman in expensive yoga clothes who can do advanced, pretzel-like poses. That image makes many people feel like yoga is not for them. A growing number of outlets in progressive and social media express the voices of people who have felt excluded from this narrow image of yoga culture. Many of them have created new niches of yoga communities to make them more welcoming and accessible for people, including "Curvy Yoga," Yoga for LGBT/queer communities, and so on. Admittedly, it may seem strange to some to modify yoga in that way. "Yoga is yoga," one woman said to me, "it is for everyone." So how, the implication goes, would we create a "queer yoga?" I agree that the principles of yoga do not discriminate. But the way yoga has been taken up in the Western cultural context has, in fact, discriminated, by reinforcing dominant cultural messages about body image, beauty, health, gender, sexuality, and race. Yoga such as "Curvy Yoga" or "Yoga for LGBT/queer communities" does not alter fundamental yoga technologies so much as modify yoga poses and yoga spaces so that they are more accessible to people with various body types. They also try to create safer spaces for people who may be self-conscious of their bodies or feel unwelcome in the traditional gym or studio yoga setting (Park 2014b, c).

Other teachers have modified yoga styles to make them accessible for people with disabilities. One prominent teacher who has done so, Matthew Sanford, argues, "Yoga doesn't discriminate, yoga poses do" (Sanford 2014). I would add that mainstream Western yoga culture does. But the benefits of yoga itself are available to anyone. Sanford, for instance, teaches how to help students have the energetic experience of yoga. He suggests that people living with disabilities start there, whereas "able-bodied" practitioners too often start with the outer form and have to work harder to get to the "real" function of yoga, which is the inner and energetic experience. By teaching the energetics of the pose, people can access the benefits whatever their body type and whatever their ability (Sanford 2014).

The point here is that the critique of the exclusionary nature of mainstream Western yoga culture is accurate. Like the criticisms I have already mentioned, they offer a prime opportunity to examine power dynamics at play. The response to those exclusions also offer the chance to see resistance at work, as people create their own more welcoming and empowering spaces. These alternatives illustrate that our positionalities shape how we experiences things, so the same space or teaching style may not feel safe for everyone. The progressive and social media that have addressed these concerns illustrate the importance of marginalized voices and the power of marginalized communities to create their own empowering spaces even as they work to transform dominant cultures. Many of these voices offer thoughtful analyses of body politics, racial dynamics, cultural appropriation, and queer gender politics as they discuss why dominant spaces feel exclusionary for them.

Finally, the perspective of Sanford and other teachers like him who are making yoga accessible to people who are differently-abled reveal that the principles of yoga are indeed available to everyone; it is how they are taken up and taught that can make them inaccessible. These very conversations make us rethink our assumptions about disability, "able-bodied," and health in a way that is very relevant to diversity classes.

There is a great deal more to say about this subject, but it is beyond the scope of this chapter. In fact there is a burgeoning community tackling these issues of diversity within social media, in so many different places that it is hard to cite them all here (Harvey 2013; Klein 2010; Park 2014a–d). My point here is that this vibrant discussion about exclusion and accessibility is yet another point of entry into the complexity of these issues. It does not mean we do not draw on the practices because they have, at times, been used in problematic ways. It means that we help students see the power dynamics at work in these complexities and we help them learn to make informed and intentional choices about what and how they practice.

Obviously, diversity courses have their own vast content to cover and probably would not have time to address each of these critiques in full. But the practices need not be avoided because of this fraught nature; instead, we can turn the situation into another practice for learning about diversity, critical analysis, self-reflection, and informed choices.

Critique #4: Mindfulness Too Often Remains in Apolitical Safety

On more than one occasion, social justice colleagues have responded to my interest in mindfulness with some skepticism. Some academics see these practices, and my particular interest in yoga, as mere exercise, rather than modes of deep inquiry. More importantly, some of them have said they do not want to "coddle" students or give them a way of avoiding the hard work of confronting their own racism, sexism, or homophobia. Implicit in these critiques is an assumption that contemplative practices are escape mechanisms that are removed from social justice analysis.

At times, these concerns are valid. Some mindfulness spaces do indeed purport a kind of "feel good" presence that perceives any analysis of sociopolitical power dynamics as a disruption to the "nirvana" vibes they prefer. As a feminist, I have repeatedly felt ostracized in yoga spaces when I raise concerns about exclusion, cultural appropriation, or oppression in how they operate. It is as if people do indeed want to use those environments as escapes.

What they miss, of course, is that power dynamics are present in the environment whether they are acknowledged or not. If the participants in a yoga studio are predominantly White, middle class, cisgendered, or homogenous in any way, one might ask why diversity is not more fully represented. If the trainings or classes are priced exorbitantly and there are no alternative options for lower-income individuals, one should question the class privilege at work. If fuller figured individuals feel shamed or ostracized in a class that emphasizes pretzel-like poses, one should question the body normativity present in the room. If modifications are not available or singled out as "lesser than," one should question the ableism that might pervade those assumptions. When power dynamics are not addressed, they become normalized and stronger. Calling them out is not "bringing them into the space," it is challenging what is already there in order to dismantle them and make the spaces more inclusive or accessible.

This response operates on the assumption that "nirvana" or peaceful coexistence can only occur if we leave conflict and hard conversations at the door. But the reality is we will never achieve peace—as individuals, as communities, or as a society—until we face the hard issues. Those very issues are what are preventing peaceful coexistence, as is our inability to engage in conflict with love and compassion. Only when we learn how to do that will we move toward peace and enlightenment.

In one of my Women's Studies courses, a biracial woman talked about coming from a place of love in her life. As she expressed this as a core value of hers, others in the class said they were often too angry to do that. Implicit in this conversation was an assumption that anger and love are mutually exclusive. And yet, many a contemplative leader has told us that we can acknowledge and even act on our anger from a place of love. His Holiness the Dalai Lama, for instance, says that anger can be a useful catalyst for change, motivating us to transform what is unjust. But one can do that, he affirms, through a place of love and compassion. The fact that so many of us think the two are diametrically opposed is part of the problem.

Both the mindfulness practitioners who think facing oppression disrupts peaceful environments and the social justice advocates who think that mindfulness practices are Pollyannaish escape mechanisms miss the fact that the deep inquiry, ability to remain in the present, and techniques for learning more compassionate and authentic ways of relating to one another are critical ways to work toward social transformation. I have argued throughout this book that we need the embodied wisdom of contemplative practices in order to truly unlearn oppression and create a more socially just world. There are mindfulness spaces that live up to this critique but that is not the form of contemplative practice for which I am calling. In fact, as much as I advocate integrating mindfulness into anti-oppression efforts, I also advocate bring social justice commitments into mindfulness efforts. The partnership, I believe, has to go both ways if either aspect is to achieve its full potential.

I am not alone in this mission. My work is deeply informed by many a social justice contemplative leader who has forged this path, including but not limited to Mahatma Gandhi, His Holiness the Dalai Lama, Martin Luther King, Jr., and even Pantanjali himself. The form of contemplative practices that I invoke draws on the work of bell hooks, Parker Palmer, John Powell, Courtney Martin, and so many others who approach their deep commitments to political change through a lens of compassionate mindfulness. Thus, this mindfulness enables us to more fully engage and remain present with the hard conversations, ultimately moving us toward a more equitable and more just society.

One Last Note: Can I Teach Mindfulness If I Am Unfamiliar with Mindfulness?

The quick answer? NO. Just as we cannot effectively teach about anti-oppression if we are not doing our own work in unlearning systems of oppression, we cannot effectively teach about mindfulness if we do not practice it ourselves. Students can sense inauthenticity. Mindfulness is an experience, so in order to teach it to others, we need to have experienced it ourselves. We cannot expect others to take the leap into the new experience if we have not done so ourselves nor can we walk them through what it will be like if we have not tried it ourselves.

This does not mean, however, that we need to be experts in mindfulness. In fact, few of us are. In mindfulness, the phrase "each breath is a new beginning" is pretty literal. We simply need to be practicing regularly. When we are, then we can use our own experience to model for students what it is like, including where we have questions, when we are unable to practice mindfulness even when we try, and how and why we turn to particular practices. Modeling our own vulner-ability and exploration in mindfulness, just as we often do when we teach about oppression, lets students see that the process itself matters, even when it does not achieve its desired goals.

We also do not have to (nor can we) be well-trained in all types of contempla-tive practices. There are far too many. We can, perhaps, have experienced many of them, but probably we focus on a couple for our own practice and learning. Those are the ones we start with so we can teach what we know. For the oth-ers, guest teachers are good options. In my own classes, I lead meditation, yoga, and *pranayama* activities, but I have invited guest teachers in to lead Tai Chi and other types of practices with which I am unfamiliar. It is important to be very clear with any guest teachers about who the students are, where they are in their practice, and what you expect of the guest talk. As someone who has been on both sides of the equation—a guest yoga teacher and a faculty member bringing in a guest teacher—a lack of clarity often makes the exercise less effective than it could be. So, if most of the students have never done Tai Chi, for instance, tell the guest teacher that. If you want the session to simply help student learn to link their breath with their movement, then perhaps a mixed-level yoga class is not the appropriate lesson; perhaps some simple dynamic arm movements linked with the breath would be more appropriate. The clearer the instructions to the guest teacher about the goal of the session, the better. It is also important to do the session with the students, whenever possible, to illustrate that you, too, are on your own mindfulness journey and that you are not asking them to do anything that you would not do. Since some of these practices can make students feel self-conscious, particularly when they are often not used to moving in the classroom, doing the practices with them can help lessen that response.

Of course, students can have responses that are much more complex that self-consciousness, so in the second half of this chapter, I will explore some scenarios that illustrate some unexpected students responses to mindfulness practices and offer some tips for handling them.

Bringing Mindfulness to Layered Discussions in the Classroom

In order to understand how contemplative practices might be both crucial and complex in the classroom, let us look at two scenarios that underscore some situations that might arise from incorporating contemplative practices in the classroom. These scenarios are hypothetical composites of my own experiences with students over the years and my research in feminist pedagogy. I will first outline the two scenarios and then analyze how mindfulness can transform these situations into invaluable teaching moments for diversity classrooms.

Scenario #1

Ted is taking an Introduction to Psychology class to fulfill a general education requirement. He is one of two students of color in the class, which is not unusual for his experience at the predominantly White institution that he attends. He often feels either invisible or hypervisible in the class. Sometimes, the teacher will make a comment about African Americans and then look to him to confirm the statement, as though he can speak for the entire African American community. His classmates are friendly enough, but he often overhears comments that he finds offensive—statements about Black men in hip hop, for instance, or disparaging remarks about President Barack Obama that imply that he is less capable because he is biracial. Some days, Ted notices half way through the class that he has tuned out the lecture as he mulls over a comment that he heard. Today, the professor tells the students that they are going to practice a mindful listening exercise, something Ted has never done before. When he is told to turn to the student to his right and begin the exercise, Ted realizes that he has landed next to a student whom he heard make a racially disparaging comment about Ted's favorite African American professor on campus. Ted was so angry when he heard that comment, and as he turned to the student next to him, he felt that rage and hurt well up again inside him. He wanted to be any-where but there but could not discretely move at this point. He determined to push through the exercise, though because he was not very open, he got noth-ing out of. He left class with no interest in trying contemplative exercises again.

Scenario #2

John is a White man and a veteran of the Iraq War who comes from a working class background. He has been on two tours and is now taking advantage of the GI bill to get his education. He feels out of place on campus—he is older than most of the students and no one else in his family has gone to college. The things his classmates talk about before class seem so unimportant to him given the things he has seen and experienced in Iraq. He knows he suffers from PTSD, but he thinks he has it pretty under control with his counseling. He makes an effort to engage with his classmate and works hard in class, but he is having a hard time in his Ethnic Studies class, which studies race relations in the United States. He understands that racism exists and that Whites have done awful things to people of color but feels that much of that is in the past. His platoon included many men of color and they got each other's backs; he knows he would not have made it back without the bond they all had. So when his teacher tells him that White men have power over everyone else in society, he feels his confusion rising. He does not feel like he has much power. He joined the military because it was the only way to escape the town he grew up in, and he never would have been able to afford college without the GI bill.

His teacher, who is also a yoga teacher, asks them to do a beginning yoga class as part of the Ethnic Studies class. Maybe he was feeling particularly sensi-tive that day because he just heard word that one of his buddies was killed by a roadside bomb. On the way to campus, a motorcycle backfired and he had a flashback. His anxiety was high when he came to class, but he figured yoga could maybe be good for him. He tried to settle in. However, the teacher kept moving around the room, so he never knew where she was and often jumped to find her too close behind him. When she touched him to give an adjustment, he tensed up and had to resist the gut reaction to lash out in self-defense. He could not lie still in Savasana and hurried out of the room when the class was finished.

These two scenarios are composites of situations that are all-too-common in the classroom. Students bring these layered experiences to any discussion of oppression, and unless we learn how to reflect upon those reactions, our teachings about diversity will remain on a superficial level. The reactions that both Ted and John exhibited are the rich ground of doing diversity work—they are what we need to explore. But there are some things the teachers could have done to make the situations more productive and less threatening for the students.

For instance, Ted's situation was partly unsettling to him because it came as a surprise. The professor could have forewarned students that the activity was going to take place, so that students could sit next to students with whom they feel more comfortable. Whether the professor knows it or not, Ted faces incremental racism everyday on campus that shapes his learning experience (David and Derthick 2013). He has developed certain survival mechanisms: in this case, shutting down and missing out on the full effect of the activity. Mindful listening requires both trust and openness, neither of which was possible for Ted, given the acts of racism he experiences.

John, too, has very complex histories that shape his experiences on campus. As more and more veterans return to school, universities have to better understand the unique needs of this population of students in order to effectively ensure their success on campus. While contemplative practices such as yoga and meditation can be incredibly effective for working with veterans struggling with PTSD, those practices are often significantly modified in a way that did not happen in John's situation (Emerson 2011). In addition, most college classrooms consist of people with a variety of experiences, so adapting the practices may be more difficult (particularly if the professor is unaware of the particular situations of each student).

In the next section, I will speak more specifically to how the teachers need to be aware of these types of responses in the students, and I will offer some principles for addressing them. In this section, I want to focus on how these scenarios illustrate the rich ground for integrating contemplative practices in diversity classrooms, if they are done thoughtfully.

The learning process in courses that teach about diversity often invokes a variety of intense emotions. People whose identities are marginalized by the systems may feel frustration, anger, sadness, or powerlessness. Sometimes, oppression works through significant acts of violence, such as hate crimes. More often, it works through daily microaggressions that accumulate over time with significant effect, often resulting in what can arguably be called oppression-based trauma ("Internalizing Racism" 2013; Williams 2013). The effects of this trauma can be very similar to PTSD, and so any activity that asks participants to turn inward and reflect is likely to bring these reactions to the surface.

Students from marginalized groups may also experience internalized oppression, such as when a gay man struggles accepting his own gay identity. As we saw in Chapter 3, internalized oppression results when a person believes the negative messages about his group that pervade dominant culture. The result can be denial of the identity, self-hatred, negative body image, depression, low self-esteem, and/ or a disconnection from one's emotions. I have, for instance, had a lesbian student who performed more masculine gender performance skip a class in which we were going to do meditation because she was so uncomfortable in her body that fifteen minutes of a body scan seemed unbearable to her. This kind of reaction is not uncommon. The usual guidance from meditation teachers to "accept your reactions without judgment," or to "drop the storyline," or to "let them pass" will likely not be enough if we do not give the students a language with which to make sense of the overwhelming feelings that might arise. This student's reaction, like Ted and John's, are not just the run-of-the-mill mind-wandering that is normal for meditation. They are actually deeply embedded coping mechanisms and wounds from oppression.

Ultimately, the meditation tools can become a compassionate way of sitting with and even healing those responses but not before the student has learned to recognize that the overwhelming reactions that arise are the result of living in an oppressive society. That lesbian student's response to contemplative activities will likely be different from the student sitting next to her who does not have the same marginalized identity location, and it is likely that the coping mechanisms that she has developed to survive will kick in (as they did—she avoided the situation by skipping class). This moment offers an invaluable teaching opportunity *if* the classroom is a safe enough space to discuss these reactions. The teacher has the opportunity to help students frame their reactions, learn to sit with them, and develop alternatives to them. This analysis is crucial if we are to understand how deeply oppression works. But they can be tricky to get at since the classroom is often not considered a fully safe place for members of marginalized groups.

Alternatively, like John, students who are characterized as members of the dominant group may feel frustration, anger, or resistance to the idea that they have privilege in a society, especially if they do not feel that they have benefited much in their lifetimes. Women's Studies classrooms often talk about how members of the dominant group (White, heterosexual, male, upper class, Western) receive benefits that are denied members of marginalized groups. Not only are people taught not to see those benefits if they receive them, but they may not be very tangible to people, especially if they are marginalized in some ways. Moreover, intersections of oppression mean that someone may gain privilege in some ways but be marginalized in others. John, remember, is White and male, but he is also working class and a veteran. The feelings of confusion he experiences are pretty common amongst the students I teach who are privileged in some ways.

Rather than characterizing their reactions as merely "resistance" that must be overcome or as a kind of clinging to oppressive systems (as their reactions are sometimes framed), I argue that these reactions are precisely the complex terrain that must be explored if we are truly to learn the self-reflection that is critical to unlearning the effects of oppression. Too often, students' reactions are talked about in terms of "resistance," but, as I discussed in Chapter 5, it would be a much more productive strategy to offer the students ways to learn to meet and process their reactions as *inevitable byproducts of systems of oppression*. Contemplative practices offer valuable tools for moving the study of oppression from a mere object of study to a deeper process that is both internal and external. They offer the tools through which to recognize, understand, and come to terms with the layered reactions students often feel when learning about these subjects. Mindfulness can help students learn to understand their own reactions and see why theirs might differ from others in the room, which is a critical step toward learning more compassionate ways to relate to one another.

Students are so often disconnected from their bodies that it is not easy to reverse the messages that we have learned from childhood. Mindfulness practices can become a valuable tool to help students more fully cultivate a sense of embodiment.

Embodied learning is generative: students become co-creators of knowledge by recognizing the body as a dynamic epistemological site. Thus, as the various reactions emerge during meditation or yoga, teachers can help students make sense of them in the context of oppressive systems that have helped produce them. We can begin to see the reactions as more than just the typical "monkey mind" but instead as inevitable byproducts of living a particular identity in an inequitable society. The combination of students with differently positioned identities and bodies in any given classroom is a vibrant and dialectical opportunity for co-creation (if a classroom is safe enough for them to have an open and honest discussion about such intense subjects; more on that in the next section). Students can then take the next step to befriend that experience and begin to unlearn the harmful cultural messages that so often barrage them. Contemplative practices can offer invaluable tools for learning, not merely intellectually, but also in an embodied way how oppression works, what its effects are, and, ultimately, how to work toward dismantling them.

When Contemplative Practices Trigger

As valuable as these tools can be to a classroom that teaches about diversity, the scenarios of Ted and John also illustrate that they are not so simply integrated. Indeed, regardless of the discipline, educators need to incorporate contemplative practices carefully. We do not know what histories our students have nor can we predict their responses to various exercises, so we need to be prepared. My experience teaching Women's Studies has taught me that certain subject matters will hit very close to home for some students, and those responses will likely become more visceral if we ask students to sink into their embodied, emotional experiences with meditation, yoga, or other mindfulness practices.

Consider these scenarios, which again are composites of various students with whom I have worked over the years, both in academic and yoga classes. Imagine how we, as teachers who are integrating contemplative practices into our classrooms, would have to adapt our practices to more effectively and safely meet their needs. I will discuss how I integrate feminist pedagogy and mindfulness practices after I trace out the scenarios.

Scenario #3

Bethany is a White woman who enrolled in a Women's Studies course to fulfill a diversity requirement. She was unfamiliar with Gender Studies and with the teacher, and had no idea that contemplative practices would be a part of the curriculum until the first week of class. She felt some discomfort, though she was not sure why. Still, this class was the only one that fit into her schedule, so she stayed in the class. In the third week, she came to class expecting to talk about the readings for that day and was surprised to find out that the class was going to do a mindful eating practice in class that day. Immediately, Bethany's anxiety rose, because she does not eat in front of people and carefully monitors her calorie intake. She already has to go to the gym for an extra hour to make up for the yogurt she ate that morning. She does not feel like she can leave the class without making a scene, but she feels waves of fear, self-hatred (though she does not yet know to call it that), and powerlessness overwhelm her as the teacher explains the mindful eating exercise. She decides that since she is trapped in the classroom, she will just numb herself to get through the activity and will go purge in the bathroom after. It would be months before Bethany acknowledges that she has an eating disorder and begins to heal from it.

Scenario #4

Jennifer is an Asian American woman who was recently sexually assaulted by a male student with whom she went out on a date her second week on campus. She has not told anyone about it because she feels so ashamed. No one notices that she has gotten more withdrawn and quiet since the event, because few people on campus knew her before the incident. She has simply shut down, keeping her eyes downcast and wearing baggy clothing. In the seventh week of her Sociology class, the teacher begins to lead them through a body scan, telling them that this meditation practice can be a helpful way of handling with the stress of the upcoming midterms. The professor turns out the lights, which makes Jennifer suddenly feel afraid. But she decides to give it a try, figuring she could use some help with stress. As she listens to the professor's voice and

(Continued)

begins to drop into her body, the fear gets stronger. Her heart rate increases, she begins fidgeting, and her body tenses up. By the time the professor has moved to the hip and pelvic area, Jennifer wants to crawl out of her skin. His voice grates on her and she wants to run from the room. When the exercise is over, she is shaking, and though the professor says goodbye to her when she leaves, he does not notice that she shies away from him and does not come to class the next day. She spends the rest of the day in her darkened dorm room.

Though this is a hypothetical composite of many students with whom I have worked over the years, the experience is all too common. In the United States, an estimated 20 million women and 10 million men have eating disorders ("Get the Facts" 2011). One in four college women report surviving rape or attempted rape ("Sexual Assault Statistics" 2013). Often, students who struggle with both situations suffer for some time before they seek out help. Each semester, students in my Women's Studies classes tell me that they have an eating disorder or have been assaulted and ask me for help. Whether or not these students talk to their other professors about their situations, they are in classes throughout campus. Their struggles can negatively affect their coursework and their overall health. They might also be unexpectedly highlighted by certain contemplative practices.

A student like Bethany would obviously have a complex response to a mindful eating exercise. As the scenario suggests, having to work with food unexpectedly in front of her peers might trigger multiple responses. At best, she may not be able to get the desired effect from the exercise. At worst, the activity can provoke overwhelming emotions and physical responses, of which the professor may remain unaware. Similarly, a student like Jennifer has likely survived the sexual assault by disassociating, so it may be impossible for her to experience her body in a body scan meditation. If she does manage to reconnect with her body, the result might be intense trauma recollections that she is not yet ready to handle. In the case of both students, these deeply unsettling responses might occur unbeknownst to the professor, who likely thinks the contemplative practices are safe and beneficial. To the students, however, the practices might have the opposite effect.

Of course, mindfulness practices can be a powerful healing tool and many treatment centers and counselors are integrating them into the programs. But to encounter the exercise unexpectedly in an academic setting when the professor has no idea that the student is struggling with disordered eating or sexual assault makes the situation much more loaded. Moreover, the professor may very well be unaware of the responses the activity triggered and would not feel qualified to deal with them anyway. Nevertheless, statistically, there is a strong likelihood that an average-sized college classroom is likely to have such a student in it.

Tips for More Intentionally Integrating Contemplative Practices

This does not mean that contemplative practices should be avoided. In fact, as I have already argued, they can be deeply valuable additions to many different classrooms. But we do need to be more mindful about how we use them. So what could the professor have done in these situations? Here are five principles I follow whenever I teach contemplative practices in the classroom. All of them are informed by feminist pedagogy.

1. **Assume that someone in the room has suffered from trauma**. I have worked with college students for more than ten years, and in any given group, it is almost inevitable that there will be survivors in the room. Rather than assume these are anomalies, I start with the assumption that they WILL be in the room and behave with the requisite compassion and calm. I always hope I am wrong about that assumption, but unfortunately, I rarely am.

2. **Prepare the students for these possible reactions beforehand**. Preface the exercises with some introductory remarks that let students know that if they have histories of any of these issues, they may experience some after-effects of those issues in their meditation or yoga practice. Even a simple warning can help prepare students for their reactions—which can be far more distressing if they arrive unannounced. Obviously, in-depth discussions of these sorts of issues may be more appropriate in a Women's Studies classroom than they would be in an Economics or Engineering classroom. But remember, the students who are talking about these experiences of violence in my classroom are also in other classes across campus; it is just that in Women's Studies, we offer a language for it. These students might be manifesting these experiences in other classes by sudden plummets in grades, excessive absences, sullen behavior, or unusual withdrawn isolation. My point is that these experiences DO affect their performance in ALL of their classes, we just might not be attributing the proper reason for the behavior. One does not have to go into a lengthy diatribe about the possible reactions to historical trauma that can arise in mindfulness, but it can be helpful to briefly name them so that students are not totally taken by surprise.

3. **Offer the option of opting out**. People heal at their own paces. It is important to allow students to self-select out of a mindfulness activity if it is necessary for them to do so. I offer an alternative assignment if the student chooses not to participate. I typically let them know before the class period where we will be doing yoga or meditation so that they can make other arrangements inconspicuously. If it is an activity that we will be doing regularly throughout the semester, or even every day, I let them know the first week of classes and ask them to talk with me if they need to make alternative arrangements. I am a firm believer that meditation and yoga can be healing activities, but students need to be ready to do so. They may not feel comfortable doing so in an academic classroom. I prefer to let students be informed

and active agents in their lives and make the choice about when it is healthy for them to participate in these activities.

4. **Provide support resources.** When I do mindfulness activities or when I teach about sexual assault, eating disorders, or other sensitive topics in my Women's Studies classes, I always warn students that these are sensitive topics that may hit close to home. I ask them to pay attention to their responses during the class session (itself a mindfulness exercise) and to take care of themselves. Connecting them with campus resources is a crucial part of this process. While we, as professors in the classroom, often do not have the skills to help students with the psychological responses that might arise from mindfulness exercises, we can and should connect them with those who can, including campus counseling services, Women's Centers, Multicultural Student Services, LGBT resource centers, Veteran's Centers and/or Health Centers.

5. **Hold the space.** As professors and campus leaders, we probably know how to claim students' attention when we want to start class and how to hold our authority as we teach. But when engaging in mindfulness practices that might create unintended triggers, we need to also hold the space with compassion, kindness, and nonjudgmentalness. Students might be startled by what can arise in mindfulness reflections, so it is particularly important for us as teachers to remain grounded and to meet students' reactions—whatever they may be—with a calm compassion and to guide the student to the proper resources on campus. Holding the space means doing our own work to maintain our center, so that we can respond as wisely as possible. Like mindfulness itself, this gets both simpler and deeper with practice.

I do not want to suggest that incorporating any meditation or yoga in the classroom will result in psychological breakdowns of our students. Of course they will not. For many of our students, it will be a new and interesting experience, notable only by its difference from traditional college lectures. But our students lead complex lives that do not stop when they walk into a college classroom. Asking them to become more present and aware is also inviting them to more fully integrate, rather than compartmentalize, their experiences. Ultimately, integrating these practices in thoughtful and intentional ways into college classrooms, particularly those that address topics of diversity and oppression, can allow for a deeper, more embodied, and transformative learning process.

Mindfulness Practices

Understanding Partial Perspectives

In groups of four, students are to go take photographs with their cell phones of the same object. Each group of four is assigned one object. They are each to take a photograph of that object at whatever angle they wish. If they wish to put a finish on it or crop it, that's fine too. The only initial stipulation is that each individual take the angle of photograph that speaks to them and that each group focus on one object.

Then, they are to share the images with one another. How are the photographs different? How are they similar? Why did each individual take the angle of shot they did or put the finish on it that they did? Does any one image tell the whole story? What about when we put the images together? Is the story complete then?

This activity helps students see the significance of partial perspectives; that every one of them sees the world through a particular lens, a lens that is shaped by their identity location. We get a more complete story by placing them in dialogue with one another.

Tree Pose

Balancing poses are an excellent way of turning inward and listening carefully to ourselves. We cannot balance if we are distracted on external stimuli. The only way to balance is to deeply connect with ourselves and pay attention to what we are feeling, what we need.

To practice tree pose, find a flat piece of ground and take off your shoes. Take a moment to ground yourself through your feet. Lift the toes on your right foot while rooting down through all four corners of your foot (the inner and outer edge of your heel, the big toe mound and the outer edge of your foot). Lower your toes but keep the rootedness. Shift your weight over your right leg and find a focal point in the distance on which to focus. Let your eyes soften on that focal point while your breathing deepens. When you feel grounded, lift your left foot up, bend your knee, and place your left foot on your ankle, your thigh, or on tip toes as you try to balance on your right leg. Lift up through your torso and the top of your head while you press your hands together at your heart. Try to keep your breathing deep and even.

As you connect inward, listen to your body. How do you need to shift your weight incrementally to maintain your balance? What external noises draw your attention and what happens to your balance when you get distracted?

When you have held tree pose for a few breaths, gently release your left foot to the floor. Pause for a moment with your eyes closed and notice what is happening for you. Repeat on the other side. Note: You can use a wall to help you balance.

The purpose of this exercise is to become adept at turning inward and really listening to what is happening for us at any given moment. We cannot balance if we are living only in our thoughts or in reaction to external events. Balance is only possible when we learn to pay attention to the nuances of our felt sense. Even if we cannot balance in tree, we can still learn that process of listening to the nuances within.

References

Ahuja, Nisha, and Toby Wiggins, Filmmakers. "Exploring Yoga and Cultural Appropriation with Nisha Ahuja." *Decolonizing Yoga*. Video, 25:25. Accessed June 21, 2014, www.decolonizingyoga.com/exploring-yoga-cultural-appropriation-nisha-ahuja.

Awake: The Life of Yogananda. Paola Di Florio and Lisa Leeman, Directors, Peter Rader, Producer. Counterpoint Films, 2014.

Barbezat, Daniel and Mirabai Bush. *Contemplative Practices in Higher Education: Powerful Methods to Transform Teaching and Learning*. San Francisco, CA: Jossey-Bass, 2014.

Carless, Will. "Yoga Class Draws a Religious Protest." *New York Times*. December 15, 2012. Accessed June 9, 2015. www.nytimes.com/2012/12/16/us/school-yoga-class-draws-religious-protest-from-christians.html.

Dark, Kimberly. "Why Feminism Belongs in the Yoga Studio." *Decolonizing Yoga*. Accessed June 21, 2014, www.decolonizingyoga.com/feminism-belongs-yoga-studio/.

David, E.J.R. and Annie O. Derthick. "What Is Internalized Oppression, and So What?" In *Internalized Oppression: The Psychology of Marginalized Groups*, edited by E.J.R. David, 1–30. New York: Springer, 2013.

Decolonizing Yoga: Where Spirituality Meets Social Justice. Accessed December 21, 2014, www.decolonizingyoga.com.

Drake, Teo. "Honoring Yoga's Sacred Religious Roots." *Roots Grow the Tree*. March 11, 2013. http://rootsgrowthetree.com/category/faith/.

Dreher, Rod. "Yoga: Exercise of Religion of Mere Exercise?" *American Conservative*. December 9, 2013. www.theamericanconservative.com/dreher/yoga-exercise-of-religion-or-mere-exercise/.

Ebrahimji, Alisha. "Is Yoga Too Religious for Schools?" CNN. August 22, 2013. Accessed June 9, 2015. www.cnn.com/2013/08/22/health/yoga-in-schools/.

Emerson, David and Elizabeth Hopper. *Overcoming Trauma through Yoga: Reclaiming Your Body*. Berkeley, CA: North Atlantic Books, 2011.

"Get the Facts on Eating Disorders." National Eating Disorders Association. 2011. Accessed July 12, 2013, www.nationaleatingdisorders.org/get-facts-eating-disorders.

Harvey, Roseanne. "Wrapping Up Sadie Nardini's 21-Day-Yoga-Adventure." *It's All Yoga, Baby*. November 26, 2013. Accessed June 21, 2013, www.itsallyogababy.com/wrapping-up-sadie-nardinis-21-day-yoga-body-adventure/.

Holpuch, Amanda. "Judge Says Yoga Does Not Promote Hinduism in California Schools." *Guardian*. July 2, 2013. Accessed June 9, 2015. www.theguardian.com/world/2013/jul/02/judge-yoga-promote-hinduism-californian-schools.

Horton, Carol A. *Yoga Ph.D.: Integrating the Life of the Mind and the Wisdom of the Body*. Chicago, IL: Kleio Books, 2012.

"Internalizing Racism." *Huffington Post Live*. Accessed July 12, 2013, http://live.huffingtonpost.com/r/segment/can-racism-cause-ptsd/519d084c2b8c2a4ebc00010d.

Karpel, Richard. "Exercise or Religion? Yoga is for Everyone." *USA Today*. May 20, 2013. Accessed June 9, 2015. www.usatoday.com/story/opinion/2013/05/18/yoga-religion-column/2158377/.

Klein, Melanie. "Feminism, Body Image, and Yoga." *Elephant Journal*. June 8, 2010. Accessed June 21, 2014, www.elephantjournal.com/2010/06/yoga-feminism-melanie-klein/.

Kremer, William. "Does Yoga Make You a Hindu?" *BBC News Magazine*. November 20, 2013. Accessed June 9, 2015. www.bbc.com/news/magazine-25006926.

Lindsay, Kelly. "Spiritual Authenticity in a Secular Context: How Modern Postural Yoga Is Searching for Legitimacy in All the Wrong Places." *Arbutus Review* 4, no. 1 (2013): 108–127. http://journals.uvic.ca/index.php/arbutus/article/view/12686/3877.

Myers, Verna. "How to Overcome Our Biases? Walk Boldly Toward Them." *TED*. November 2014. Accessed June 9, 2015. www.ted.com/talks/verna_myers_how_to_overcome_our_biases_walk_boldly_toward_them.

Park, E. K. "Diversity in the Western Yoga Community" *Yoga and Diversity Introduction*. Online Video, 13:09. February 12, 2014a. Accessed June 21, 2014, www.globalmindbody. org/articles/yoga-and-diversity-introduction.

———. "Yoga and Diversity: Gender and Sexual Identity." Part II, *Yoga and Diversity Series*. Online Video. 15:01, February 28, 2014b. Accessed December 21, 2014, www.global mindbody.org/yoga-and-diversity-gender-and-sexual-identity/.

———. "Yoga and Diversity: Size and Body Image." Part III, *Yoga and Diversity Series*. Online Video, 13:22, April 5, 2014c. Accessed June 21, 2014, www.globalmindbody .org/articles/yoga-and-diversity-size-and-body-image.

———. "Yoga and Diversity: People of Colour." Part IV, *Yoga and Diversity Series*. Online Video, 12:20, April 26, 2014d. Accessed December 21, 2014, www.globalmindbody. org/yoga-and-diversity-people-of-colour/.

Powell, John A. *Racing to Justice: Transforming our Conceptions of Self and Other to Build an Inclusive Society*. Bloomington: Indiana University Press, 2012.

Rajghatta, Chidanand. "Yoga Passes Secularism Test in U.S." *Times of India*. July 4, 2013. http://timesofindia.indiatimes.com/world/us/Yoga-passes-secularism-test-in-US/ articleshow/20901632.cms.

Sanford, Mathew. Yoga Workshop. Minnetonka, MN, January 8, 2014.

Schultz, Colin. "Yoga a 'Distinctly American Cultural Phenomena,' California Judge Decrees." *Smithsonian Magazine*. July 2, 2013. www.smithsonianmag.com/smart-news/ yoga-a-distinctly-american-cultural-phenomenon-california-judge-decrees-5739356/?no-ist.

"Sexual Assault Statistics." *One in Four*. Accessed July 12, 2013, www.oneinfourusa.org/ statistics.php.

South Asian American Perspectives on Yoga in America. Accessed June 9, 2015. http:// saapya.com/about-saapya.

Syman, Stefanie. *The Subtle Body: The Story of Yoga in America*. New York: Farrar, Straus and Giroux, 2011.

Tisdell, Elizabeth J. *Exploring Spirituality and Culture in Adult and Higher Education*. San Francisco, CA: Jossey-Bass, 2003.

Vitello, Paul. "Hindu Group Stirs a Debate Over Yoga's Soul." *New York Times*. Noveber 27, 2010. www.nytimes.com/2010/11/28/nyregion/28yoga.html?scp=1&sq=hindu%20 group%20stirs%20a%20debate%20over%20yogas%20soul&st=cse&_r=1&.

Williams, M.T. "Can Racism Cause PTSD? Implications for DSM-5," *Psychology Today*. Accessed July 12, 2013, www.psychologytoday.com/blog/culturally-speaking/201305/ can-racism-cause-ptsd-implications-dsm-5

Yoga & Body Image Coalition. Accessed December 21, 2014, http://ybicoalition.com.

"Yoga Beyond Asana: Hindu Thought in Practice." Hindu American Foundation. December 21, 2014. Accessed June 9, 2015. www.hafsite.org/media/pr/yoga-hindu-origins.

7

BUILDING EMPOWERED, COMPASSIONATE COMMUNITIES

We cannot solely be concerned with our own well-being without recognizing the interconnectedness with all different communities, and we cannot see the issues of marginalization and oppression in a variety of communities as separate and apart from individual issues of trauma and well-being.

—Khouri and Hicks-Peterson (2015)

In a true dialogue, both sides are willing to change. We have to appreciate that truth can be received from outside of—not only within—our own group . . . we have to believe that in engaging in dialogue with another person, we have the possibility of making a change within ourselves, that we can become deeper.

—Thich Nhat Hanh qtd. in hooks (2003, xvi)

Unlearning oppression means existing in a place of uncertainty and resisting habitual ways of being in the world in order to create alternative, more socially just communities. We cannot merely relate to each other in the same old ways and hope to produce a more equitable and compassionate world. We cannot be satisfied with merely interrupting ideologies of oppression because of how deeply we hold its imprints in our hearts and our bodies. Instead, we need to find new ways of being with one another, which also entails being with ourselves with more honest and profound presence. This process requires vulnerability, openness, an ability to sit with discomfort, and a willingness to do our own work of unlearning oppression. While this can be a scary process, it can also be a transformative one.

Social justice work has to happen at the collective level of institutionalized change: altering our laws, our practices, our criminal justice systems, our educational systems, our media portrayals. It *also* has to happen at the level of the individual, as we unlearn prejudicial ideologies and oppressive ways of being. In order to do so, we need to uproot the ideologies and historical traumas that are deeply embedded in our sense of self. Doing so requires an awareness of our individual responses to power, oppression, and privilege, and that requires an embodied unlearning that mindfulness helps facilitate. As teachers in social justice courses, we would serve our students much more effectively if we helped them learn the mindfulness skills to do just that.

Many of these qualities are evident in the following mindfulness practice, which is adapted from a workshop by Dr. Kerrie Kauer, who adapted it from an activity led by the yoga and social justice nonprofit organization Off the Mat, Into the World (Kauer 2015).

Embodied Connection Practice

Do this practice in an open space with enough room for participants to freely move around. Ask students to walk freely around the room, being mindful of not colliding with others but otherwise not interacting with others. Students with mobility limitations can do the practice seated, swaying in their seat when the music is playing.

Begin playing music and invite students to move walk around the room. Each time the music pauses, have them stop, turn to the person closest to them, and do the one of the exercises below. After giving the students a couple minutes to engage the activity, invite them to shake it off as you begin playing the music and have them move freely around the room again. After a minute or so, pause the music and move onto the next activity. Start playing the music.

Pause and look into the eyes of the person in front of you. Recognize that this person has hopes, dreams, and people she/he/ze loves.

Pause. Think of a time when you felt disempowered by oppression. How did that feel in your body? Embody that feeling in your body, your facial expression, and how you relate to others. When the music begins, move around the room carrying that disempowerment.

Remember a time when you felt empowered and strong in your identity. Embody that feeling in your body, your facial expression and how you relate to others. When the music begins, move through the space embodying that empowerment.

Remember what it feels like to experience racism, sexism, homophobia, classism, transphobia, ableism, xenophobia, or ageism. Embody that experience while moving around the room.

Remember what it is like to feel joyful and empowered. Move around embodying that experience. When the music stops, turn to the person closest to you and share your experience of the last two practices.

Walk around the room and notice the people you are passing and the assumptions you have. Stop, turn to the person next to you and share three assumptions you had about them.

Pause. Look into the eyes of the person in front of you. Recognize that this person has experienced loss, oppression, and suffering.

Pause. Look into the eyes of the person in front of you. Recognize that this person has learned and probably internalized limiting definitions of themselves and others.

Pause. Look into the eyes of the person in front of you. Acknowledge that this person wants to be deeply seen, heard, and understood.

Before you end the practice, pause the music one more time and have the participants turn inward and reflect on their reactions for a few moments. Then come back to a seated arrangement and reflect on their responses as a group. What was hard for them? How did their bodies feel differently when they were empowered or disempowered? Did they "see" their colleagues any differently when they recognized that they, too, have suffered from oppression in some way? What do we do with these realizations? How might they shape how we relate to one another? (Kauer 2015).

What I appreciate about this activity is that it invites participants to cultivate compassion for our own histories of trauma and those of our colleagues. It helps us compare the embodied effects of oppression to an empowered embodiment. It invites us to really *see* ourselves and our classmates. In doing so, it reveals our connection to one another. This relationality and mutual accountability is what it will take to forge more socially just communities.

Mindfulness practices can take the form of introspective, individual activities, such as *pranayama* (yogic breathing) or quiet meditation, but they can also be much more interactive, such as the one described previously. They invite us to become deeply aware of our experiences, our thoughts, our feelings, and our relations to others. They teach us how to remain present in the moment of intense responses, so that we can more intentionally choose how to engage. And they help us cultivate compassion and healing, which is so necessary at both the personal and the collective levels.

Throughout this book, I have discussed how oppression affects us on a cellular level. It is embodied in our very selves and our communities. We cannot oppress one another in isolation, though, paradoxically, system of oppression create both alienation and isolation. Systems of oppression have distorted the humanity in all of us, albeit in different ways. They have poisoned our connections and understandings of one another.

But there is hope, and it lies in our basic humanity, our desire for a better world, and our interdependence with one another. We are connected to one another and we need each other, which is ultimately what will motivate us to cultivate more empowered, authentic, and kind ways of being. The mindfulness work we do as individuals has a ripple effect in shaping the communities of which we are a part. Mindful practices help us learn to more compassionately relate to one another. When we unearth oppressive ideologies from our very sense of self, we can heal into healthier, whole human beings. As we do so, we can bring our full selves to our community and transform our relations with one another.

This book has been focused on the college classroom, offering ways to help individual students become conscious of how they are responding to social justice material and helping them become more intentional about how they process those reactions so that they can make more empowered choices. Those individual student responses occur in the classroom community, which offers opportunities for us to learn to be more accountable and compassionate toward one another. My hope is that by modeling how to create empowered and transformational community relations within the classroom, we can help students learn how to continue this work outside of academia, long after the completion of the semester or even the conclusion of their college career. As this partnership between mindful education and anti-oppression pedagogy continues to grow, we can further explore how to move this learning beyond the individual, beyond the classroom, and into cultivating sustainable, just communities.

We all have an investment in changing oppressive systems. We all have work to do. And we all have something powerful to gain in this transformation into more compassionate and socially just communities: nothing less than our full dignity, our fully empowered humanity.

References

hooks, bell. *Teaching Community: A Pedagogy* of Hope. New York: Routledge, 2003.

Kauer, Kerrie. Yoga and Body Image Coalition Workshop. Minneapolis, MN, February 7, 2015.

Khouri, Hala and Tessa Hicks-Peterson. "The Trauma of Injustice." Off the Mat, Into the World Workshop, March 5 and 10, 2015. Accessed March 10, 2015. www.offthe matintotheworld.org/trauma-of-injustice.

INDEX

Note: Page numbers with *f* indicate figures